Carnal Crimes

John Dunning has had a varied and adventurous career, including service in the US Navy and the Shanghai Municipal Police. He spent four years in a Japanese POW camp during the Second World War and then worked in American intelligence. He subsequently became a journalist, travelling to China and Europe. Now a full-time writer, he lives in Luxembourg. He is the top-selling author of murder stories for *True Detective* magazines and has written over a thousand accounts of true crime.

Also in Arrow by John Dunning

Deadly Deviates
Madly Murderous
Mindless Murders
Murderous Women
Mystical Murders
Strange Deaths
Truly Murderous

CARNAL CRIMES

John Dunning

First published 1988

9 11 12 10

First published 1988

Random House, 20 Vauxhall Bridge Road, London SW1V 2SA

Random House Australia (Pty) Limited
20 Alfred Street, Milsons Point, Sydney,
New South Wales 2061, Australia

Random House New Zealand Limited
18 Poland Road, Glenfield
Auckland 10, New Zealand

Random House South Africa (Pty) Limited
PO Box 337, Bergvlei, South Africa

Random House UK Limited Reg. No. 954009

A CIP catalogue record for this book
is available from the British Library

ISBN 0 09 957340 7

Printed and bound in Great Britain by
Cox & Wyman Ltd, Reading, Berkshire

CONTENTS

INTRODUCTION

Heaven knows what this book will end up being called, but my original title was *Sex Crimes*. This may have been somewhat redundant. By straining a little, it is possible to argue that all crimes are connected, in one way or another, with sex.

Aside from the obvious rapes and sex murders, there are many crimes against persons and property which are sexually motivated. Spouse murders spouse to enjoy an undisturbed relationship with whatever sex. Accountant cooks books for glorious nights in Tahiti with seductive typist. Even the dashing bank robber rarely puts all of his booty into food, drink and safe investments.

Compiling a book of sex crimes is, therefore, a simple matter. There is hardly any other kind.

A minor problem is selection. Sex is a field of human endeavour in which staggering ingenuity is shown. Everything within the realm of the physically possible and many things that are not has been and will be attempted repeatedly. The more imaginative of such efforts are often disgusting and sometimes lethal which, however, does nothing to deter their enthusiasts who do not find them disgusting, but quite the contrary. As had been said by me, if no one else, one man's sex is another man's perversion.

Of course, neither 'disgusting' nor 'perversion' form a part of the vocabulary of modern, right-thinking persons. Homosexuality, flagellation, bondage, scatophagy, zooerastia, all are 'alternative life styles', respectable and respected.

Socially and, perhaps, politically the concept of unconventional sex is unobjectionable. From a practical point of view, it leaves something to be desired.

Physiologically, sex is friction of the sex organs leading to a glandular reaction and the ejaculation of semen. Under normal circumstances this may result in pregnancy. It is enjoyable so that it will be performed enthusiastically, thus providing for many pregnancies. In most life forms, sexual pleasure is the bait for the trap of reproduction.

Humans, being very clever, have learned to extract the bait without springing the trap so that the greater part of human sexual activity is simple pleasure without reproduction.

If sex is performed purely for pleasure, how the pleasure is obtained is unimportant. As entertainment, sex is almost invariably superior to television, less hard on the eyes and egalitarian as some forms, at least, are difficult to commercialize.

Biologically, however, people confining themselves to other than heterosexual intercourse become automatically the last of their line and a society made up of such individuals would perish within a generation. There is no case known to science of reproduction resulting from the union, however romantic, of two persons of the same sex.

Alternative sex practices are not yet widespread enough, even in very liberated societies, to greatly affect population figures. It is true that most of the Western European countries have a negative birth rate, but this is probably due to an excessive attachment to expensive machines and the fact that real earning power has decreased to the point where wives cannot afford the time off from work to have children.

With respect to crime, the sexual eccentrics appear to be, with some exceptions, less prone than the orthodox. If you are preoccupied with such questions as to whether you should buy you and your lover matching moustache cups for your anniversary, or where you can find some one to beat you to a howling pulp while wearing net stockings and a pig mask, you scarcely have time to think of, let alone commit, crimes.

The exceptions are, however, ghastly. Sadists, rapists, homicidal psychopaths and the like do almost nothing but think of crimes and commit them.

Although extremely dangerous, these individuals are often lumped in with the non-violent, regarded as victims of an unfair society and considered to be normal or, if not, capable of becoming so. For social and political purposes only, that is. Legally, they are as mad as hatters and, consequently, not responsible for their actions.

In enlightened European societies, such persons who may have given vent to a symbolic cry for help by disembowelling someone are provided with skilled psychiatric counselling and released – not infrequently to disembowel someone else. This, naturally, reinforces the original diagnosis of mental incompetency and precludes trial or incarceration for any length of time, which results in further disembowelments.

The repetition can become tedious for police and crime writers, although not for victims. Fortunately, police officers and crime writers are almost never regarded as sex objects by even the most perverted and do not, therefore, fall into a high-risk category.

Nearly everyone else does and it serves them right. If, as enfranchized adults, they persist in voting into office persons advocating the release of violent criminals, they must expect to be exposed to violence. Unlike the criminals, they cannot escape their responsibility through a plea of mental incompetence, justified though it may be in many cases.

The sole group without responsibility for these unnecessary hazards within society is the one which suffers the most. Children have no vote. They are unable to defend themselves physically. They rarely go armed. Their parents cannot protect them and the State will not. The result is a movable holocaust.

At this moment, throughout the world, appalling

numbers of small children are being beaten, forced into prostitution, raped, murdered and subjected to tortures which would make the Marquis de Sade turn pale. Some will survive. Others not. All will be quickly forgotten other than by close friends and relatives.

Gallons of printers' ink are blubbered over daily for the plight of people in obscure corners of the world who are not getting enough to eat, but the torture-death of a child is rarely worth more than a paragraph.

While celebrities howl and dance to raise millions for feeding people who do not, however, seem to eat a great deal better for it, no one appears to be greatly concerned over the dangers to women and children in our society. Starvation is unpleasant, but it is vastly preferable to being ripped open for sexual purposes by a psychopath.

It is true that some of these crimes cannot be avoided. For close to a hundred years, western societies have carefully preserved all individuals, however terrifying their genetic stock, and have permitted them to breed freely. It would be truly remarkable if there were not large numbers of psychopaths and mental incompetents.

Psychologists are right; violent sex criminals are insane and they are not responsible for their acts, but where the psychologists have been repeatedly and tragically proven wrong is in their belief that they can consistently do something about this.

Although some sex criminals do respond to treatment, others do not and it is the inability of the psychologists to distinguish between the two which leads to continuing slaughter.

There is only one sure way to prevent such repetitions of violence. Persons who have been found incompetent to stand trial for an act of violence against a woman or a child must be removed permanently from society.

If the tax-payers do not object – and experience has shown that the modern tax-payer will put up with almost anything – they may be housed, fed, clothed and entertained in great luxury, but they must be isolated from their potential victims and they must not be allowed to breed.

Persons who have killed a woman or a child for sexual reasons must be killed, quickly, painlessly and without appeal.

For those who find this attitude biased, I hasten to assure that although I like women just fine, I am not particularly fond of children who are, as a rule, scruffy, noisy and poor conversationalists. I do not, however, think they should be killed as do, apparently, those opponents of capital punishment willing to risk any number of lives to avoid the far fewer potential errors of justice.

Such suggestions invariably meet with shrieks that capital punishment does not deter crime. This may be true, although I believe that there are statistics to contradict it, but the question is not one of deterrence. It is one of removing from society a proven dangerous element.

There is *no* known case of an executed offender repeating the offence, but there are *many* known cases of cured offenders repeating their offences.

Shooting rabid dogs does not deter other dogs from becoming rabid. We continue, however, to shoot rabid dogs.

But the human is not an animal! When he (she, it) kills children, he (she, it) is.

Unfortunately or, perhaps, fortunately, you will see no more of sex crimes involving children in this book. Most of the magazines for which I write do not print child sex murders. They find it too trying on the nerves of editors and readers. Perhaps they are right. Such horrors are disturbing to the sensitive, caring people that we all are and, as it is unlikely that anything will be done to spare the children, the least I can do is spare your feelings.

I

FREE RIDES TO THE DEVIL'S MOOR

For seventy-five miles, from Bremen in the south to Hamburg in the north, the low-lying land between the estuaries of the Weser and the Elbe is as flat as a parking lot and wet with swamps. This is moor country, wild, sparsely populated, beautiful at times, disturbing and sinister at others.

The moors have names and one of the largest, which lies a few miles to the north of Bremen, is called the Devil's Moor. No one now living knows why, but it has been called that for a long time.

On the night of Thursday, March 8, 1984, a handsome and very muscular, young man was preparing to rape an eighteen-year-old girl on the Devil's Moor.

It was a night suited to evil-doing. Early spring in northern Germany is not noted for clement weather and the temperature was near freezing. Sweeping in from over the chill waves of the North Sea, less than thirty miles to the northwest, a bitter wind rattled the dead stems of last year's reeds and ruffled the deep, dark waters of the ponds. An occasional break in the ragged, black clouds fleeing helter-skelter inland over the empty moors flooded the landscape with pale-yellow light from a lop-sided half-moon.

'Take off your clothes,' whispered the man, his voice tense, barely controlled.

Gisela Braun could see little choice but to obey. She knew where she was and she knew who was sitting next to her in the front seat of the brown Datsun. Some girls who had sat where she now sat had been raped. Others had been raped and murdered. Her entire attention was concentrated on remaining in the first group.

If she knew who the driver of the brown Datsun was, she did not know his name or anything else about him other than what he did to girls. To the media, he was the 'Devil's Moor Murderer' and he was suspected of eleven rapes of which four had ended fatally. All this had happened within the past thirty months and in the open country between Bremen and Hamburg.

Gisela did not know that it had been eleven. Not even the police did. Many rapes are not reported. Some bodies are never found. Only one person knew all the details and only one would ever know them.

What both Gisela and the police did know was that the Moor's Murderer was a compulsive sex psychopath. The police, however, knew other things as well.

They knew, for example, that the 'Devil's Moor Murderer' owned a car, for his victims were invariably hitchhikers. They knew that the sole qualifications for a victim were that she be female, pretty and young. Hair colour, size, manner of dress, general appearance were not important to him as they often were to compulsive killers. Perhaps, the age group was. The oldest victim had been twenty, the youngest seventeen.

They also knew that he was capable of orgasm which was not the case with all rapists. They knew that he was not unconventional sexually. He raped vaginally and in the so-called missionary position. They knew these things from the results of the autopsies of the victims and from the testimony of the survivors.

What no one knew was why he killed some and not others. And, when he did kill, he killed savagely.

Eighteen-year-old Britta Schilling, thought to be his first victim, had been stabbed twenty-seven times with a large, sharp, single-edged knife. That had been on the night of October 30, 1981, a Friday, and Britta, like many girls of her age, had spent the evening in a discotheque.

Discotheques in West Germany are often located out in the country as they are not popular in residential areas. Britta, who lived with her parents in a small village some five miles away, did not own a car and between the discotheque and her home there was no public transport even during the daytime, let alone at one o'clock in the morning. Britta, therefore, hitchhiked.

That night of October 30th was not the first time that she had hitchhiked and she was, by no means, the only girl to do so. The roads were literally lined with nubile, teenage females, all prepared to get into the car of the first stranger to come along.

For a sex psychopath, it was a sort of giant cafeteria. You drove leisurely along and made your choice of a gorgeous blonde, a sulty brunette or a flaming red-head. In the meantime making certain, of course, that no one saw her get into your car. Granted, it was dark and few persons would be able to recall the make or colour of the car or take note of the licence plate number, but there was no point in taking chances.

'The Devil's Moor Murderer' had taken none so far. Of the eight surviving rape victims, not one had been able to provide the police with any specific information on the car or its driver other than that he was young, muscular and handsome. This, presumably, made the experience somewhat less distasteful than had he been old, scrawny and ugly. None of the eight survivors had resisted.

The police approved of this dishonour-before-death attitude wholeheartedly. Indeed, they urged incessantly in all of the media that victims co-operate and, if possible, take note of any details about the rapist, his car and his clothing which might help to identify him.

Why the survivors had taken only the first part of the police advice was a mystery and, in the case of Britta

Schilling, there was reason to believe that she had not followed any of their recommendations at all.

Britta's body was not found until November 6, eight days after the murder, although the police had been looking for her since the morning of October 31st when her parents reported her missing. They had not looked in the Devil's Moor because, at that time, they had no reason to believe that Britta was there. A good many young girls reported missing in West Germany are found in their boyfriends' beds, in alternative life-style communes or, less frequently, in whorehouses, either domestic or Middle Eastern.

Britta was, therefore, found by chance. The autumn weather had turned crisp and clear and this brought hikers out to the moors. One of them stumbled over Britta's body. It was in poor shape, having been exposed to sun, insects, birds and small animals for over a week, and Dr Wilhelm Kartheiser, the medical expert attached to the Bremen Police Department of Criminal Investigations, was not able to determine much from the autopsy.

As the body was largely naked and there was minor laceration of the genitals, it was thought probable that Britta had been sexually assaulted. Whether the operation had been concluded to the satisfaction of the rapist, could not be determined. By this time, any semen present in or on the body would have broken down into acid phosphotase and, indeed, acid phosphotase was found to be present in the vagina. It was, however, only an indication as the substance is not only a product of the chemical breakdown of semen, but occurs naturally in the body as well.

As might be expected of a pretty, liberated girl in a progressive country, Britta had had no hymen to rupture. Whether she had resisted the rape or not; she had resisted the murder. There were self-defence cuts on both hands and forearms and three of her fingernails were broken. Unfortunately, she had apparently broken them on his clothing for there were no traces of skin or hair under the unbroken ones.

The case was investigated by the Bremen Police who began with the theory that the murderer had been someone Britta had met at the discotheque. Sex psychopaths interested in meeting young people often frequented such establishments. There had been none in that particular discotheque on that specific evening it seemed, for the police were eventually able to identify every person who had been present and they were all local teenagers like Britta herself.

The police had not entirely completed this task when a second incident took place on the Devil's Moor.

The victim this time was Karin Franck, a pretty girl one year younger than Britta. Like her, she was sexually experienced, but, unlike her, she survived. Otherwise, the circumstances were very nearly identical.

Karin had been hitchhiking home from a discotheque shortly after midnight of November 9th, which was a Monday. The weather had been clear but chilly. Girls who look like Karin seldom have difficulty in obtaining rides and she was not surprised when a car stopped soon after she had taken up her station beside the road.

As she clambered gratefully in, she noted that the driver was young, handsome and clean-cut. She did not notice how he was dressed, the colour of the car or the make.

When the car passed the turn which would have taken her home, she protested and the young man silently showed her a weapon which she thought looked like a large hunting knife. It was only three days after the discovery of the body of Britta Schilling and the newspaper stories of the murder were very clear in Karin's mind so she raised no further objections.

The man drove straight to the Devil's Moor, but at some distance from where Britta's body had been found. There, he stopped the car, told Karin almost formally that he was going to have intercourse with her and ordered her to remove her clothing.

The terrified girl complied without protest. She did not doubt for an instant that this was the man who had killed Britta Schilling and she doubted scarcely less that he was going to kill her.

The man then opened the door on the passenger side to make more room and raped her, arriving at his climax very quickly.

Karin thought that he was still holding the knife and she was amazed when, instead of thrusting it into her cringing body, he silently pushed her out of the car, started the engine and drove away without turning on the headlights.

On the verge of hysteria and hardly able to believe that she was still alive, Karin crawled off into the darkness and crouched in a clump of reeds with her fingers in her mouth to keep from screaming. She was afraid that the man would come back. He did not and, after a time, it occurred to her that she was becoming very cold. She did not have a stitch on her, not even her shoes, and she was, she thought, a long way from any human habitation.

Karin was not superstitious, but this was, after all, the Devil's Moor where another girl had been savagely murdered only ten days earlier. So far, she was physically unharmed, but there was little point in surviving the rape only to die of exposure in the moor. Or, of blundering into quicksand or drowning in some deep, muddy pool. It was very dark and, frightened as she was, she dared not run wildly off. She had to find the track and hope that if she followed it, it would lead her out of the moor and not further in.

Had Karin lost her head, she too would probably have died in the Devil's Moor, but she did not and, gibbering with cold and fear, she felt with her bare feet for the car tracks, found them, remembered the direction in which the car had driven off and, after a walk which she would remember for the rest of her life, arrived at a paved road where she was picked up by a carpenter on his way to work at six o'clock in the morning.

The carpenter wrapped her in a car rug and drove her home where her parents immediately called the police.

Karin was able to provide them with very little information. She had paid scant attention to either the driver or car when she was picked up as she had been picked up a good many times before and she was sleepy and anxious to get home. And, once she had realized the danger she was in, she had been too frightened to think of anything other than saving her skin.

Nevertheless, the circumstances and, particularly, the scene of the crime were sufficiently similar to those in the Britta Schilling murder that a murder commission was formed.

Such commissions are common in series crimes which take place over a large area. Depending upon the importance of the cases, they may consist of anything from a half-dozen detectives up to as many as a hundred or more investigations' officers, technicians and specialists. These are drawn from various criminal investigations departments in the area and the commission may remain in existence for many years if there has been no success in identifying the perpetrator or perpetrators.

In charge of the actual investigation work of this commission was Chief Inspector Walter Scharneck, a solidly built man with a broad, calm, smooth-shaven face and a handsome head of black hair streaked with grey. Normally attached to the Department of Criminal Investigations of the Hamburg Police, he was regarded as one of West Germany's leading experts on sex-motivated homicides.

His assistant and second in command was Inspector Max Burger, Chief of the Bremen Police Rural Homicide Division, who had conducted the investigations into the murder of Britta Schilling and the rape of Karin Franck. A lean, heavily tanned man in his mid-forties with striking, pale blue eyes set deep on either side of a hooked knifeblade of a nose, he had had wide experience in the investigation of series crimes.

Finally, there was short, plump, but remarkably agile Dr Wilhelm Kartheiser, the medical expert who had performed the autopsy on the body of Britta Schilling and had questioned Karin Franck on the details of the rape. Blond, bullet-headed and wearing gold-rimmed spectacles, the doctor was one of those fortunate people whose profession was his main interest in life as well.

These were the key members of the murder commission. Over them were commissioners from the Hamburg and Bremen Police and, under them, an as yet relatively small number of detectives, specialists and technicians. More would later be added and, before the investigation finally came to an end, the full commission would number nearly a hundred people.

At the moment, however, only the two inspectors and a half-dozen detectives were active. There was not much to investigate and they were mainly concerned with trying to confirm the police theory that this was the beginning of a series of psychopathic sex crimes.

In order to do this, they were engaged in identifying every male that either girl had known or with whom she had come into recent contact. Far more rapes are committed by friends or even relatives of the victims than by total strangers.

Although Karin had said that she did not know the rapist, she could have reason to conceal his identity and even if she had not known him, this did not necessarily mean that he did not know her.

The investigators barely had time to determine that the rapist had indeed been a stranger to Karin and that the theory of a series was presumably correct when, on December 3rd, the 'Devil's Moor Murderer' provided further confirmation with a third crime. This time, it was neither late at night nor had the victim been visiting a discotheque.

Ilse Blumenthaler was twenty years old and worked as a sales clerk in a downtown Bremen store. She lived, however, with her parents in a village outside the city and, on the evening in question, she had had to work late and had missed her bus. The buses did not run very often and, rather than wait for nearly an hour, Ilse advanced to the side of the road and held out her thumb.

Considering that she had read all about the Britta Schilling and Karin Franck cases in the newspapers, this was a foolish thing to do. Ilse was a very beautiful girl with an almost startling figure.

After a relatively short wait, a car slowed, pulled in to the curb and the driver reached across to push open invitingly the door on the passenger side. Climbing in, Ilse noted that he was young, handsome and neatly dressed. Any apprehension she might have felt from reading the newspaper reports vanished. With this one, there was obviously nothing for a girl to fear.

The man drove fast and silently in the direction of the Devil's Moor. Either he was not given to idle conversation or he did not want to risk being identified later by his voice. Most Germans speak with a regional accent.

He did not show Ilse the knife. It was not necessary. The instant he turned off the main road, she knew who he was and where he was going. And she came within a hair's breadth of fainting from sheer terror for, although older than either Britta or Karin, Ilse was still an intact virgin.

Fear can greatly improve the memory. During that terrible ride, Ilse found that she could remember almost verbatim everything she had read of the Britta Schilling and Karin Franck cases and the detail which impressed her the most was that Karin had co-operated and had escaped with her life.

Ilse did not want to lose her virginity to a sex maniac, but that was certainly preferable to death. Her only hope then was to follow the advice of the police, not to resist, to pretend to enjoy it, even to ask for another date with the rapist. In that manner, a girl could sometimes escape the worst.

But how was she to pretend to enjoy being raped? How could she hide the physical pain or the disgust and resentment she would feel at this horrible, forced intimacy?

Besides, how did a girl act when she was enjoying it? Having had no experience in the matter, Ilse simply did not know, although she seemed to recall vaguely something about moaning. So she would moan. That should not be difficult. She would probably feel like moaning anyway, although not from pleasure.

For the rest, the key principle was 'co-operate' and she clung to it desperately, obediently removing her clothing, but leaving on her stockings and shoes. It did not occur to her that the man might find that erotic. She was merely remembering that Karin Franck had had to walk a long way to the road.

Despite all her determination, she was unable to bring herself to part her thighs to him and he forced them open, entering her urgently, brutally and without lubrication. She screamed as her hymen burst, but the pain did not last long for the unexpected realization that he was deflowering a virgin brought on the man's climax instantly and he jerked, gasped briefly and withdrew.

Moments later, Ilse found herself standing in the middle of the moor in her shoes and stockings with the blood running down the insides of her thighs and the sound of the car motor dying away in the distance. Her entire body was trembling violently and she was crying, but she was no longer afraid. She did not think she was going to be murdered and everything else had already happened to her.

Although it was not yet eight o'clock, in these northern latitudes, it was already dark and the sea wind was beginning to sigh and chatter in the reeds. She had no idea of the direction of the road and, with shaking legs, she began picking her way along on her high heels in the direction of the glow which represented the city lights of Bremen.

It was cold, but not so cold that she would freeze to death. She hurt and she was bleeding, but it was not serious. She was relieved. She had survived it.

In fact, she was still in considerable danger. The moor was treacherous in places and, had she strayed from the track, she could have sunk into soft mud or drowned. She did not know this however, and plodded patiently on until she eventually reached a house where she was let in and the occupants, horrified by her blood-streaked legs, called the emergency ambulance and the police.

Ilse was taken to the hospital in Bremen where it was determined that aside from her ruptured hymen, she had suffered no serious physical injury. Her nervous system was, however, badly shaken and although her parents were notified and rushed to the hospital, she remained there until the following day under sedation.

She was being given her breakfast when Inspector Burger appeared and asked if she was prepared to answer questions. He had been at the hospital the night before, but the doctors had not let him speak to her.

Ilse answered to the best of her ability, but her answers were of little value to the police. The man had been young, handsome, muscular and quick on the trigger. The only words he had said were, 'Take off your clothes'. She had not noticed any dialect which meant that he was probably local.

'Unquestionably the same man,' said Inspector Burger. 'Well, two rapes and one murder so far. It's definitely a series.'

'Two rapes and one murder that we know of,' said Chief Inspector Scharneck. 'We'd probably better run a check on all missing females in the age group for the entire area.'

Considering that the area included Bremen with a population of six hundred thousand and Hamburg with a population of over two million, it was hardly strange that a lot of girls were missing.

The commission spent all of the rest of December 1981 and January 1982 trying to determine whether any of these had met the same fate as Britta Schilling, but with such inconclusive results that, when Heike Schnier disappeared on the afternoon of February 9th, the police doubted that she had fallen victim to the 'Devil's Moor Murderer'.

Her parents were sure of it. Heike was only seventeen, but she was working and on that evening, she had, like Ilse Blumenthaler, missed her bus. No one could be found who had seen her hitchhiking, but there was no other form of transport available and Heike had hitchhiked before.

Nearly as pretty as Ilse Blumenthaler, she was less chaste and had had therefore less reason for the resistance which the police thought made the difference between rape and murder.

There were, however, other reasons for resistance as the investigators soon learned from Heike's parents, friends and colleagues at work.

Heike, it seemed, was a girl with a fanatical belief in the principle of equality between the sexes and she had often said that she would rather die than submit to force. Her parents thought that was what had happened.

Inspectors Scharneck and Burger were most optimistic. A search of the Devil's Moor had uncovered no body and no new incident in the series had been reported for over two months. It was possible that the psychopath had left the area or met with an accident. Automobile traffic in West Germany is dense and even sex maniacs get run over.

Their optimism did not last long. On March 4th eighteen-year-old Herta Schmits, set out to hitchhike home from an evening at a discotheque. She was picked up by a handsome, muscular, well-groomed, young man, taken to the Devil's Moor and raped twice in succession, the second performance not resulting in orgasm.

There followed the now familiar naked trek across the moor to the road where the unfortunate Miss Schmits was picked up by a motorist, described as being in his early forties with brown hair, brown eyes and a thick moustache, who raped her a third time. However, he did drive her home afterwards and because the indignant victim had noted his licence plate number, he was arrested the following day and, nine months later, sentenced to two year's imprisonment. His only comment was that pretty girls standing naked beside the highway could expect nothing more.

He was not, however, the 'Devil's Moor Murderer' and he was therefore of no interest to the commission who, by this time had other problems for, on March 24, the remains of Heike Schnier had been found by a hiker on the Devil's Moor.

Too much time had passed for Dr Kartheiser to determine whether she had been raped or not, but cool weather had preserved the body to some extent and he was able to report that Heike had been stabbed thirty-six times with what was probably the same knife that had killed Britta Schilling.

'The indications,' said the doctor, 'are that when he begins stabbing, he goes into a sort of frenzy. More than half of the wounds would have been fatal. She was nearly disembowelled.'

'She resisted?' said Chief Inspector Scharneck.

'Definitely,' said the doctor. 'She must have fought like a tiger.' Nails broken on both hands, defence cuts on both forearms and hands, heavy bruising of arms and torso. She marked him. No question about it. Unfortunately, any scratches will have healed by now.'

Britta Schilling, Karin Franck, Ilse Blumenthaler, Heike Schnier, Herta Schmits and then, on the evening of May 22, 1982, eighteen-year-old Angela Marks disappeared. She had been on a shopping expedition in Bremen that Saturday and had missed her bus.

'And despite everything, they continue to hitchhike,' said Inspector Burger. 'Talk about Russian roulette!'

'It's the somebody-else-but-not-me philosophy,' said Chief Inspector Scharneck. 'Statistically, they're right, of course. There are thousands of girls hitchhiking in the area and how many has the 'Devil's Moor Murderer' taken? Five. Or six, if you count this one. There are more run over by bicycles.'

This was, perhaps, not literally true, but the fact remained that there had been no discernible reduction in the number of lovely, young hitchhikers. The police warnings had had practically no effect.

Following Angela's disappearance, the Devil's Moor was thoroughly searched, but it was a big place with many pools, swamps and beds of reeds. Nothing was found. The case was tentatively classed homicide and added to the Devil's Moor murder file. If Angela had merely been raped, she would have been home by now.

Elsbet Warnecke got home more quickly than most of the others. The eighteen-year-old student was raped on the Devil's Moor by a handsome, vigorous, taciturn, young man only a mile from her own home. She had been hitchhiking.

Elsbet, who knew all about the police recommendations and was public-spirited, tried to trap the murderer by pretending ecstasy and begging for a repeat performance the following day. The man made no comment and did not appear for the date, a wise decision on his part as the scene of the rendezvous was swarming with plainclothes police.

Elsbet was raped on July 10, 1982 and, nine days later, so was Gerda Oppelmeier.

Gerda was seventeen years old and, like all of the other victims, pretty. She had, of course, been hitchhiking.

'It is incredible,' said Chief Inspector Scharneck, 'that with all the publicity this has received, everything continues as usual. Girls keep on hitchhiking. He keeps on raping and killing them. Not one can describe the car. You would think that rape and murder were a normal part of everyday life.'

'Well, to an extent, they are,' said Inspector Burger. 'However, the series is beginning to attract some attention. People are going out to the Devil's Moor on weekends to view the scenes and I understand that some one is planning organized tours with a guide. The Moor's Murderer is gradually becoming a tourist attraction.'

'That may be our only hope,' said Chief Inspector Scharneck sarcastically. 'He'll get so much publicity that he'll turn himself in so he can write a book.'

Actually, the publicity seemed to have the opposite effect and, following the Oppelmeier rape, there were no further incidents for nearly a year. Or rather, there were no incidents which could definitely be ascribed to the 'Devil's Moor Murderer'. There were, of course, no end of rapes and some murders, but either they were solved or the *modus operandi* was totally different.

Once again, the police began to hope that something terminal had befallen the 'Devil's Moor Murderer', but the commission was not disbanded nor did the investigations cease – which was fortunate for on June 6, 1983 seventeen-year-old Ruth Gruenert was raped and left naked in the Devil's Moor. She had been picked up by a young man driving what she thought was a Japanese car, although all she could say about the colour was that it was dark.

Miss Gruenert had not been sexually inexperienced, but she suffered from a somewhat fragile nervous system and she had read and heard a great deal about the'Devil's Moor Murderer'. She had been utterly convinced that she was going to die and, even after being picked up and brought to the hospital in Bremen, was so hysterical that she required months of psychiatric treatment.

The experience had not been very satisfactory for the murderer either. Miss Gruenert had been in such a state that, although he had penetrated her, for the first time, none of his semen was recovered from the victim's vagina.

'Possibly a bad sign,' commented Dr Kartheiser. 'There is a sort of progression in these perversions of the sex act. He may be requiring an increasingly stronger stimulus to arrive at his climax and this could end in mutilation, torture and all sorts of nasty things.'

It was not a prospect likely to cheer the investigators, but, once again, there was a respite with no further incidents up until December 20 when the remains of Angela Marks were found in the Devil's Moor. These consisted of nothing more than a skeleton and a little hair, but Angela had suffered a broken arm as a child and she had had several dental fillings so that a positive identification was possible. Dr Kartheiser was also able to determine that she had been stabbed for the knife had cut into her ribs in several places and had actually severed one of them. No clothing was found and she was presumed to have been raped.

Six days later, on December 26th, there was another disappearance, but this one did not trouble the officers of the commission for they did not know about it.

With the exception of the 'Devil's Moor Murderer' no one did. The victim was a person who was inclined to disappear anyway.

Twenty-year-old Martina Volkmann was a girl with an unusual hobby. She liked to go on long trips in trucks. As she was pretty, willing and not without talent, she found little difficulty in persuading truck drivers to take her with them.

Martina's parents did not, therefore, usually know even what country their daughter was in.

She had last set out from her home in Bremen-Vahr on the morning of December 26th, saying that she was meeting a truck driver who had promised to take her with him to Sweden. Her parents had the impression that the meeting was to take place in Hamburg and that it might be some very considerable time before they saw their daughter again.

They would never see her again. Martina's body was so savagely mutilated when it was found near the bypass at Tostedt, a small town to the south of Hamburg, that the parents were not permitted to view the corpse and identification was made by means of the fingerprints.

As the body had not been found on the Devil's Moor, but thirty miles to the east, and, as Martina had not only been stabbed a total of fifty-seven times but strangled manually as well, the murder was not referred to the commission, but investigated locally. The local police concluded that Martina had fallen victim to a sex psychopath because, although she had been naked only from the waist down, she had been raped. But they were unable to identify him.

In the meantime, the commission was occupied with other matters. On January 4, 1984, Sigrid Poeltz were raped and left naked on the Devil's Moor. She was seventeen and had been a virgin. She described her attacker as having a military manner and said that his car was dark brown.

A month later, on February 4th, much the same thing happened to twenty-year-old Anneliese Schreiner. She had been hitchhiking home from an evening in a discotheque when she was picked up by an attractive young man who drove her to the Devil's Moor, forced her to strip, raped her and left her naked in below freezing weather.

'It's a miracle that none of them froze to death,' said Inspector Burger. 'That makes eleven now. I wonder when he'll make it an even dozen.'

The inspector did not know about Martina Volkmann. Nor did anyone else. However, Gisela Braun was, on that night of March 8th, not the twelfth victim, but at least the thirteenth, an unlucky number for some, as it later turned out.

Unlike some of the previous victims, Gisela was not a

virgin nor was she skilled in the martial arts of judo, karate, kung-fu or aikido. She was not even a particularly ardent supporter of the principle of sexual equality. What she was was a badly frightened girl who had heard all about the 'Devil's Moor Murderer' and who realized clearly that her life was at stake.

However, in contrast to the other victims who had sought safety in co-operation, Gisela, for no reason that she was later able to offer, decided to stall for time.

'I don't mind doing it with you,' she said, 'but I'm bit worked up. Let me smoke a cigarette first. It always helps me to get in the mood.'

It was a fair offer and the 'Devil's Moor Murderer' accepted, gallantly lighting Gisela's cigarette with his own lighter.

His good manners were not rewarded.

Gisela took a long drag on the cigarette and, as the end glowed red as a ruby in the dark, with a quick movement she pressed it into the man's left eye.

The 'Devil's Moor Murderer' screamed in pain and clutched at his face. Gisela tripped the door handle, sprang out of the car and ran off into the darkness.

At this point, the 'Devil's Moor Murderer' made his first and only mistake. Instead of driving away immediately with the headlights switched off, he turned them on in a vain attempt to locate his tormenter. And, as the headlights went on, so too did the little light over the licence plate at the back. Crouched beneath a clump of bushes, Gisela saw clearly the number and the name of the manufacturer, Datsun.

She had abandoned her purse in the car and she had nothing with which to write, but, picking up a twig, she scratched the number into the dirt beneath the bush. The specialists from the commission found it and photographed it that night.

Gisela had waited until the killer gave up and drove away and had then run all the way to the nearest village where she telephoned the police. As the commission had been maintaining a flying squad round the clock for over two years, the response was instantaneous. The area was cordoned off, teams of officers and dogs went in and two helicopters with floodlights began criss-crossing the moor.

The murderer was, by this time, gone, but it hardly mattered for Gisela had noted the licence plate number of his car and this would be traced.

By nine o'clock the following morning it had been and, an hour later, Inspector Burger took into custody twenty-four-year old Thomas Rath, a sergeant in the West German Army, stationed at Fallingbostel twenty miles to the east of Bremen.

Rath had a badly burned eye, but he had not been blinded. He offered only token resistance to interrogation and eventually confessed to all of the rapes and murders of which he was suspected and the rape and murder of Martina Volkmann for which he was not. He confirmed the police theory that he only killed when the victim resisted and said that his sole motive for the crime was that he liked sex with young girls.

This was regarded as a not entirely satisfactory explanation. Rath really was a very attractive, young man and, sexual morality in West Germany being something short of Victorian, could have had sex with as many young girls as he could stand. Moreover, he was already living with a twenty-two-year-old dental technician who was astounded to learn that her companion was the 'Devil's Moor Murderer' and who told the police that Rath had always seemed sexually completely normal to her.

He did not seem normal to the court and, after listening to testimony from the psychologists who had had Rath under observation during the pre-trial detention, the judges concluded that he was too dangerous ever to be allowed his freedom and sentenced him, on April 26, 1985, to confinement for the remainder of his life in an institution for the criminally insane.

2

BRIGHT NEW MORALITY

In the southwest of France, some fifty miles inland from the Mediterranean, the Tarn river, a modest stream, meanders rather aimlessly about, passing through the Gorges du Tarn and eventually arriving at the town of Albi.

The Gorges du Tarn are famous and often compared to the American Grand Canyon. Albi is less so, but it is a pleasant place to live. Although it numbers less than fifty thousand inhabitants, it is the largest community in the area.

On the morning of Wednesday, June 15, 1983, two men were drinking coffee and smoking black tobacco cigarettes at a pavement café in the centre of the city. Although it was still early, the sun was already blinking down through the leaves of the plane trees and bringing an ochre glow to the ancient façades of the buildings surrounding the small square. The air was cool, almost liquid, heavy with the promise of the midday heat to come.

'I was rather surprised that they got that much,' said one of the men. 'The circumstances – '

He was a young man, not yet thirty, and he was handsome with shining, straight black hair, large slightly tilted, black eyes and a fine, black moustache. This being the south of France, his complexion was olive.

' – were no excuse for cold-blooded murder,' said Inspector Jules Mazurin, completing the sentence differently than Detective Sergeant Pierre Gregoire had intended. 'The court was lenient because they're women.'

Although older and heavier than his assistant, he had much the same colouring and general appearance. However, he was not handsome and he had no moustache.

The trial for the most spectacular murder ever to take place in Albi had ended the day before and the officers, who had investigated it, were discussing the results.

Actually, there had not been a great deal to investigate. The duty desk sergeant in the charge room at police headquarters had received a telephone call at three-fourteen in the afternoon of Friday, November 27, 1981, from a woman who said she had just shot her brother-in-law. The duty sergeant did not know exactly what to make of this. Albi is not a place where many people shoot their brothers-in-law, but there are some crazy or drunk enough to think they have.

The address given by the woman was 19 rue Timbal which was in the centre of town and only a short distance from the police station. The sergeant, therefore, dispatched two of his standby patrolmen to investigate. There was no point in alerting the Department of Criminal Investigations until he had reason to believe that a crime had taken place.

However, after the patrolmen had left, the sergeant had second thoughts and called the ambulance. If someone really had been shot, he might not be dead and he would be held responsible for failing to send medical assistance.

Traffic conditions in the narrow streets of the old town were difficult, so the patrolmen on foot arrived before the ambulance and immediately reported back that there was, indeed, a man lying in a pool of blood in the living room of an apartment on the first floor of the bulding at 19 rue Timbal. They did not know whether he was dead, but he looked it and they had been unable to detect a heartbeat. They had found the door to the apartment standing open, but no one was inside.

The sergeant ordered them to remain at the scene and take into custody anyone who turned up. He then reported to the Department of Criminal Investigations that he had a confirmed shooting and possible homicide in the rue Timbal.

The report had brought out Inspector Mazurin and Sergeant Gregoire who, when there were any homicides to investigate, constituted the Homicide Squad. They had hurried to the scene where they had found the ambulance just leaving. The paramedic who had come with it had examined the victim and had found him dead of what appeared to be gunshot wounds. The ambulance crew had consequently withdrawn, as the body could not be disturbed until it had been seen by the coroner.

Albi coroner Dr Clement Sabatier was immediately summoned, and, having carried out an examination of the corpse, reported that there were three gunshot wounds, one in the chest, one in the back and another in the head. He did not know whether the first two were fatal, but the one in the head was.

While the inspector had been waiting to hear this report, Sergeant Gregoire had been making a cautious survey of the apartment and had located papers identifying the dead man as Jean-François Abram. According to this identification, he had been married, since 1972, to a woman named Liliane Lavis, three years his senior, and was the father of four children, all under the age of eight.

'If he had a wife, then he may have had a sister-in-law,' said the inspector. 'The woman who called said she'd shot her brother-in-law. See what else you can find. We want the sister-in-law's name and address.'

The sergeant continued with his investigations and the inspector went off downstairs to summon the police ambulance so that the body could be taken to the morgue.

'You'll want the autopsy immediately?' said the coroner.

He was a large, hairy man with a bald spot on the top of his head and the rolling, slightly clumsy gait of a bear. Although the coroner of a small community, he had had vast experience in examining corpses because the residents of Albi, as elsewhere in Europe, had greater faith in their driving skill than was warranted.

'I'd like the bullets,' said the inspector. 'The rest doesn't matter. I don't see how there could be anything to help the investigation.'

'Will there be one?' said the doctor, who knew that a woman had called to say she had shot her brother-in-law.

'Has to be officially,' said the inspector. 'There'll be a trial and the court will want to know the circumstances. Shouldn't be too complicated. These are simple working-class people.'

He could not have been more mistaken. Professionally and intellectually, the occupants of the apartment in the building at 19 rue Timbal might be relatively simple, but their relationships and attitudes were complex beyond even the understanding of a criminal investigations officer.

To begin with, it appeared that an improbable number of people had been living in the apartment. Listed with the building registry were Bernard Lavis, sixty-one, Marcel Fournier, fifty, Paulette Fournier, fifty-two, Jean-François Abram, thirty, Liliane Abram-Lavis, thirty-three, Jocelyne Bidon-Lavis, twenty-eight, Alexis Lavis, twenty-four and six children, four of whom were the Abrams' and two surnamed Bidon who were apparently Jocelyne's. This made a total of seven adults and six children living in a four-room apartment.

One of the rooms which was very small had been shared by Jocelyne and her brother Alexis who, it seemed, was an avid pornography fan for he had literally covered the walls from floor to ceiling with obscene pictures. There was only one bed.

Another, slightly larger room had been the nursery where the six children had slept together on mattresses nearly covering the floor.

The rest of the adults had apparently slept wherever there was room to creep in.

None of these people were present when the police arrived, but following the removal of the body, they began slowly drifting in and were promptly taken off to police headquarters for questioning.

All proved to be gratifyingly co-operative, including the murderess Jocelyne Bidon-Lavis, who said, yes, it was she who had telephoned from a café, and handed over a rather expensive, new rifle which she said was the murder weapon. She and Liliane had bought it in the Mamouth department store, a popular chain in France, on Monday with the government's child allowance money. It had cost eight hundred francs, not counting the ammunition.

'But why did you want to kill your brother-in-law?' asked the inspector. 'Was he threatening you?'

'Oh no,' said Jocelyne. 'It was a favour to my sister. She's always been very good to me and, a week ago Thursday, we were talking about Jean-François and Liliane said, "I'm good and sick of Jean-François. One of these days I'm going to plant a knife in him." And I said, "Don't be foolish. You might not kill him. What you need is a rifle." But she said she didn't know how to shoot a rifle so I said, "Well, I'll do it then." '

'Were you not aware that it is against the law to shoot people?' said the bemused inspector.

'Oh I suppose so,' said Jocelyne. 'You can't do anything today without the government sticking its nose in.'

She was an attractive woman, slender, fine-featured and with slightly wavy, blonde hair reaching to well below her shoulders.

Liliane, her sister, looked nothing like her, being stocky, round-faced and wearing her dark brown hair short and tightly curled.

Both women had been raised in an orphanage as had all four of the children of Paulette Fournier, formerly Paulette Lavis. Bernard and Paulette had divorced in 1965 and she had married Fournier in 1978.

It appeared at first that Paulette had been sharing an apartment with both her new and former husband, but, although this had been the case for some time, Bernard was no longer there, having died the preceding year.

According to the police and court records, Bernard had been rather too fond of his children. He had been sentenced to two years in prison in 1959 for raping Liliane who had been eleven at the time. The sentence had been light because Liliane had told the judge that she had not objected and that she had not been a virgin at the time anyway.

Bernard had barely got out of jail when his wife filed charges again, this time for raping Jocelyne who was even younger than Liliane had been, but who offered the same excuse for her father's incestuous actions as had her sister. Bernard, who made no effort to deny the charges, had been sentenced to three years for the second offence, but had only served two before being reunited with his family.

His feelings towards Paulette had, however, undergone a change and the following year they divorced, she confessing before the judge to adultery with an immense number of men whose names, she said, she could not remember. She admitted freely that she had been so engaged since the day of her wedding which, she thought, might account for the fact that there was little family resemblance among her children.

In the meantime, most of the children had got out of the orphanage and Liliane, the oldest, had begun a professional career, during the exercise of which she was on several occasions arrested for soliciting and rolling drunks.

In 1972, she had met Jean-François as a client and they had soon married. Her change in status had had no influence on her way of life, however, and she had since divided her time between the cultivation of alcoholism and the entertainment of male strangers while Jean-François was at work, the sole difference being that she no longer charged for her services.

One of her more recent lovers, twenty-two-year-old Didier Jonquiere, was contacted and confirmed largely what Liliane herself had said concerning her married life.

He had come to 'relieve himself', as he put it, with her in the afternoons and, on one occasion, had been surprised by Jean-François coming home unexpectedly. He had had to flee the apartment naked, but Jean-Paul had thrown him his clothes from the window and had said they would discuss the matter the following day. Didier had avoided him since, although he still came to relieve himself with Liliane. He did not like her very much, he said, but she did not charge and he was unemployed and could not afford anything better.

Jocelyne's family life had been similar. After leaving the orphanage, she had gone to live with an uncle in nearby Toulouse, but had soon run away and had taken up with an older woman who taught her what little she still did not know about sex and put her to work as a prostitute. As she was fifteen years old at the time, she was soon picked up for soliciting and spent a number of years in and out of various detention centres.

In 1977, she had met thirty-one-year-old René Bidon, a corporal in the French Army, had born him a son and had married him, in that order.

Shortly after, the corporal was posted to the French island of Guadeloupe where Jocelyne became a mother for a second time in January of 1978. At the end of the tour of duty, the family returned to France where the marriage broke up because of problems with in-laws.

True to family tradition, Jocelyne had, according to her own admission, rarely failed to entertain a casual lover whenever her husband was out of the house for so much as a quarter of an hour, but she also believed in the feminist double standard and, when she surprised René in bed with Liliane, she divorced him and went home to mother.

Although similar in character and interests, Jocelyne and Paulette did not get on well and in November of 1980, Jocelyne left and went to live with Liliane.

The sisters had always been close and Jocelyne did not hold Liliane's frolics with René against her. It was, as she told the inspector, no more than what she would have done herself under the circumstances. In fact, it was what she had done for she confessed that she and Jean-François had also engaged in intercourse, but, she justified, only occasionally.

She denied indignantly the suggestion that she had been intimate with Alexis, although she admitted that they had shared a bed the sheets of which, the police laboratory reported, were stiff with sexual secretions. The traces of sex, said Jocelyne, came from Liliane and the friends whom she was in the habit of entertaining there during the afternoons.

This part of her statement was corroborated by Liliane and by Didier Jonquierre who said that it was in Jocelyne's and Alexis's bed that he had 'relieved himself' with Liliane's assistance.

Alexis chose not to make a statement on the subject, citing grounds of possible self-incrimination. He had been living in the apartment when Jocelyne moved in with her two children and there had been no other place for her to sleep, he said.

Bernard Lavis, in poor health and with none of his former vigour, was also living in the apartment at the time and being tenderly cared for by his former victims,

Liliane and Jocelyne, who appeared to be sincerely attached to him. Later Paulette and Marcel had moved in as well and Bernard had died happily in the arms of his reunited family, so to speak.

'I don't understand these people,' remarked the perplexed sergeant. 'Sexually depraved, but good-hearted. Mrs Abram never turned a relative away no matter how crowded the place was.'

'Depravity no longer exists,' said the inspector. 'They're merely modern. Sexual promiscuity is all the rage nowadays. I'm surprised that the children weren't involved as well.'

The sergeant threw him a quick look, but the inspector's normally somewhat bland face was expressionless.

'Well, the oldest is only eight,' said the sergeant slowly, 'and . . .'

'Just the right age!' exclaimed the inspector. 'Wasn't Jocelyne eight when she had her little fling with her father?'

'Nine,' said the sergeant dryly. He had grasped that his chief's enthusiasm for the new morality was not entirely sincere.

As a matter of fact, the sexual aspects of the case irritated the inspector as he felt that they tended to draw attention away from the main issue. For him the offence was homicide, deliberate, premeditated homicide, and he was basically concerned with preparing a case which would result in a conviction without extenuating circumstances or diminished responsibility. In this, he was being ably assisted by the accused themselves.

Liliane had repeated independently, almost word for word, what her sister had said concerning their conversation prior to the murder of Jean-François. She had been good and fed up with him. She had said she was going to plant a knife in him one of these days and she had meant it. She had found the rifle a good idea and had gone with Jocelyne to buy it. She would have done the shooting herself, but she had had no experience with guns whereas Jocelyne's husband was in the army so she knew about such things.

'But why did you want to kill your husband?' said the inspector. 'Didn't you want a divorce? I thought you said you were fed up with him.'

'I was,' said Liliane. 'I was glad he filed for divorce. If he hadn't, I would have.'

'So, you were in agreement on the divorce and he was leaving,' said the inspector. 'Why kill him?'

Liliane shrugged her shoulders. She did not know. It had seemed like a good idea at the time. She was annoyed with Jean-François . . .

'What worries me,' the inspector told the sergeant, 'is that they might get off on a plea of mental incompetence. What kind of a motive is that? She was annoyed with him!'

He need not have worried. Liliane and Jocelyne were maintained under psychiatric observation for nearly a year and, at the end of that time, the doctors were in complete agreement. The sisters had known exactly what they were doing. They had known it was illegal. They had acted deliberately, wilfully and they were completely responsible for their actions.

What they had not known was that it was wrong. Citizens of the modern world with no moral standards, no religious ethics, no accepted rules of behaviour, they lacked the basis for a concept of right and wrong. All that counted was doing your own thing. Their thing had been as much sex as flesh and blood could bear, alcohol in numbing quantities and financial dependence on social welfare and petty crime.

The inspector waxed philosophical. 'Actually, all of them are better adjusted to society than you and I,' he told the sergeant. 'They're the vanguard of the future. Another generation and everybody will be like that. Look at Jonquiere, he's a perfect example of twenty-first century man.'

'I don't believe it,' said the sergeant stoutly. 'This will

never happen in France. Other countries, perhaps, but not France.'

'Albi is in France,' said the inspector. 'If it can happen here, it can happen anywhere.'

Whether in earnest or not, he was right. A new type of crime, committed simply because there was no reason not to by people with no standards of behaviour whatsoever, was beginning to appear in Europe. And would undoubtedly spread for, although politicians might live in the fairy-tale world of ideology, criminals were often practical people who had long since grasped that they ran little risk in the commission of their crimes.

Police forces were overworked and understaffed and many criminals remained at liberty. And, even if apprehended, tried and convicted, the criminal still had little to fear. Capital punishment had been abolished and jail sentences were trifling. Even if a jury handed down a heavy sentence, it was never fully served.

The most savage killers were declared not responsible for their acts by reason of their very barbarity and were sent for short stays in psychiatric clinics. The worse the crime, the less the chance of serving any seriously inconvenient sentence for it.

These were facts well-known to the police of larger cities, but this was Albi and the inspector fully expected to see Jocelyne, if not Liliane, sent to prison for life.

What Jocelyne and Liliane expected was hard to say. Neither appeared to suffer from exaggerated feelings of guilt and both had told doctors and police that they enjoyed their way of life and hoped to continue it. Although they realized that they were incriminating themselves and each other, they were amazingly frank in describing the details of the murder.

They had bought the weapon, a thirty-calibre hunting rifle, on Monday and, having loaded it, had put it under the mattress of the bed shared by Liliane and her husband at night and various other persons at other times. The mattress had either been a good one or Jean-

François had been a sound sleeper for he had not noticed the gun.

On the afternoon in question, Liliane and Jean-François had been having one of their nearly permanent arguments and Jocelyne had gone into the bedroom and returned with the rifle.

'He understood at once that it was for him' said Jocelyne in her confession. 'He tore open his shirt and said, "Go on. Shoot! I would as soon be dead anyway. Then, I can visit my father."

'I couldn't shoot him when he was looking at me so I asked him to turn around. He turned around and I shot him once in the back. He fell over slowly sideways and I went up and shot him again in the chest.

'He still wasn't dead and I thought, well, maybe this isn't such a good idea after all. I went to see mother and Alexis and Marcel, but they all said that it was none of their business, I had started it, now I would have to finish it off.

'Liliane said she would like to help, but she didn't know what she could do so I went to the neighbours on the same floor. There was nobody home in one apartment and, in the other one, Mr Poussin said I had best call the police.

'So I went back to the apartment and shot Jean-François in the head. He had been groaning and sort of twisting around on the floor, but then he stopped.

'I went off to call the police and everybody else left too. I guess they didn't want to stay in the apartment with Jean-François.'

The details of the confession were corroborated by Liliane, by Paulette and Marcel, by Alexis and by the neighbour, fifty-two-year-old Gerard Poussin. None of them appeared to find anything remarkable about it.

Stranger yet, Paulette, Marcel and Alexis admitted that they had known of Jocelyne's and Liliane's intention of murdering Jean-François and they insisted that Jean-François had known it too. The inspector found this hard to believe, but they had no reason to lie about it and he was forced to accept that, as Liliane and Jocelyne had once consented to be raped by their father, Jean-François had consented to be murdered by his wife and sister-in-law who was also his mistress.

Whatever the case, it was premeditated murder and the inspector was dismayed when, at the trial on June 13th and 14th of 1983, the prosecuting attorney called only for the modest term of twenty years' imprisonment for both sisters.

Neither offered any defence for having murdered Jean-François and both admitted to having planned the crime in advance. Nor was either sister able to suggest any motive which might constitute an extenuating circumstance.

This unheard-off acceptance of responsibility and absence of excuses so impressed the judges that they came to the conclusion that the defendants could not possibly be in their right minds and handed down sentences of only fifteen years' imprisonment to each one.

The remaining members of the family, who were guilty by their own admission of having foreknowledge of the murder and doing nothing to prevent it, were not charged.

3

A GIRL TO LOSE YOUR HEAD OVER

A city of seven hundred and fifty thousand inhabitants generates a lot of trash. And, where there is a lot of trash, there are scavengers. For the not overly fastidious, there is a living in what others throw away.

Genoa, Italy, is a city of seven hundred and fifty thousand inhabitants and Damiano Moscatti was one of the scavengers who lived from its trash. There was nothing shameful in this. Moscatti, who was approaching forty and had been a scavenger for nearly twenty years, worked hard, possessed a fund of professional knowledge and made a good living. He owned his own modest home. There was money in the bank. His two children were in secondary school and would attend university.

It was, therefore, with a light heart that Damiano Moscatti went trundling off to the main municipal dump in his little, three-wheeled truck on Monday morning, July 25, 1983. Business was good. The weather was beautiful. Even the scenery was a delight.

Not the view of the dump, of course, but the city and the harbour below. Genoa, one of the more important Mediterranean seaports, lies on the vast, blue gulf of the same name. Behind it, the land rises sharply to the mountains of the coastal range through which the Bisagno river rushes downward to the sea. It is an old and moderately honourable city, steeped in the history of two thousand years.

Discreetly located on the outskirts to the north of the

city, the dump, although scenically less attractive, was financially more rewarding. Moscatti parked his truck and went to work.

But not for long. He had barely begun when, kicking aside a cardboard carton which had contained a video recorder, something rolled out and lay staring up at him with an expression of the utmost horror. Moscatti stared back with the same expression. The object was a human head.

Public dumps are one of the more favoured places for disposing of the bodies of murder victims and, in twenty years of professional activity, this was not the first corpse that Moscatti had discovered. It was, however, his first discovery of a disembodied head.

The discovery of dead bodies is something that few become accustomed to and, despite his past experience, Moscatti was shocked, horrified and nauseated. He ran back to his truck and went clattering off down the road in the direction of the nearest public telephone booth. In such cases, the only thing to do was call the police.

There are a lot of police in Genoa. Like any port city, it has its share of crooks and gangsters, its prostitutes and pimps, its psychopaths and sex deviates. The police are needed.

It was, therefore, only a very short time before a patrol car arrived at the telephone booth to find Mascotti waiting and followed his truck up to the dump where he pointed out the head lying amidst the refuse. The patrolmen asked if he had moved it, checked his identification, sent him off about his business and radioed the dispatcher at police headquarters that the report of a human head in the dump as confirmed.

The duty homicide squad for the northeastern sector of city left immediately. Or, at least, the key members of it did. These were Inspector Luciano Panzoni, officer-in-charge, Sergeant of Detectives Silvio Bracco, his assistant, and Dr Andrea Invernati who was a police expert in forensic medicine.

There were, of course, a great many other detectives, specialists and technicians attached to the squad, but they had first to assemble their equipment and the vans which they used were not as fast as the inspector's car.

The advance squad found the officers from the patrol car standing at the edge of the dump, guarding the head. Their orders were not to approach it and they had not. Damiano Moscatti had gone home. He was not feeling very well and he rightly suspected that the police would be less than enthusiastic over his continuing to scavenge while the investigations were going on.

While Dr Invernati examined the head without disturbing its position, the inspector listened to the report by the senior of the patrolmen concerning Moscatti's description of his discovery of the head and his explanation of what he had been doing at the dump.

'You personally saw his identity card?' said the inspector.

The patrolman had not only seen it, he had kept it.

'Get a statement from him when we go back to town, Silvio,' said the inspector. 'And give him back his card.'

The sergeant nodded. He was a stocky, little man with a broad, cat-like face and a scanty, brown moustache across his long upper lip.

'What do you make of it, Andrea?' called the inspector. 'Is it recent?'

'Fairly, I think,' said the doctor. 'I can't tell a great deal because of the flies.'

Although the dump was not used for garbage, there was a certain amount of organic material in the rubbish and there were great swarms of flies. The head was a crawling mass of them, two and three deep.

'Get some plastic out of the car and we'll see if we can cover it over until the photographer arrives,' said the inspector to the sergeant. 'We don't want to move it until we have a record.'

The sergeant fetched a metre-square sheet of plastic

from the car and, with the help of the patrolmen, drove off most of the flies and covered the head.

'Relatively young man,' commented the doctor. 'Looks like a clean cut. Sword or something similar.'

The doctor was a slender, swarthy man with an enormous, drooping, black moustache and gold-rimmed spectacles which looked as if they did not belong on his face.

'A little variety,' said the inspector. 'Nice for it not to be a gun or knife all the time.' He also wore gold-rimmed spectacles, but they went well with his face which was smooth, plump and, generally, expressionless. People who did not know his profession, usually took him for a bank executive.

No one said anything more. They were waiting for the rest of the detail to arrive after which there would be a great deal of hot, dirty, unpleasant work. A part of a body found in a dump means that the entire dump may have to be gone over for the rest of it. Fortunately, it was not the case this time. The body was found less than six feet from the carton which had contained the head. It had been buried rather carelessly under cardboard and general rubbish.

Body and head were photographed in place and the locations marked on a scale map of the area. They were then wrapped in plastic, placed on a stretcher and carried to the police ambulance for transfer to the morgue.

Dr Invernati went with them. The sergeant went off to return Damiano Moscatti his identity card. And the inspector went back to his office. At the scene, a sweating crew of junior detectives and apprentice technicians searched through the rubbish for potential clues, cursing the flies.

The head and body arrived at the morgue at a little after eleven o'clock and, at a quarter to twelve, the doctor telephoned the inspector to suggest they have lunch together as he had a number of things concerning the corpse to report. The inspector was in agreement and they went to a restaurant called Il Melograno which was not far from the station and had a clientele made up almost exclusively of regulars.

'To begin with,' said the doctor, digging into the antipasto, 'the head and the body go together.'

It was the first question that had had to be asked. The fact that body and head had been found near each other in the dump was no proof that they had ever been joined.

'They were separated by a sharp, heavy blade during the early evening of July 23rd,' continued the doctor. 'He was alive at the time.'

'Heavy?' said the inspector, raising his glass to peer into the ruby depths of the Barberesco.

'Would have to be,' said the doctor. 'The head was severed with a single blow.'

'Well, quick, at least,' said the inspector.

'Not at all,' said the doctor. 'The man was tortured horribly with a live electric wire on the most sensitive parts of the body and, particularly, the genitals. He may have been unconscious when he was killed. The agony would cause most people to faint.'

'Good God!' said the inspector, putting down his glass. 'So that's why the corpse was naked. I thought it was to avoid identification.'

'He was bound hand and foot with wire,' continued the doctor, 'probably to a chair. I can't say how long the torture went on, but it must have been some considerable time. He lost control of his bladder and his bowels and there was non-sexual ejaculation resulting from the electric shocks to the testicles.'

'It might have been better to discuss this after lunch,' said the inspector, looking thoughtfully at his plate. 'No identifying marks, I suppose?'

'None,' said the doctor. 'He was a man in his late twenties, handsome, in good health, a garage mechanic . . .'

'The hands,' said the inspector. 'Did you get a lab test?'

The doctor nodded.

'The lab identified automobile grease and oil,' he said. 'Too much for him to have been simply tinkering with his own car. It's ingrained into the skin and under the fingernails.'

'Well, that's helpful,' said the inspector. 'We should be able to identify him. We have the fingerprints and I dare say you can fix up the face well enough for a portrait.'

The doctor could, but the young man was, in fact, identified that afternoon from the police missing persons' files.

He was twenty-eight-year-old Gianfranco Logozzo, owner of a small garage in Sestri Ponente, a suburb seven miles to the west of the city. He had been reported missing by his fiancée, Bettina Commecci, on Sunday morning after he had failed to keep a date with her on Saturday evening.

Miss Commecci came to the police morgue, made an official identification of the corpse, which was covered entirely except for the face, and became hysterical. She was an exceptionally beautiful girl, nineteen years old.

'And rich,' said the sergeant. 'Her father is the Commecci who owns all the hardware stores. Logozzo was a lucky man.'

'He doesn't strike me as lucky,' said the inspector. 'Get some people onto this and let's see what kind of a person he was that somebody would torture him to death. Nothing at the dump, I suppose?'

'Nothing,' said the sergeant. 'They didn't even find his clothes.'

The investigators poured into Sestri Ponente and began asking questions. Within twenty-four hours, they had uncovered not one, but a dozen motives for the murder of Gianfranco Logozzo.

'This bird was the biggest Don Juan in Sestri Ponente and, maybe, all Genoa,' reported the sergeant. 'If half what they say about him is true, he made Casanova look like a monk. Women were scratching each other's eyes out for a date with him. We're getting up a list.'

'Of boyfriends, husbands, brothers,' said the inspector. 'The logical suspects I suppose, but why now? Hasn't he been at this for some time?'

'Since he could walk, I imagine,' said the sergeant, 'but I'll check it out.'

Gianfranco had been at it for some time. Not since he could walk, but for a long time just the same. Curiously, the boyfriends and brothers did not seem to hold it against him and the husbands had had no reason to. Gianfranco had not dated married women.

'Nor seriously engaged ones either,' said the sergeant. 'A remarkably ethical sort of Don Juan.'

'When did he get engaged to Miss Commecci?' said the inspector.

'On June 1st,' said the sergeant.

'Then, I think you may find that there was somebody else who wanted to marry her,' said the inspector.

'She's a lovely girl,' said the sergeant a little dreamily.

'Her father has money,' said the inspector.

His assessment of the situation proved to be correct. Before encountering Gianfranco, Bettina Commecci had been much attached to twenty-six-year-old Luigi Cantarelli, a handsome, young man who had failed his university studies, been kicked out by his parents because of it and was managing to live without working or other visible means of support.

'Miss Commecci was just about his only hope,' said the sergeant. 'He told his creditors they were getting engaged and he would be the director of one of the Commecci stores. Probably would have been too, if Miss Commecci hadn't taken her car in to be fixed.'

'And met Gianfranco,' concluded the inspector. 'All right, we'll concentrate on Cantarelli. There won't be many with a better motive.'

There were none or, at least, none that the investigators could locate. No one else had suffered such a material loss.

'Even so,' said the sergeant, 'I don't think we can completely exclude an emotional motive. It wasn't simply a matter of eliminating Logozzo. He was torturned and that means the murderer hated him personally.'

'I take it you don't think much of Mr Cantarelli as a suspect,' said the inspector.

'I don't,' said the sergeant. 'The man's shiftless and weak. He'd pick your pocket or swindle you, but I don't think he has the guts to torture a man for hours and chop off his head.'

'Then look elsewhere,' said the inspector. 'You may be right. Anyway, we have no case against Cantarelli. The fact that he had a possible motive is no evidence.'

The sergeant began to look elsewhere, not personally, but with the detectives under his command. He did not abandon the Cantarelli lead and a detail continued with attempts to trace his whereabouts at the time of the murder, but the main thrust of the investigation was now directed towards identifying other Gianfranco conquests.

Privately and without mentioning it to the inspector, the sergeant had developed his own theory of the case. As with the inspector's theory, it was based on Logozzo's engagement to Bettina Commecci, but her father, rather than her discarded fiancé, was the suspect.

Commecci was not a man to be trifled with and Bettina was his only daughter. He was not a snob, so he would not have objected to an engagement with a simple mechanic, but he might have taken violent exception to infidelity by his future son-in-law and Gianfranco was a born tomcat. Supposing that he had succumbed to the blandishments of one of the countless women who were throwing themselves at him and Commecci had learned of it?

The sergeant did not think that Commecci had personally tortured and beheaded his prospective son-in-law.

He did not have to. He was rich and the rich can have such unpleasant jobs done for them.

A hired executioner would have been a professional, meaning that he belonged to the underworld and, if so, some one in the network of police informers should know who he was.

To the sergeant's delight, the inquiries produced quick results. Yes, said the informers. Gianfranco Logozzo had been murdered by a member of the Genoa underworld and his name was Urio Boninsegna.

Keeping such information to himself would have been hazardous to the sergeant's career and he immediately reported to the inspector what he had done and what he had found out.

The inspector was pleased. He too did not think Cantarelli much of a suspect. Boninsegna was much better for there was a voluminous file on him in the police records section. Unfortunately, it contained nothing to make him a likely suspect in a torture murder.

Now thirty-seven years old, Boninsegna had had a long and undistinguished career as a smuggler, dealer in stolen goods and, most recently, procurer. He was, it seemed, none too skilled in his chosen line of work and almost invariably ended up getting caught, but, because the offences were on a petty scale, he rarely received a heavy sentence. His last prison term had been for four months and he had been released on June 1, 1983.

'He's passing famous in the underworld,' said the sergeant, 'but not because of his criminal career. On July 17, 1977, he married a local prostitute in a big, formal wedding. The bride was all in white. The bridesmaids were whores and the guests were streetwalkers, pimps, smugglers and petty crooks. Seems to have been a success. They're still married.'

'Small wonder,' said the inspector. 'They sound like a great team. Any ideas as to why Boninsegna did it?'

The sergeant shrugged.

'Money, I suppose,' he said. 'Why else? He's a sort

of journeyman crook. If Commecci offered him a reasonable fee, he'd accept. The problem is how we're to prove it.'

'Put some pressure on his wife,' said the inspector. 'A professional prostitute wouldn't want any trouble with the police. What's her name anyway?'

'Maria Totaro,' said the sergeant, 'but she's professionally known as La Cicciolina. Thirty years old and registered as a prostitute since 1973. Blonde, beautiful, knows what she's doing. Drives a metallic blue Fiat for business purposes and has a small villa at 188 Corso Firenze. Good business woman.'

'La Cicciolina,' said the inspector. 'Little Fatty. Common enough name for a whore. Well, have the Vice Squad pick her up and we'll see what she has to say. Is she fat?'

'Only in the right places,' said the sergeant.

La Cicciolina was picked up and held briefly on soliciting charges. She was not questioned directly about the Gianfranco Logozzo murder, but efforts were made to determine her feelings towards her husband who had now retired from the smuggling business to devote himself to full-time procuring.

The only thing that could be determined was that she was attached to Urio although the police had information that he had beat her like a carpet following his release from prison.

'Which is rather mysterious,' said the sergeant. 'He was sent to prison on a smuggling charge shortly after they met and before they were married. She paid his lawyer and came to see him every visiting day.

'When he got out, she tried to recycle him as a pimp. She'd never had one before. He wouldn't and got himself sent up a couple of other times. This last one was for receiving stolen goods. She always paid for the legal fees, brought him cigarettes and socks while he was in jail and kept her nose to the grindstone.'

'That is mysterious,' said the inspector. 'The man's

downright ungrateful. Where does La Cicciolina go for her car repairs?'

The sergeant gave him a startled look.

'I'll find out,' he said slowly, the significance of the inspector's question beginning to register.

Until cessation of business due to the death of the owner, La Cicciolina had taken her car to Gianfranco Logozzo's garage.

'Very interesting,' said the inspector. 'Bring them both in, interrogate them separately and search the villa.'

Neither La Cicciolina nor her husband were unacquainted with the police or ignorant of their rights under the law. Their only response to the questioning was a demand for legal representation. This was, of course, granted, but in the meantime, a warrant had been obtained and the technicians from the police laboratory were going over the villa at 188 Corso Firenze by the square centimetre.

In most of the rooms they found nothing more than the professional equipment of a working prostitute and housewife, but, in the living room, they recovered traces of blood from the floor, the carpets and, above all, a heavy, wooden chair. Tests showed that the blood was human and of the same blood group as that of the late Gianfranco Logozzo.

There was more. Hidden under the floorboards of a shed behind the house was a heavy machete with a thirty-inch blade. It too bore traces of blood.

'But the strangest thing of all is a sort of doll made out of wax that was on the living room mantelpiece,' said the sergeant. 'It's stuck full of pins.'

'Voodoo, witchcraft,' said the inspector. 'She was trying to kill Logozzo by witchcraft.'

'And, when it didn't work, she used the machete,' said the sergeant.

Actually, she had not and this soon became known when Maria and Urio, confronted with the evidence of their guilt, decided to make a clean breast of the murder.

‘It was my fault,’ said La Cicciolina. ‘I am too sentimental. Urio was in jail and I was lonely. I took my car in to the garage and I saw Gianfranco. He was so beautiful. I said, “Look, I’ll give you credit.” He didn’t say anything and the next time I came, I said, “To hell with the credit! For you, it’s on the house!”

‘He accepted my offer and it was wonderful. I still loved Urio, but Gianfranco was something else. Such feeling! Such technique!

‘Then Urio got out of jail and, of course, some rotten bitch told him about Gianfranco and me.

‘Urio was angry and he beat me up very bad. I didn’t have any excuse for what I had done and so I said I hadn’t wanted to do it, but Gianfranco had bewitched me. Urio believed that and we worked out a scheme to punish Gianfranco for what he’d done to me.

‘I’d given him a lot of presents, jewellery and so on, and I went to see him and said he should bring the presents back to the house. His future father-in-law was rich enough to give him better ones.

‘He agreed because he’d heard that Urio was my husband and that he was out of jail. He said if he’d known I was married, he wouldn’t have touched me.

‘He came to the villa that Saturday evening at around six o’clock and Urio offered him a drink. After the drink, he asked him if he would take a look at the car and, when he bent over the engine, Urio hit him over the head with a club and knocked him out.

‘We took him into the living room, fastened him to a chair and punished him for what he did to me.’

‘All undoubtedly true,’ said the inspector, ‘but the real reason that you tortured and murdered Gianfranco Logozzo was that he had dropped you when he became engaged to Miss Commecci.’

La Cicciolina remained silent.

Her husband corroborated her confession and added further details concerning the murder itself.

Maria, he said, had told him that Gianfranco had

bewitched her so they had to kill him by witchcraft. He had stripped the ends of an electric wire which he had plugged into the mains and wherever Maria had stuck a pin into the rough wax figure of a man, he had touched the wires to Gianfranco's body.

Gianfranco had screamed and pleaded for mercy.

'Why are you doing this to me?' he groaned. 'It's true, I did sleep with Maria, but so have half the men in Sestri Ponente.'

'So why did you do it to him?' said the inspector. 'What he said was true. Your wife is a professional prostitute.'

Boninsegna stared at him blankly.

'I don't know,' he said hoarsely. 'I don't know.'

La Cicciolina knew. She was seriously annoyed over Gianfranco's engagement to Bettina Commecci and would have continued the torture longer. Urio did not have as strong a stomach and, taking pity on the victim, chopped off his head.

The jury may have interpreted this as a kindly gesture for, on June 15, 1984, they sentenced Urio to the modest term of twenty years' imprisonment. La Cicciolina, being of the weaker sex, got off with fifteen.

4

LOVE MATCH

Sometime during the summer of 1978, Alfred Schwaiger fell in love.

It was about time. A large, handsome, powerfully built man with a heavy, drooping, black moustache, he was twenty-seven years old and still not married – which did not mean that he did not know what he was missing. A man with an exaggerated sex drive and the capacity of a prize bull, his experience in the tender passion was roughly equal to that of an eighty-year-old Turkish sultan. In matters of the heart and many other organs, there was nothing that Alfred did not know and little that he had not tried.

The object of his devotion was, however, more than a match for him. Roswitha Treppler, was only four years older than him; but she had packed what would have been for another woman a lifetime of experience into those four years. Roswitha was capable and not infrequently achieved fifty orgasms within a period of less than twenty-four hours.

Not with Alfred, of course. Despite feminist belief in physical equality between the sexes, the man who can equal a woman sexually has not yet been born. Alfred was, no doubt, aware of this sexual discrimination against the male, but he did not know about Roswitha's fifty orgasms.

Therefore, or perhaps, none the less, after a respectable interval of three years' reflection, Alfred and Roswitha were wed on June 10, 1981, in the Church of

Our Lady in Steyr, an Austrian town of some forty thousand population, located at the confluence of the Steyr and Ens rivers seventeen miles to the south of the Danube.

Roswitha, who had been living in a suite in the most expensive hotel in Steyr, now moved into Alfred's modest home at 41 Mozart Strasse. Undoubtedly blinded by love, it did not occur to Alfred to wonder how she had paid the hotel bill. The daily rate roughly equalled his weekly salary and Roswitha was neither working nor rich.

Curiously, although her expenses had actually been reduced, Roswitha took a job in the offices of a metal forming company not long after her her marriage.

The company was not in Steyr, but in Traun, a small community on the edge of the city of Linz, twenty miles to the northwest. Alfred, who was a representative for a textile firm, often dropped her off in front of the building. Sometimes, her colleagues would be waiting and waving to her from the pavement. The company did not seem to have many female employees.

Alfred and Roswitha settled down to a married life less boring than is often the complaint of couples who have been living together for over three years. Although a terrible cook and a worse housekeeper, Roswitha knew how to nurture the magic in a marriage. When Alfred returned home from work, he usually found her stark naked; or in a variety of stimulating costumes; waiting in what could be described as a provocative posture on the bed.

The encounters which followed lasted most of the night and, had Alfred not been able to eat in restaurants and catch a few naps in his car, he would, unquestionably, have died of malnutrition or lack of sleep, if not exhaustion.

The compensations were, however, such that he was more than willing to overlook his bride's inadequacies in housewifely skills.

Alas! The joys of matrimony were to last but a scant four months before one of Alfred's friends, a colleague named Bruno Happert, drew his attention to an advertisement in a Linz newspaper.

The advertisement offered sexual services which was nothing exceptional. Indeed, the entire page was filled with such advertisements. Like many other European countries, Austria has, for some time, been gripped in the hysteria of sexual liberation.

'Bury yourself in the loins of my concupiscence,' read the advertisement in slightly overblown, German poetic style. 'Drown in the waves of my lust. Where? At 10 Quincke Strasse in Traun. Or telephone 07229–2337.'

'And?' said Alfred, handing the newspaper back to Bruno.

'It's not free. It's a whore.

'Do you notice anything about the telephone number?' said Bruno.

Alfred took back the paper and looked at it.

'It's mine,' he said in a mystified voice. 'But I don't live in Traun.'

'You must get some unusual telephone calls,' said Bruno.

Troubled by a bizarre premonition, Alfred drove to Traun and sought out the building at 10 Quincke Strasse. It was a whorehouse.

Alfred had a chat with the owner.

'Yes, indeed,' she said. 'Roswitha Schwaiger is my star girl. Some of the others are prettier and younger, but none of them take the interest in their work that Roswitha does. She is so popular that the clients often line up on the pavement at the other end of the alley to wait for her.'

Alfred walked to the other end of the alley. It opened out in front of the metal forming company where he had so often dropped Roswitha off at her supposed place of work. Where he was standing had stood the small crowds of alleged colleagues, waiting and waving to Roswitha as she got out of the car. It had occurred to him at times that they had an oddly impatient air about them, but he had ascribed it to Roswitha's popularity.

He had not been wrong. Roswitha was exceedingly popular in the whorehouse in Quincke Strasse and in their home in Steyr where she continued her activities in her free time. By her standards, a full-time job in a brothel was barely enough to whet a healthy girl's appetite.

Alfred was upset by these discoveries, but, on reflecting that there was always the possibility of a misunderstanding of some kind, decided to put Roswitha to a test. He enlisted the services of his friend, who had met and knew Roswitha, and asked him to call the telephone number listed in the advertisement.

Bruno called and, with Alfred listening in on an extension, found himself engaged in commercial negotiations with his friend's wife.

Roswitha was cheerful but businesslike. Her basic fee, she said, was five hundred schillings, but there was a discount of ten percent for steady customers which meant, at least, two visits a month. He could come either to the Quincke Strasse address in Traun or to her home in Steyr, whichever was more convenient. She worked only by appointment and she did not make house calls. She suggested a trial service at a low, introductory price.

'My name is Bruno Happert,' said the scandalized friend. 'Do you know who I am?'

'Yes,' said Roswitha, 'but I can't make it any cheaper.'

Alfred went home and beat Roswitha to a howling pulp. This was not, he said, the way he had envisioned married life.

The indignant Roswitha went to the police where she filed charges of assault against Alfred. She was examined by Dr Anton Siebenaler, the elderly, bearded medical officer attached to the Steyr Police Department of Criminal Investigations, who peered at her through his gold-rimmed spectacles and reported that she had a black eye, various contusions and abrasions and that two of her teeth were loose. She was not seriously injured and, to judge from her skinned knuckles, her husband had not had things entirely his own way.

Interviewed by Inspector Josef Huckemeyer, a stocky, thick-waisted man with very little neck and a high complexion, Roswitha explained almost naively the cause of her dispute with Alfred.

'But,' she said, 'he knew that I was highly sexed when he married me and besides, who believes in the old-fashioned bourgeois moral standards any more? This is the 1980s and if a girl can make a little money on the side, the husband should be grateful. I am not the only working wife in Steyr.'

'And probably not the only one working at that particular profession,' sighed the inspector.

Mrs Schwaiger had gone home and he was speaking in the privacy of his office with his assistant, the young, blond, muscular and deceptively alert-looking Detective Sergeant Franz Polter.

'But not with the husband's knowledge, I should think,' said the sergeant. 'This is too small a place. A man would make himself a laughing stock. What action are we taking?'

'We?' said the inspector. 'None. He'll get a notice to appear in the municipal court. The judge will read Dr Siebenaler's report and our transcript of Mrs Schwaiger's statement, ask Schwaiger what he has to say and fine him a few hundred schillings.'

'And that will be the end of it,' said the sergeant.

'Not entirely,' said the inspector dryly. 'Sooner or later, he'll probably kill her.'

'Wouldn't divorce be more logical?' said the sergeant.

'Relationships like that aren't logical,' said the inspector. 'They're emotional. If he was logical, he'd have divorced her already. Instead, he beat her up and they're probably making love at this minute.'

However, the inspector was wrong. The relationship

between Roswitha and Alfred Schwaiger was not as simple as he imagined.

To begin with, Roswitha did not mind being beaten up as much as some others might. She was masochistically inclined and she liked her lovemaking rough. This tendency dovetailed marvellously well with Alfred's tastes for he was inclined to moderate sadism. Although not the type of psychopath to pour molten lead into the natural orifices of his beloved, he did enjoy slapping her around a bit.

And Alfred was not as much of an old fogey as Roswitha maintained. He did not exactly approve of his wife working in a whorehouse, but he was prepared to put up with it. Roswitha was his dream girl and he was not going to give her up simply because a few dozen other men were making use of her body.

Moreover, his feelings were reciprocated. Roswitha had known at least a thousand men, socially and in the biblical sense of the word, but never before had she been tempted to enter into matrimony with any of them. At the age of thirty-five, she was marrying for the first time.

In other respects, the inspector was right. The Schwaigers would eventually end up as a homicide case and he would have to deal with it, although the amount of investigation would be negligible.

It would be during the course of this investigation that the name of Peter Berger would turn up.

Peter was only twenty-three and remarkably handsome so that he could have had all the sexual entertainment he could stand for nothing. However, for no reason that he or anyone else could explain, he preferred to patronize the whorehouse in Quincke Strasse. In so doing, he quickly came into contact with Roswitha Schwaiger who, although married and presumably in love with her husband, fell madly in love with Peter too.

The result was a considerable saving for Peter as Roswitha, never rigidly commercial in her dealings, charged him only the percentage paid to the house and asked nothing for herself. She also babied him, showered him with presents and wrote him long, passionate love letters in the same florid style which she used for her advertisements.

Overlooking the fact that she was already married, she proposed that they marry and flee the country. She was, she said, capable of supporting him in style anywhere there were men with money.

Peter was not willing. He pointed out that, while he greatly admired Roswitha and was enormously impressed by her skill and enthusiasm, there was a considerable difference in their ages and that it was illegal under Austrian law to be married to two men at the same time. He was, however, very polite and expressed, guardedly, undying love. Peter did not want to lose his discount in Quincke Strasse and Roswitha was the most talented practitioner of the sexual arts whom he had ever encountered.

Later, there would be reason to believe that Roswitha had not been entirely sincere in her dealings with Peter. She admired his physical beauty and she enjoyed sex with him, but, had he accepted, she would, probably, not have run off with him.

Roswitha was, like many whores, sentimental and Peter represented her ideal, more a symbol than a real person.

Alfred was a real person and, as she continued to engage in sexual intercourse with regiments of paying and free-complimentary admirers, he continued to beat her like some one else's Oriental carpet.

In the four-month period from November of 1981 to February of 1982, Roswitha appeared no less than seven times at the Steyr police station to swear out charges of assault against her husband, but, by the time of the final complaint, not even the first one had come before the court.

As it turned out, none of them ever would. For a fatal change had taken place in the strange character of

Roswitha Schwaiger. She had ceased to be a masochist and had become a sadist. And a far more cruel sadist than Alfred who was now to learn what real suffering was.

Although not academically qualified, Roswitha knew more things about male psychology than Freud ever dreamed and she set out to torture her husband in the precise manner that would hurt him the most. This man for whom the greatest pleasure in life was sex, she would render impotent.

The paradise of returning home from work became hell.

It was not that Roswitha was no longer waiting for him on the bed, naked and heavy with the ecstasy of her afternoon's lovers, but that she was still eager, lusting and joyously receptive. She was. Always.

But, when he tore off his clothes and flung himself upon her, she rejected him, fought, bit, scratched and, if he overpowered her by sheer force, lay motionless and unresponsive as a wooden doll.

Later, she would tell him stories of her countless lovers and clients who were so much more skilled in the art of love, so inexhaustably virile, so monstrously endowed. Much of what she said was not true and Alfred knew that it was not true, but the psychological effect remained the same.

It was not long before Roswitha had no need to fight off Alfred's advances. He was no more capable of sex with her than with a warthog. And with no other woman either. Roswitha had deliberately turned Alfred into a sexual cripple.

Impotence often gives rise to sadism. The sufferer, desperately seeking relief from the torment of sexual pressure, turns to more intense forms of stimulation.

Alfred's treatment of his wife became increasingly violent, eventually reaching a point where she feared for her life.

As for Alfred, he undoubtedly feared for his reason.

What had begun as a happy, unconventional, marriage had degenerated into the blackest horror of which the human mind could conceive.

And yet, neither of the mutually tortured and torturing emotional Siamese twins was able to seize upon the obvious means of deliverance – separation and divorce.

'They love each other and they hate each other,' said Inspector Huckemeyer to the sergeant following Roswitha's seventh appearance at police headquarters.

He and the sergeant had gone to have a talk with Alfred Schwaiger and the inspector had bluntly suggested divorce.

'You and your wife are killing each other,' he said. 'This is no marriage. You should separate before something worse happens.'

Alfred had told him curtly to mind his own business. He would answer to the charges before the court, but it was not up to the police to provide him with marriage guidance counselling.

'And there's nothing we can do about it?' said the sergeant in dismay. 'We just have to wait until he kills her?'

'I'm afraid so,' said the inspector. 'You can't arrest people for what you think they might do. Anyway, I may be wrong. There are couples who go on like this until their golden wedding anniversary.'

The sergeant thought it highly unlikely in this case and it saddened him. He had come to take a personal interest in the affairs of the Schwaigers. Police work in a community the size of Steyr is dull. The Sex Athletes, as the Schwaigers were unofficially known to the police, were the only interesting case to come along in years.

The climax came on the night of February 6, 1982, a Saturday, and neither the inspector nor the sergeant was on duty at the time.

It had been a black winter's day, cold, overcast and with a savage wind sweeping down from the high alps to the south. The winter solstice was barely six weeks past and darkness had fallen at five o'clock. At seven o'clock, it began to snow, not soft, white flakes drifting gently downwards, but hard, gritty kernels driving like birdshot before the wind to rattle against the window panes.

'Meet me in Mozart Strasse,' said the inspector's voice from the telephone. 'It's finally happened.'

It was not necessary to say what number in Mozart Strasse; nor what had happened. The sergeant knew.

When they arrived at the house, two patrol cars and Dr Siebenaler were already there. He had not been on duty either, but his house was only two blocks away and he had been the first to be alerted.

Two of the patrol car officers were in the front hall of the house and they reported that the doctor was in the bedroom examining the corpse. They had been the first at the scene, but it had obviously been too late even when they arrived and the ambulance had not been summoned.

The inspector and the sergeant went silently into the bedroom where the doctor was bending over the naked body on the bed. There was a fantastic amount of blood. The sheets appeared to be covered with it entirely and there was more on the floor and splashed on to the walls. It was fresh, red and glistening so that the impression was that of being in a slaughterhouse in full operation.

'Three stab wounds,' said the doctor, straightening up as the inspector and the sergeant entered the room. 'All through the heart, I think. Butcher's knife apparently, but I don't want to remove it until we get the body to the morgue.'

The inspector bent over to look at the wooden handle of the knife sticking stiffly up from the left side of the chest.

'Rammed in to the hilt,' he remarked. 'Well, all right; let's get on with it.'

He left the bedroom and, followed by the sergeant,

entered the living room where Roswitha Schwaiger was sitting on the sofa between the two patrolmen from the second car. She was totally naked and smeared with blood and she looked devastated, but she was not crying.

'Get her a dressing gown or something, Franz,' said the inspector. 'Are you prepared to make a statement, Mrs Schwaiger?'

Roswitha shrugged her shoulders.

'What can I say?' she muttered in a small voice. 'I killed him. Is that what you want?'

'Among other things,' said the inspector. 'I must caution you on your right to remain silent. You do not have to answer my questions, but, if you do, anything you say will be taken down and may be used against you. You are entitled to legal counsel if you wish it. Are you still prepared to make a statement?'

Roswitha shrugged again.

'It makes no difference,' she said tonelessly. 'Alfred is finished. I am finished. Everything is finished. Ask me whatever you want to.'

'What happened exactly, Mrs Schwaiger?' said the inspector, taking the little tape recorder out of his pocket and setting it on the table. 'Please speak into the tape recorder and begin by identifying yourself and stating the time and date.'

Roswitha complied. 'I am Roswitha Schwaiger, born Treppler, resident at Mozart Strasse, Steyr,' she said. 'It is nine-thirty in the evening of February 6th; 1982.

'Approximately an hour ago, I killed my husband, Alfred Schwaiger, by stabbing him three times in the chest with a butcher's knife. He was asleep at the time.

'The stabbings took place over a period of fifteen or twenty minutes as he did not die immediately, but kept rolling around on the bed and crying, 'Why are you stabbing me?' I did not answer him. When he stopped moving, I called the police.'

'Did you fetch the knife from the kitchen while your husband was asleep?' asked the inspector.

'No,' said Roswitha, standing up so that the sergeant could drape the dressing gown he had brought from the bedroom around her shoulders. 'I have been taking it to bed with me every night for three weeks now. Sometimes I put it under the pillow. Sometimes I kept it under my left arm pit.'

'But, if your husband was asleep, then you were not quarrelling,' said the inspector. 'Why did you kill him? Had you been fighting?'

'No more than any other time,' said Roswitha. 'I just thought, well, I will kill him now and that will be the end of it. So I did.'

'The knife is from your kitchen?' said the inspector.

'No,' said Roswitha. 'I bought it to kill him with.'

'Take her to headquarters and tell the desk that the charge will be homicide with premeditation,' said the inspector.

The following Monday, Roswitha Schwaiger was formally indicted for the murder of her husband and ordered bound over for trial.

The autopsy had, by then, been completed and the results confirmed what Roswitha had said. Although stabbed three times directly through the heart with the six-inch, single-edged butcher's knife, Alfred Schwaiger had taken nearly twenty minutes to die.

Roswitha Schwaiger never retracted or altered in any way her confession to the murder; nor was she ever able to offer any explanation as to why she had committed it in cold blood and not during one of the many violent quarrels with her husband.

On November 10, 1982, she was brought to trial, pleaded guilty as charged and, on November 12th, was sentenced to twenty years' imprisonment, having been accorded some extenuating circumstances because of the unusual nature of her marriage and the fact that her husband had beaten her.

She accepted the sentence apathetically, commenting

only that she would be too old to practise her profession when she got out of prison.

In the meantime, she sits in her cell writing interminable, poetic love letters to Peter Berger, who never replies.

5

THE JOLLY JUNKMEN OF DIJON

Christine Loubert sat in the house trailer and wept. It was the morning of Friday, May 15, 1981 and Alain was gone. It had been midnight of the preceding night before she had finally accepted that he was not coming back.

'Going out for a pack of cigarettes,' he had said. 'Be back in a minute.'

But that had been at nine o'clock in the evening. She had thought, at first, that he had run into an acquaintance and had gone for a drink, but, by midnight, even that hope had evaporated.

Alain had left her. She was alone.

Her situation could not have been worse. She had no money at all. There was almost nothing to eat in the trailer. The anaemia sapping her strength had left her too sick and weak to work and, in any case, what kind of work could a thirty-five-year-old woman with no particular training expect to find in France in 1981?

Had it not been for the economic depression and massive unemployment throughout Europe, she and Alain would never have been in such a position to begin with.

It had started off so well too. A real-life story of a maiden in distress rescued by the knight in white armour. Of course, physically, Alain Villemers was not much like a knight. He was three years younger than herself and he was only slightly bigger, but he was gentle and tender and hard-working, everything that her husband had not been.

Above all, he had not been an alcoholic. Her husband had been and, when he returned home drunk, which was nearly every night, he had beaten her, raped her and maltreated her to the point where she thought he would kill her.

That had been in the Grand Duchy of Luxembourg, only a little more than a hundred miles north of Dijon where she was now stranded.

She had finally found the courage to leave him and was sitting in a café, sipping a soft drink and wondering what she should now do with her life when Alain came to her table and asked politely if he might sit down.

He was, it turned out, a pipe-fitter on construction projects, a very desirable profession, although it required him to move continually from one construction site to another.

At that time, in January of 1976, finding new construction jobs had been no problem. Alain was working at a site in the south of Luxembourg, but he already had his next job lined up at Strasbourg in the French Alsace less than sixty miles away.

When Alain left Luxembourg, Christine went with him. They were not, of course, living in any cramped house trailer then, but in near-luxury apartments. Alain's job paid very well.

From Strasbourg, they had gone to Rouen in the west of France and then south to Fos-sur-Mer, on the Mediterranean, near the city of Marseille.

There, the good life had come to an end. When the job at Fos-sur-Mer began to draw to a close in December of 1980, Alain set out confidently to find another and discovered that there were none. Socialist mismanagement had devastated the economy and no one was building anything.

Fortunately, he and Christine had savings and they decided to invest them in a car and a house trailer.

'Then,' said Alain, 'we can go to a job anywhere

without paying for transport or rent. Sooner or later, somewhere, construction work is going to start again.'

The savings had been enough to cover a reasonably comfortable, if small, trailer, but only a second-hard car. It was the failure of this machine that would destroy their plans, end their love affair and subject Christine to greater suffering that she could have ever imagined.

No one suspected that at the time, however, and there was great rejoicing when, at the end of January, Alain returned to the trailer with the fantastic news that he had been offered a job in Liège at the magnificent salary of ten thousand Belgian francs a month.

Ten thousand Belgian francs was, at this time, the approximate equivalent of a thousand pounds and the job was big enough to last for a long time. All that was needed was to get there. From Fos-sur-Mer on the Mediterranean to Liège in the north of Belgium is close to seven hundred miles. Could the car make it?

It was the car or nothing. The savings had all gone on it and the trailer. There was barely enough left for petrol and food until the first pay cheque.

They set bravely off on February 4, 1981 and, sixty miles from Fos-sur-Mer, near the town of Avignon, the car broke down. The garage said that it could be repaired, but not for as little money as they still had.

Alain sold it for junk and was hunting around for work of any kind so that they could buy another when he ran into a persuasive, young man named Simon Grunthal who owned a car and who was prepared, out of the goodness of his heart, he said, to tow the house trailer up to Liège. Alain could refund him his expenses when he got his first pay cheque.

Now, neither Alain nor Christine was exactly naive. No one who has worked on construction sites for close to twenty years retains a childlike innocence. Neither cared very much for Grunthal's appearance or manner. He looked, in fact, very much like a hippie as he wore a long and dirty beard, had a gold ring in his left ear and dressed in a decidedly eccentric fashion.

On the other hand, there was no real alternative. What work Alain had been able to find brought in so little that the job in Liège would be over before they could save up enough to buy another car.

On February 8, 1981 they set off in Grunthal's car, pulling the trailer behind them. It was a good car, not beautiful or even clean, but mechanically robust. By the evening of February 10th, it had pulled the trailer all the way to Dijon where they parked in a trailer camp called The Nomades and went to bed.

When Alain and Christine woke up the following morning, Simon Grunthal was gone and so was everything they owned which had the slightest value. With an astonishing display of deft stealth, he had cleaned out the trailer even while they were sleeping in it.

Alain and Christine, who had been accustomed to a rather luxurious way of life, now found themselves without a penny, without transport and with nothing saleable. Moreover, Dijon, a city of some one hundred and sixty thousand people, was not the most promising place in the world to look for work.

The sole bright spot in the picture was that the rent for the space at The Nomades trailer park was extremely cheap. There was a reason for this. Located well outside the city limits in a vast prairie of weeds, junk and rubble, the trailer camp was nearly filled with the rusting carcasses of junked cars and the only other trailers were occupied by junkmen and scavengers.

Desperate for enough money even to feed themselves, Alain struck up an acquaintance with the junkmen and was able to earn a pittance cutting up old cars. From his position as a highly paid construction specialist, he had sunk to the lowest, most miserably paid work in France.

Such conditions place a strain even on the most harmonious of associations and the magic began to go out of Alain's and Christine's common-law marriage.

Christine became ill. She had suffered from anaemia in the past and it now returned, leaving her weak, tired and apathetic.

And to add to all of their other misfortunes, the spring of 1981 arrived late, cold and wet in Dijon. For days on end, the rain poured down, turning the raw dirt of the camp into a morass of deep, sticky mud in which shoes were lost and the pale, sickly children of the junkmen became trapped like flies.

Peering through the curtain of rain streaming down the pane of the trailer window at the sea of mud, the rusting cars and the heaps of rotting refuse on that morning of May 15, 1981, poor, sick, tired, lonely and despairing Christine Loubert thought that she was in hell.

She did not know how good she had it.

Christine was not peering through the window to admire the view. Someone had knocked on it and she now saw through the wet pane the slightly distorted features of thirty-three-year-old Georges Stephan, one of the junkmen for whom Alain had sometimes worked.

'Tell Alain to come out,' yelled Georges. 'We need him to help get a motor out.'

Christine opened the door of the trailer.

'He's not here,' she said. 'He's gone.'

'When's he coming back?' said Georges.

'Never, I guess,' said Christine sadly. 'He left yesterday evening.'

'You mean he's run off and left a nice girl like you?' said Georges. 'You'll have to go to your friends.'

'I haven't any friends,' said Christine despondently. 'And I haven't any money. And I haven't anywhere to go. I don't know what's going to become of me.'

'Nothing,' said Georges firmly. 'You're not without friends. We'll take care of you here, you can bet on that. Here, what you need is a glass of hot mulled wine. Come out to the edge of the road and I'll pick you up there in ten minutes. Don't be afraid. We'll all come.'

Christine was not afraid. She knew Georges and she knew he was married with at least four children and probably more. Nearly all the junkmen were married, although, perhaps, not officially. It did, however, occur to her as somewhat off that Georges had asked her to walk through the mud out to the road. He could as well have picked her up at the trailer.

In her present state of mind, however, she was not going to argue. She would have accepted an offer of friendship from the devil. Little did she realize that she had.

She had barely arrived at the road four hundred yards away when a rusty wreck of a Citroen pick-up truck drew up beside her. Georges was in it and so was his brother, François who was twenty-three, but also married.

Crammed into the little cab were two other men, Sylvain Hallais, the driver, who was thirty-one, and Eugene Satory, thirty-five. Christine had seen them before and knew that they were junkmen although she did not know their names.

It seemed impossible to squeeze yet another person into the little truck, but Christine was very thin and was threaded through the open spaces, so to speak.

The truck set off for the outskirts of Dijon with the junkmen in high spirits and singing. Christine was less exuberant. Her contact with the junkmen, who were not given to unnecessary washing, was rather more intimate than she might have wished. All of them were wearing wet working clothes and the atmosphere within the cab was similar to that of a small and greatly overcrowded goat shed.

Fortunately, the ride was not long and they were soon safely ensconced in a dirty, little bar which looked exactly the sort of place that junkmen would patronize, but where, oddly, they did not appear to be known.

Enormously relieved and comforted to find herself unexpectedly surrounded by friends, Christine reflected that white knights always seemed to turn up when she was most in need of them and overlooked the dirty, brutal, unshaven faces becoming ever more flushed with alcohol. By the time that she had had two glasses of hot, spiced wine, she even found that the junkmen did not smell all that bad. Perhaps, she should have remembered her husband, whose face had often looked very much like these, but, in her weakened physical condition, the hot wine went quickly to her head and she lost track of the proceedings.

Later, she would recall more hot wine, another ride in the truck and, finally, the smooth, hard boards of a narrow bench on which she fell gratefully asleep.

She awoke with a shriek of pain. Something thick, hard and hot was stabbing into her very vitals. Opening her eyes, she saw that a total stranger was lying on top of her and realized, with horror, that she was being raped.

Confused and terrified, she tried to resist and found that she could hardly move at all. Hands were holding her in an iron grip and, as she raised her head, she saw that it was the Stephan brothers holding her arms and the driver of the truck holding her left ankle. Someone was holding the right one too, but the man lying on top of her blocked her view so that she could not see who it was.

Christine began to scream and a heavy hand slapped her twice across the face with such force that her tongue and lips were cut on her teeth and the blood began to run from the corners of her mouth.

Christine stopped screaming and forced herself to relax. She had been raped often enough during her married life by a drunken brute to know that resistance only stimulated greater sadism.

The whole thing had been planned, she now realized. Georges had told her to come out to the road because he did not want witnesses to see her getting into the truck. They had taken her to a bar where there were not known so that they could not later be identified. They had deliberately made her so drunk that now she did not know even where she was. She was completely at their mercy.

The man grunted to his climax and rolled off her body and she saw that she was being held, naked and spread-eagled on a mattress in a small room with wooden plank walls, exposed rafters and bare roof boards.

She recognized the man holding her right ankle as Joseph Satory, although she still did not know his name, and he now turned the ankle over to the man who had just raped her and took his place.

There was less pain this time. Her muscles were relaxed and the semen from the first rape provided lubrication. She was, however, so nauseated, so sickened by the smell and the contact of the drunken monsters who were taking their lewd pleasure from her body against her will that she vomited up the wine.

The stomach acids bit savagely at the cuts in her lips and tongue and a mixture of wine and blood clogged her nose and throat. For a long moment, she could not breathe and she thought she would choke. Then, the body's automatic defence mechanism reacted with a fit of coughing that expelled the obstruction and the air rushed back into her lungs.

She was not going to die; at least, not immediately. With the clarity that comes to those in mortal danger, she understood that her torturers would not let her die because that would end the entertainment.

And they wanted the entertainment to last. They were five, strong, young, healthy men. From one-thirty that afternoon when Christine was brought to the shack until nine that evening when the junkmen went home for dinner, she was raped some twelve or fourteen times, a rough estimate as no one had actually kept count. Least of all, Christine who, after the sixth or seventh sexual assault, was only barely conscious. When she could think at all, it was only to reflect that she was as good as dead.

After what the men had done to her, it was impossible that they would let her live.

The Stephans, Satory and Hallais went off at nine o'clock to have dinner with their families, leaving her with the forty-six-year-old owner of the shack, François Schatz.

The shack was located near locks on the Canal de Bourgogne outside Dijon and, Schatz being the host, it was he who had been accorded the honour of the first rape.

He was an immensely strong man, but he was not overly ambitious. Rather than go to the trouble of tying Christine up for the night, he gave her as violent a beating as he judged necessary to leave her too weak to run away. His judgement was good. Two of Christine's ribs were broken and she had suffered such severe bruising of the pelvic region that she could barely stand.

By morning, she was suffering badly from the broken ribs, the blackened eyes, the flattened nose, the cuts lips and the bruises which covered her entire body, but the injuries to her pelvis had become less painful and she could stand and even walk.

This was fortunate for Schatz who, grumbling that there was no bread in the house, thrust some money into her hands and told her to go buy some. If she was not back in ten minutes, he would come after her and kill her.

Christine, who did not doubt his word for a minute, struggled into her clothes, left the shack and hobbled across a field to where she could see a small store. She was in a state of shock and, although there were people in the store to whom she could have appealed for help, she simply bought the bread and returned to the shack.

Her appearance had, of course, been noticed, but the district was one in which the sight of a badly beaten and, presumably, drunken woman was not unusual.

Back at the shack, the guests were arriving. All of the previous day's merrymakers were present and they had brought with them three young comrades – Joseph Satory's brother Eugene who was twenty-one, a third Stephan brother, Joseph who was twenty, and Leon Jacquin who was only sixteen, but physically mature enough to join in the festivities.

The party began in typical French fashion with a meal, preceded, accompanied and followed by wine and, if the food was not grand cuisine and the wine not of the finest vintage, there was a great deal of both.

The meal was prepared and served by Christine who, out of fear that she might dirty her clothes in doing the cooking, had been urged to remove them. She was also urged to partake, particularly of the wine as it was thought that this might result in a little more co-operation during the latter part of the entertainment.

Christine, who believed herself within hours of death, neither ate nor drank. She knew what was coming and she did not want to choke on her own vomit. Being beaten to death was preferable.

It appeared that her preference was to be granted for the beating began immediately after dessert. Without even waiting for coffee, Schatz seized her, hammered her half unconscious with his fists, threw her on the table and raped her to the cheers and laughter of the other diners.

Such a demonstration has a stimulating effect on people who have drunk a great deal of wine and the other seven immediately followed Schatz's example.

By the time they had finished, Schatz was ready again and the process continued until nine in the evening when the guests went home for dinner with their families. They left in high spirits, promising to meet again the following day and bring any friends they might run into.

Poor Christine – naked, aching, dripping with semen and blood – did not even hear them. Her sufferings had reduced her to the level of a cornered animal, but it was precisely this that would prove to be her salvation.

Humans have not come to dominate the world because

they give up easily. Stripped of the veneer of civilization, they are as cunning as foxes, filled with a burning will to survive and the most dangerous life form that the planet has ever produced.

Christine Loubert was too hurt and sick to be dangerous, but she was cunning and she was filled with an insane lust for revenge. She was determined to live if for no other reason than to see the junkmen punished for what they had done to her.

Schatz, somewhat exhausted by his efforts and, perhaps, confident that his guest no longer had the strength to flee, had neither tied her up nor beaten her helpless. Possibly, he had been reassured by her obedient return after buying the bread. In any case, he paid no attention to Christine and went matter-of-factly to bed.

Crouched in a corner and wary as an animal, Christine waited until nearly midnight and, when Schatz's snores finally began to fill the shack, slipped quietly out the door, struggled painfully through a barbed wire fence and stumbled off across the fields. She was nearly naked. Schatz had thrown her slacks and blouse on the bed and was sleeping on top of them. But she was not concerned with modesty. All that mattered was escape.

In the distance, she could see the flashing lights of one of the village fairs which travel around Europe from early spring to late autumn and she ran limping towards them. The rain had finally stopped and there would be people at the fair who could help her.

But would they? She should have realized that they would not.

Christine was a mess. Both her eyes were blackened and her entire face was turning green and blue with bruises. Her mouth was swollen and cut. Her hair was sticky with filth. She was dressed in only a few torn and dirty rags and she had no shoes. She also stank beyond belief.

Women who allow themselves to get into such a condition in France, and sadly there are not a few, are generally avoided by the more fortunate and the fair-goers turned away from Christine, ignoring her appeals for help and not even answering when she asked for directions to the nearest police station.

The impression that she made was not improved by the fact that she was gibbering with fear so that she sounded as if she were drunk. She was terrified that Schatz might awake at any moment and come across the fields after her. For all the help that she had received so far, she did not doubt that he could beat her within an inch of her life and drag her back to the shack without anyone raising a finger.

She was on the point of leaving the fair and crawling off into the protecting darkness when she felt a hand fall on her shoulder. Christine gave an involuntary shriek of terror, but the owner of the hand was not one of the junkmen but a pretty, seventeen-year-old girl who was, inexplicably, at the fair alone.

Beatrice Cabonnet was not a militant of the women's liberated movement, but she was soft-hearted and she had been moved by Christine's appearance and obvious distress. For a few moments, she could not believe what Christine was stammering out. France was a civilized country. Such things did not happen in France.

But the proof of Christine's story was all too clearly visible on her face and body.

'Come,' said the appalled Beatrice. 'We'll find a policeman.'

They found two. Most fairs have a team of patrolmen assigned to them as the fair-goers have a tendency to get into fist fights.

The officers had nearly as much difficulty in believing Christine as had Beatrice, but they were finally convinced and followed her to the shack where they took François Schatz into custody.

That same night, a detachment from the Dijon Police Department of Criminal Investigations came out and went over the shack thoroughly, finding ample confirmation of Christine's statements.

The three Stephan brothers were arrested the following morning and, by Tuesday, all eight rapists were in the detention cells and blaming each other.

Although all claimed that Christine had been consenting, the medical evidence was against them and they were eventually persuaded to confess with the result that, on April 9, 1982, the three Stephans, the two Satorys, Hallais and Schatz were sentenced to fourteen years' imprisonment each. Leon Jacquin, who was legally a minor, was sentenced to ten years' juvenile detention.

In the meantime, Christine had been fed, washed, clothed and provided with medical treatment by the Dijon Department of Social Welfare and had returned to the trailer. Removing the tablecloth to shake out the crumbs from her first meal, she found a note under it which Alain had left before his departure. It read simply, 'I've got to get out of this for a while and clear my head. I'm going to mother's place in the Dordogne. If you still love me, follow.'

Christine had neither the money nor the strength to follow, but the social welfare officer arranged for her to telephone and, when Alain heard what had happened, he rushed back to Dijon, filled with guilt for having left Christine alone.

Christine and Alain are now at an undisclosed construction site somewhere in France or perhaps, Belgium, and are more united than ever.

The trailer still sits, sinking slowly into the the mud of The Nomades trailer park, surrounded by the rusty wrecks of junked automobiles. There are no other trailers there now as the junkmen who owned them are all in jail and their families have gone elsewhere. It continues to rain a great deal.

6

DUAL PURPOSE BABY-SITTER

November 23rd, 1986 was a Sunday and, although the weather was overcast, chilly and threatening rain, thirty-two-year-old Marten Schey decided to go fishing. He would have to return to his job as a carpenter's helper the following day and, by the next weekend, the weather could well be worse.

Schey worked in Brussels, the Belgian capital, but he lived in Willebroeck, a town of some twenty-five thousand inhabitants almost exactly halfway between Brussels to the south and Antwerp to the north. The distance to one or the other was a matter of fifteen miles.

Western Belgium is relatively low-lying and there are many canals. One of these runs through Willebroeck and it was in this canal that Schey proposed to fish.

He set off for a place on the canal called the Verbrande Brug, a name meaning the Burned Bridge, and, by nine o'clock, was preparing to cast his line into the distressingly murky waters. However, there was to be no fishing that day for, at that moment, the body of a large, well-dressed man came floating down the canal on its back.

It was barely awash with limbs and head submerged beneath the water and only the swollen torso rising out of it. The hands were not visible and the arms were twisted behind the back.

Schey promptly laid down his fishing pole on the towpath and set off at a brisk trot in the direction of the nearest café. It would be open even on a Sunday morning and he would be sure of finding a telephone there.

The response to his call to the ordinary police, fire department and ambulance emergency number was so swift that he barely had time to get back to the canal when a patrol car arrived, followed very shortly by two more. The area between Brussels and Antwerp is heavily populated and prosperous, and the public services are good.

While one team of officers went off to look for a boat, the others got out lines from the cars and tried casting them over the body with such success that, by the time the team with the boat returned, they had already drawn it in to the bank and were trying to lift it out of the water. This proved to be extremely difficult and the reason became apparent as the hands came into view. They were tied behind the man's back with a thick, orange, nylon rope to which was attached a heavy concrete building block.

The officers immediately drew back from the corpse and one of them went to the car to radio headquarters that they were at the scene of a homicide.

The report was inaccurate. As the body had been drifting down the canal, the murder had obviously not taken place there, but somewhere upstream.

It was, however, unquestionably homicide and the dispatcher at the station in Willebroeck at once alerted the Brussels Homicide Squad. For the Brussels Police, the report was a matter of routine. Urban Brussels has a population of over a million and there are, perhaps, double that number in the suburbs and smaller communities surrounding it. Even on a Sunday morning, there were several investigation units on duty.

The one which went to Willebroeck consisted initially only of an inspector of detectives, a sergeant of detectives and a medical officer. They were not supposed to carry out an investigation, but to determine the circumstances so that a decision could be made as to how much investigation would be needed.

Many homicides require little or no investigation. The

identity of the victim is known. The identity of the murderer is known. The motive and the circumstances of the murder are known. The task of the police consists mainly of making a record for the use of the court.

In this case, the results of the initial survey were inconclusive, although, in the opinion of Dr Raymond Pecheur, the man had not died of drowning and certain marks on the throat could indicate strangulation.

'He's been in the water for some time,' said the doctor, a quiet, smooth-cheeked man with neatly parted, straight, brown hair, who looked and was highly competent.

'Decomposition of the internal organs has released enough gas to bring him to the surface despite the cement block.'

'Lucky that he didn't get caught up in the screws of some barge,' said Detective Sergeant Marcel Despons, kneeling beside the corpse and going through the pockets of the clothing. 'Ah! Here we are.'

He took out an expensive leather wallet from the inside pocket of the jacket and handed it to the inspector who opened it, extracted a personal identity card and handed the wallet back to the sergeant to hold.

'Jan de Bruyne,' read the inspector. 'Engineer. Born 1951. Resident 31 rue de la Peulisbaan, Brussels. That's expensive property. I doubt there's a house there worth less than five million.'

'There's close to fifty thousand francs here in the wallet,' said the sergeant, thumbing through the soaked banknotes. 'Well, it wasn't robbery.'

He was a lean, handsome man with a small, carefully trimmed moustache and long sideburns. Although his eyes were a bright blue, his hair was almost black.

'No, it wasn't robbery,' said the inspector, hunching his huge shoulders in an unconscious gesture of launching himself into the investigation. 'Family matter perhaps. I see no point in calling out the full squad.'

'Nothing here for them to investigate,' agreed the doctor. 'Wherever he was killed, it wasn't here.'

The inspector nodded and lumbered off heavily in the direction of the car to call for a police ambulance to transport the body to the morgue.

The ambulance had been alerted at the time of the first report and, therefore, arrived quickly. The body was wrapped in plastic and, with the cement block still attached, taken away. Dr Pecheur went with it.

The inspector and the sergeant returned to their car and drove to the rue de la Peulisbaan which was a beautiful residential street winding through the moss-covered rocks of a sort of enchanted forest to the north of the city not far from the town of Mechelen. A restricted number of expensive homes had been built along it.

At number 31, the officers found Mrs Rosa de Bruyne, the lovely, thirty-two-year-old widow of the dead man, and their two small children.

Her face, at first puzzled, took on a look of alarm when the officers identified themselves.

'Is it about Jan?' she demanded. 'Is he all right? There hasn't been anything happen . . . ?'

'I'm afraid that your husband is no longer with us,' rumbled the inspector gravely. 'We . . .'

Rosa de Bruyne's hand flew to her mouth. She gave a choking gasp and the colour drained out of her face as she stared wide-eyed at the inspector over her fingers.

'Perhaps, you should sit down, Mrs de Bruyne,' muttered the inspector uncomfortably.

His broad features had turned pink, the colour nearly matching the sandy-red of his receeding, sparse hair, and he fumbled awkwardly with fingers as thick as sausages. There was nothing the inspector found more distasteful than notifying next of kin, for which reason he never delegated the task to his assistant.

Mrs de Bruyne turned on her heel and led the way into the spacious living room with the enormous, custom-built sofas and armchairs. Collapsing on to one of them, she covered her face with her hands and bent forward until the backs rested on her knees. For several minutes, she remained silent and almost motionless, her body racked by spasms of suppressed sobbing.

'A car accident?' she said finally, raising her tear-stained face.

'Uh, not exactly,' said the inspector. 'I'm afraid your husband was murdered.'

Rosa de Bruyne's mouth fell open and she stared at him with an expression of total disbelief.

'But why?' she cried. 'Why would anyone murder Jan?'

That was, of course, the question that the inspector and the sergeant had to answer, but they received little help from Mrs de Bruyne.

Her husband, she said, had been missing since, probably, Monday, November 17th. She, herself, had not seen him since the night of Sunday when he had gone away in response to a telephone call. She had not been surprised. Jan was often called out at night for something in connection with concrete, she did not know what.

He was an internationally-known expert on concrete and had invented a new kind with special properties. His company, a large construction firm in Antwerp, not infrequently pulled him out during the night on some problem or other in his field. Jan had not minded. He was obsessed with concrete. It was his job and his consuming interest.

She had not been alarmed when he did not turn up on Monday. His work took him to construction sites all over Europe and he was often gone for days on end. On Tuesday morning, however, she had called the firm to ask where he was and had been told that they had seen nothing of him since the preceding Friday. She had immediately called the police to report him missing.

Asked if he had had any enemies, she replied, 'Not unless it had something to do with concrete.'

The officers returned to Brussels, convinced now that

they faced a difficult investigation, but still with no reason for bringing in the full squad of technicians and specialists. There was nothing for them to investigate.

Upon his arrival at the office, the inspector telephoned the morgue and was told by Dr Pecheur that the cause of death had, indeed, been strangulation with something smooth and tough such as a leather belt.

'It was two people,' said the doctor.

'Two?' said the inspector. 'How did you arrive at that?'

'The belt was drawn very tightly around his neck, not knotted but looped, and it would be impossible for one person to pull so hard on both ends simultaneously,' said the doctor.

He added that he had found no signs of a struggle and thought that de Bruyne might have been drugged at the time. The body had been in the water for approximately a week.

'In short, he was killed on Sunday night after he was called out,' said the inspector 'Contact the company, Marcel, and see if they telephoned him on Sunday.'

The company had not.

'Oh damn! It's one of those things,' said the inspector in dismay. 'Leading a double life or something. We'll have to identify his girlfriend. Put about six men on to it.'

The sergeant put six men to tracing the personal background of Jan de Bruyne and was soon able to determine that the sole love of his life had been concrete.

He had taken his engineering degree in concrete at the Technical University of Alost where he had also met his future wife whom he had married in 1976.

Mrs de Bruyne, who came from a wealthy, middle-class family in Willebroeck, had taken her degree at Alost as a dietician, but was currently working as a teacher at the Buso School in nearby Vilvoorde.

De Bruyne had been a man truly obsessed with concrete. Far from having a secret love interest, he had done almost nothing other than work with, on and in the substance. In his company, he was regarded as a genius.

'Professional jealousy?' suggested the inspector upon hearing the sergeant's report. 'Some other great lover of concrete?'

'We'll take a look,' said the sergeant, 'but it's not the sort of thing that many people find fascinating and I gather that de Bruyne was so much head and shoulders above everybody else in the field that he had no competitors.'

'He had somebody who didn't like him,' said the inspector. 'Better take a look at Mrs de Bruyne then. She's an attractive woman and she may not have appreciated his lavishing more attention on concrete than on her.'

The inspector was, of course, thinking of a possible lover for Rosa de Bruyne and the sergeant soon found out that one existed.

'Passionate, red-hot love affair,' reported the sergeant. 'The only thing is, it isn't a man. It's the baby-sitter.'

'A girl?' said the inspector, cocking a bushy eyebrow. 'She was having a love affair with a girl baby-sitter?'

'Well, she's not exactly a girl any more now,' said the sergeant. 'She's twenty-four years old. But she was in her teens when the affair started. It was a scandal in the Buso School.'

'Where Mrs de Bruyne teaches,' said the inspector. 'One of her pupils?'

The sergeant nodded. 'Pupil, lover, baby-sitter, in that order,' he said. 'It's been going on for over five years.'

'Ask Dr Pecheur to step over here, will you?' said the inspector.

What the inspector wanted to know from the doctor was whether two women could have pulled hard enough on a belt to have strangled Jan de Bruyne. The man had been husky with a neck like a bull.

The doctor was unable to answer the question. He had, he pointed out, not seen either Rosa de Bruyne or Myriam van der Wildt, her lesbian lover.

'They would have to have above average strength,' he said. 'Of course, if he was unconscious at the time, which he probably was as there's no indication that he tried to defend himself . . .'

'No trace of drugs in the body, I suppose?' said the inspector.

'None,' said the doctor. 'We ran stomach, intestine and blood analyses. All negative. However, after a week in the water, there are many drugs, including some common sleeping pills, that would no longer show up.'

The inspector turned the doctor over to the sergeant with instructions to arrange for him to see Mrs de Bruyne and Miss van der Wildt.

'Mrs van der Wildt,' corrected the sergeant. 'That's her maiden name, but she's a widow.'

'At twenty-four?' said the inspector. 'Don't tell me something mysterious happened to her husband?'

'I don't know,' said the sergeant. 'We haven't finished with her yet.'

Dr Pecheur was taken to see Rosa de Bruyne and Myriam van der Wildt and infuriated the inspector by saying that he was unable to express an opinion. Neither woman was very large, but they might be stronger than they looked. In any case, if de Bruyne was unconscious, they could have kept on pulling for a long time.

This lack of precision upset the inspector because it made obtaining an indictment difficult. He did not doubt for an instant that Rosa and Myriam had murdered de Bruyne, probably because he stood in the way of their love, but he had to be able to convince the examining magistrate that they were capable of it. If the medical opinion on that point was not clear, the magistrate might be inclined to grant the accused the benefit of the doubt.

'The trouble with things like this,' growled the inspector, 'is that they're hard to prove. We believe that the motive for the murder was a homosexual relationship between Mrs de Bruyne and Mrs van der Wildt, but if it came to a trial they'd say, "Why that's not true. We're simply good friends." And what evidence could we offer that they aren't?'

'Well, there was a lot of gossip at the school,' said the sergeant, 'but hearsay is no proof. I doubt very much that we could get anybody to actually testify that Mrs de Bruyne and Mrs van der Wildt were lovers. It's not the sort of thing you can find witnesses for.'

The sergeant had been able to relieve the inspector's mind on one point. Myriam van der Wildt's husband really had died an accidental death. He and Myriam had been married in 1982 when she was twenty and he was twenty-six. They had had no children, but the marriage appeared to be reasonably happy. Then, on February 12, 1986, he had taken a curve on a country road near Mechelen in his Porsche at what the police estimated was close to a hundred miles an hour. Tests later showed that it was possible to hold a car through the curve at a maximum of just over sixty. The Porsche had struck a tree, turned over five times and caught fire. Belgians are generally regarded as the worst drivers in Europe and Myriam's husband had upheld the national tradition.

The de Bruynes had not driven such high performance cars, but had had matching GTI Rabbits – his green, hers red.

De Bruyne's car had been missing since his disappearance and it now turned up near the town of Lot nearly ten miles to the southwest of Brussels.

The inspector went out personally to look at it. It was undamaged and the doors were unlocked, but there were no keys in the car. Incredibly, a considerable quantity of valuable photographic material and engineering instruments lay openly in the back seat and had not been stolen, although the car was parked in an exposed turn-out on a main road.

Specialists from the police laboratory and fingerprint

experts were going over the car and they reported that they had found one latent print on the steering wheel which was not that of Jan de Bruyne.

'It looks as if the wheel and gear shift were wiped,' said the fingerprint man, 'but he missed one.'

'Probably she,' remarked the inspector. 'We'll have to arrange to get Mrs de Bruyne's prints without her knowledge.'

This was easily managed. The sergeant called on Mrs de Bruyne and showed her a large, glossy photograph which he said was of a suspect in the murder of her husband. He wanted to know if she recognized him. Mrs de Bruyne took the picture, looked at it carefully and handed it back saying that she had never seen the man in her life.

The sergeant had not expected that she would have. The picture was that of a child molester who had died over ten years earlier. The important thing was that she left nearly a full set of fingerprints on the glossy photograph which he now carried carefully back to the fingerprint department.

It took the experts only a few minutes to make the comparison. The print from the steering wheel of de Bruyne's car was not his wife's.

A similar ploy was used with Myriam van der Wildt. The print was not hers either.

For twenty-four hours, the investigation came to a complete halt while the inspector tried to think what he should do next. He was still convinced that Rosa de Bruyne and Myriam van der Wildt were guilty, but he was further than ever from being able to prove it.

At the end of that time, he went to see the head of the police laboratory and asked him how much difference there was in cement construction blocks. The technician said there was quite a lot. The cement was much the same, but the sand and gravel were natural substances and varied from batch to batch. In addition, the proportions of the materials in any one mix varied slightly. Generally speaking, it was possible to determine whether blocks came from the same batch.

Whereupon, the inspector obtained a court order and sent the sergeant with a half-dozen detectives to the de Bruyne house where they recovered from behind the garage nine cement blocks of the same size as the one which had been attached to de Bruyne's corpse. A coil of orange nylon rope similar to that with which his hands had been tied was also found.

Cement blocks and rope were brought to the police laboratory where six of the blocks turned out to be identical in composition to the one used to weight the corpse.

Even more conclusive, it was possible to show that the rope attaching the block to his hands had been cut from the coil in the garage.

Rosa de Bruyne was arrested and formally charged with suspicion of homicide. She denied the charge and demanded to see her attorney who succeeded in obtaining her release on bail.

In the meantime, Myriam van der Wildt had been arrested and had also denied any connection with the crime. As there was no evidence against her, she was released, but almost immediately re-arrested and held without bail.

The investigators, checking every set of fingerprints they could find, had obtained those of her twenty-two-year-old brother, Marc, and one matched the print taken from the steering wheel of de Bruyne's car.

Taken into custody and charged with murder, Marc immediately confessed and implicated his sister and Rosa de Bruyne.

Rosa, he said, had promised him a hundred thousand francs, the equivalent of two thousand dollars, to kill her husband and he and his sister had done the job.

His confession was read to Myriam who promptly broke down and added her confession. She and Rosa had been lovers since she was in her teens and a pupil at the Buso School. Rosa had been lonely and bored with her marriage and had said that the only way she could hope to interest her husband would be to have herself cast in concrete. Myriam had been neither lonely nor bored, but she was bi-sexual and she found Rosa attractive.

The affair had not ceased with Myriam's marriage. Her husband, she told the investigators, had been bi-sexual too and an enthusiastic participant in group sex activities.

Following his death, she had gone to live with a young, bi-sexual couple named Pitt and Laura de Kamp, all three sleeping in the same bed and indulging in veritable orgies.

Rosa, tied down by her husband and children, had not been able to join in and had not, in any case, wanted to. Although bi-sexual, she was not attracted to group sex. Rather, she was wild with jealousy and had nagged her husband to let her hire Myriam as a live-in baby-sitter.

Jan, who did not suspect his wife's relationship with her old pupil, agreed and Myriam moved in at the end of July.

There followed three months of great happiness. Then, at the end of October, Jan, whose comings and goings were erratic, had caught them naked and in the act of making love in the living room and had thrown Myriam out. He did not particularly object to his wife having sex with other women, he said, but he thought it a bad example for the children.

'Rosa was indignant,' said Myriam, 'because she had never let the children watch and we decided to kill him.'

They had worked out a plan with Marc who had always been very close to his sister and was game for anything.

Rosa was to grind up a dozen tablets of the strong sleeping pill, Temesta, and mix them with Jan's dinner on the evening of Sunday, November 23rd. Myriam and Marc would arrive at nine o'clock, by which time it was assumed that he would be sleeping soundly enough to be killed.

Everything had gone according to plan. Rosa had mixed the sleeping pills into Jan's yoghurt, and, the dose being strong enough to fell an ox, he had barely made it into the bedroom before falling asleep.

Myriam and Marc had arrived punctually, but had gone into the bedroom alone as Rosa refused to take part in the actual murder. Having decided that strangulation would be the best method, they wrapped one of Rosa's stockings around de Bruyne's neck and taking hold of the ends on either side, pulled as hard as they could.

De Bruyne had temporarily stopped breathing, but the stocking had broken so Marc had climbed on to his chest, and sitting astride him, had attempted to strangle him manually.

He had not been strong enough so Myriam had taken off her belt which they wrapped around his throat and again pulled on the ends from either side. It had taken a long time, but, finally, de Bruyne had ceased to breathe and they were no longer able to detect a heart beat.

Having tied his hands and attached the cement block in the garage, they drove him in Myriam's car to Willebroeck.

After throwing the body into the canal, they had returned and Rosa had put Jan's engineering instruments and his cameras into his car which Marc had driven to Lot, Rosa and Myriam following in the other GTI Rabbit. The idea was to make it look as if he had been attacked somewhere away from the house.

Even after the confessions of the van der Wildts, Rosa de Bruyne continued to protest her innocence, but, shortly before Christmas, gave up and confirmed the accuracy of their statements.

On March 20, 1987, all three were found guilty of murder and conspiracy to commit murder and sentenced to life imprisonment.

Thomas Rath *(Free Rides to the Devil's Moor)*

Jocelyne Bidon-Lavis *(Bright New Morality)*

Maria Totaro *(A Girl To Lose Your Head Over)*

Urio Boninsegna *(A Girl To Lose Your Head Over)*

Karl Groiss *(The Lady Doth Resist Too Much, Methinks)*

Andrea Schoenbichler *(The Lady Doth Resist Too Much, Methinks)*

Roswitha Schwaiger on the way to her trial *(Love Match)*

Above: Ibrahim Allam in court *(Personal Service Business)*

Dahlia Allam setting hearts athrob among the jurors *(Personal Service Business)*

7

ENTERTAINMENT DISTRICT

Ilse Bormann ascended quickly the narrow, dirty, ill-lit stairs to the second floor of what called itself a hotel in the Bahnhof Strasse of Frankfurt am Main.

It was seven o'clock in the evening of Tuesday, July 8, 1986 and she was dressed in her working clothes, a transparent blouse, open to the waist, a mini-skirt extending an inch below the crotch of her underwear, black fishnet stockings, black high heels and a pair of black lace underpanties containing less material than a lady's handkerchief.

Ordinarily, Ilse would have been followed up the stairs by a customer, fat or lean, young or middle-aged, clean or dirty. Competition in the tangle of narrow streets and alleys between the Kaiser Strasse and the main railway station, ironically called the Entertainment District, was fierce. You took what you could get.

This visit was, however, not ordinary. The hotel was not Ilse's place of business. It was that of her friend, thirty-two-year-old Rosemarie Novak.

Rosemarie was in the same line of business as Ilse and she had not appeared at her usual stand that evening.

In this jungle of a city of seven hundred thousand inhabitants, a failure to appear for work was ominous. Frankfurt was tough. A prostitute's life was dangerous.

Ilse had first telephoned to Rosemarie's apartment which was not the same as her place of business. She had been hoping that her friend was merely sick, but no one answered the ringing telephone.

Now, sick at heart, she was climbing the stairs to the dingy, little room, half fearing what she would find, half hoping she would find nothing. However, even before she pushed open the door, the premonition came over her so strongly as to extinguish hope.

As she had feared, Rosemarie lay lifeless on the bed. She was wearing her stockings, a garter belt, her high heels and nothing else. Unlike Ilse, she was a natural blonde and her skin gleamed pale as marble beneath the feeble ceiling light.

Ilse put her fingers in her mouth and began to cry, hard, choking sobs that hurt her throat. She had known Rosemarie well. For over five years, they had stood together in the streets of Frankfurt, in the cold of winter, in the slashing rain of spring, in the clammy fogs of autumn and the sticky heat of the summer that now was. She had been a good comrade, a faithful friend.

Crossing the room, she laid her hand on the skin between the jutting breasts, hoping against hope to feel a heartbeat, but there was none and the flesh beneath her fingers was cold and hard.

Snivelling softly, Ilse Bormann made her way back down the stairs. There was a tavern on the corner where she would be able to telephone the police.

Dead whores are, as a rule, reported anonymously to the police, if they are reported at all, but, when the patrol car arrived, the officers found Lisa Bormann waiting. She was no longer crying and she led them without a word to the room where Rosemarie lay.

The officers checked vainly for signs of life and, while one remained at the scene, the other went back down to the patrol car to report to the dispatcher at police headquarters, only a few blocks away, that an apparent homicide had taken place in Bahnhof Strasse. He took Ilse Bormann with him and kept her sitting in the patrol car. The homicide squad would want her statement on the discovery of the corpse and anything else she knew concerning the victim.

One of the duty homicide units arrived shortly. It consisted of Inspector of Detectives Paul Becker, a man of completely average appearance with medium-brown hair, medium-brown eyes and a neatly trimmed moustache; Sergeant of Detectives Ulrich Bronsen, who was tall, thin, haggard-looking and wore glasses; and one of the department's medical specialists, Dr Gerhardt Reich, who was young, dark and wore a full beard and moustache.

While the inspector and Dr Reich ascended to the second floor, the sergeant tape-recorded a statement from Ilse Bormann, checked her personal identity card and sent her off about her business.

Ilse did not, however, do any business that night. Instead, she removed her make-up, changed her clothes, went to a bar where she was not known and drank herself unconscious. Having known the victim personally, Ilse was, of course, more deeply affected than the police officers for whom the affair was largely routine.

Prostitutes, because of the nature of their work, are often murdered. In some cases, by psychopaths who subject them to unbelievable tortures and disembowel or dismember their bodies.

Rosemarie Novak had been spared that. She was not mutilated and her body displayed scarcely any signs of a struggle.

'She had assumed the position for servicing the client,' said the doctor, 'who lay down on top of her, took her throat in his hands and strangled her to death. It's almost impossible for a woman in that posture to defend herself and she would have lost consciousness quickly.'

'Intercourse before or after?'asked the inspector. 'Did he achieve orgasm at all?'

The questions were important. The murderer was, presumably, a sex psychopath and there might be a file on him in the police records section. The ability or lack of it to complete the sex act was an essential characteristic of the profile which could help to identify him.

'We'll see,' said the doctor, inserting the blades of the speculum between the lips of the dead girl's vagina.

He probed with rubber-gloved fingers, withdrew his hand and rubbed the finger tips together.

'Commercial lubricating cream,' he said. 'There's no trace of semen in the vagina and, as the cream hasn't been disturbed, there was apparently no penetration. Maybe incapable of erection.'

'All right,' said the inspector. 'You can let me have the rest in the autopsy report. Can you give me an estimate of the time?'

'Sometime last night,' said the doctor. 'I'll be able to pare that down a good deal when I get her to the morgue.'

While the doctor had been carrying out his examination of the body, the sergeant had come up to the room, taken an appraising look and gone down to summon the specialists standing by at headquarters and the corpse transporter, a low, two-wheeled, metal trailer towed by a police car.

This arrived quickly and the crew got out a stretcher, but did not bring it upstairs. The body could not be moved until the technicians had finished their work around it.

One of these was engaged in photographing the corpse and the room as found, while others were going over the floor and bed, almost the only article of furniture in the room, in search of potential clues. As these could be almost anything, they were finding a great many which they labelled and placed in plastic sacks for transfer to the police laboratory.

Having had much practice, the specialists worked quickly and the body was soon taken down to the corpse transporter and driven away to the morgue.

By eleven o'clock, Dr Reich was ready with a preliminary, verbal report and he came to the inspector's office to make it.

'He not only strangled her, he broke her neck,' he

said. 'Enormous pressure. The man has very strong hands. In other respects, rather less so. No semen. No penetration. He's marked, probably on the shoulders. Small fragments of skin under the nails on both her hands. Caucasian, brunette. Time was ten-fifteen of Monday evening, plus or minus twenty minutes.'

'But no signs of torture?' said the inspector, frowning. 'He didn't beat her? No bruising?'

'Nothing,' said the doctor. 'I don't think he is a psychopath. If he is, he's one that's not in the books. People killing for pleasure take their time about it. This one walked in, climbed on to the girl, killed her and walked out. I doubt that he was in the room for ten minutes. Was she robbed?'

'No,' said the inspector. 'That's just it. She didn't keep any money on her, of course. No professional does. But she'd collected from him in advance and the money was still there in her handbag. He didn't even open it.'

'How do you know it was from him?' said the doctor. 'Maybe she did carry change.'

'Her girlfriend, the one who found the body, says she charged a hundred marks for one time straight, no frills,' said the inspector. 'There was a hundred marks exactly in her handbag and the lab says the only prints on the bag are hers.'

'Hard to figure then,' said the doctor. 'It wasn't aberrant sex. It wasn't money. Must have been something personal.'

'That's the angle we're working on now,' said the inspector.

They did not work on it long. Rosemarie Novak's life had not been exactly an open book, but there were no great secret passions in it either. No one had had a personal reason to murder her.

The inspector did not like this at all. It was bad enough to have a murderer running around Frankfurt who had had a motive, however irrational, for his crime. A murderer who had had no motive whatsoever meant that anybody could be murdered at any time.

'Still, there probably is some kind of a motive,' he worried. 'We just don't understand it.'

'Sheer blood lust,' said the sergeant in a deep, gloomy voice. 'Records said there was nothing like this in the files nationwide.'

'Don't try to cheer me up,' said the insepctor. 'If you look at it right, there is a pattern of sorts. The victim was female, blonde and a prostitute. I predict that he'll kill again and that the victim will be female, blonde and a prostitute.'

He would achieve a score of two out of three. The woman who was murdered on the night of Saturday, August 9th, was female and a prostitute, but she was a long way from blonde.

'A Thai national,' said the sergeant. 'Came to Germany six years ago, apparently with the intention of peddling her body and that's what she's been doing ever since. Cute girl and very exotic. The accountants say she left a huge estate.'

Thirty-four-year-old Thi Ramanalonda had met exactly the same fate as Rosemarie Novak and under almost identical circumstances. Even the hotels were very similar and they were less than three blocks apart.

Thi had practised her trade in the same Entertainment District as Rosemarie and had probably known her, by sight at least. She had surely known of her murder.

There must, therefore, have been a few ghastly seconds when she realized who was lying on top of her and whose hands were closing relentlessly around her throat.

She had managed to tear free for an instant for there was blood on her mouth of a different blood group than hers. Although she had sunk her teeth into one of those deadly hands, it had not saved her. Her throat was crushed, her neck broken, just as had been the case with Rosemarie Novak. In her unopened purse, the investigators found four twenty-mark bills. The Orientals tend to undercut the market price.

'You agree that it's the same man?' said the inspector.

'Oh, I think without question,' said the doctor. 'No semen. No penetration. He killed her and got out. Was the time close enough to clear your suspect?'

The question was directed at the sergeant who had been checking out the alibi of sixty-four-year-old Harold Kramer, one of Thi's most faithful admirers. It was he who had discovered her body and had summoned the police.

'Yes,' said the sergeant. 'He's clean. Didn't really consider him much of a suspect, but he does have unusually large, strong hands.'

'That's a possibility we've overlooked,' remarked the inspector. 'Tell the records section to run a computer check on stranglers with unusually strong hands.'

The initiative was not very successful. Most stranglers have strong hands, but there were none listed in the computer's memory who killed quickly and without apparent motive.

'The only thing really in common is that they were both prostitutes,' said the inspector. 'I think we'll find that the future victims will be too.'

Neither he nor anyone else connected with the investigation doubted for a moment that there would be future victims. Two so similar murders within a period of five weeks was evidence enough that a series had begun.

There was no speculation over how long it might continue. The killer was obviously going to be hard to trace. He had probably had no previous contact with his victims. He spent too little time with them for there to be much hope of witnesses. He had chosen them at night and from a group where contacts with strangers was normal. His motives were not known and, perhaps, not understandable to others. And he displayed no identifiable eccentricities in his crimes.

'It could be anybody in Frankfurt,' said the sergeant with glum exaggeration.

As the murders of Rosemarie Novak and Thi Ramanalonda had happened so near to each other in time and place, the police were keeping an apprehensive eye on the Entertainment District for September.

So were the prostitutes. There were a half-dozen incidents. A prospective client with peculiar mannerisms was shot but not seriously wounded by a nervous hustler. Another was kicked painfully in a part of his anatomy that rendered impossible the transaction in which he had been engaged. Two others were beaten unconscious by pimps. Business in the railway station district was seriously affected.

But none of these unfortunates was the killer. All could easily establish alibis for the times of the murders. And September passed without a homicide.

October did not. There was a murder and the victim was a prostitute. She was, however, killed more or less unintentionally by her pimp for failing to hand over her full receipts. As their relationship was known and as he had left his fingerprints in blood on her handbag, he was quickly apprehended and persuaded to confess. He was, in fact, filled with remorse. The girl had not only been his sole source of income, but he had been sincerely fond of her, he said. He was indicted on a charge of unintentional homicide and ordered held for trial.

By this time, most of November had passed and the police were becoming mildly optimistic.

'Something's happened to him,' said the inspector. 'Got sick and died. Was run over by a truck. Cleared out of the area altogether.'

'He'd have had to clear out of Germany,' remarked the sergeant. 'Wiesbaden is keeping tab on cases with a similar *modus operandi* anywhere in the country. None reported so far.'

Wiesbaden, a few miles to the west, was the location of the central police registry.

'I would prefer the truck,' said the inspector. 'If he's left the country, he could come back. What did Dr Reich say when you spoke to him?'

'That, if he isn't back in operation by the end of the year, he's probably gone for good,' said the sergeant.

November ended with no further reports of murders of prostitutes in Frankfurt. The girls in the Entertainment District began to relax. Business was good again and Christmas was coming. Even whores enjoy the holiday season. The weather is often bad for standing around on street corners, but the clientele is in an expansive mood and inclined to be generous.

However, not everyone who makes a living lying down on the job has to stand in the cold streets. Some are employed by business firms and enjoy more dignified working conditions. One such business in Frankfurt is called Erotika and, like any other firm, it has employees, offices and a heavy advertising and public relations budget.

Erotika does not, however, provide any services on its own premises, but sends its employees to the customer. Hence, the heavy advertising and the two full-time female employees with husky, soft voices who answer the half-dozen telephone lines.

In charge of this not negligible operation was a surprisingly young woman named Helen Gibbert who was listed on the organization chart as Directress.

On the morning of December 2nd, Directress Gibbert arrived at her office at the usual hour of eight and began a survey of the preceding night's operations. Much of Erotika's business was done at night.

As the preceding night had been a Monday, business had been rather slow and Miss Gibbert noted almost immediately that operator Ulrike Thoma, professionally known as Iris, had not turned in her receipts from a call made to an address in Kaiser Strasse at ten-thirty the night before.

This was strictly against company regulations. It was

dangerous for the girls to be carrying sums of money on them and the offices were kept open throughout the night so that they could get rid of it.

Even if Iris had been retained all night long and had got off only early in the morning, she would still have been required to drop the payment off at the office before going home.

Directress Gibbert, therefore, immediately picked up the telephone and called Miss Thoma's apartment. There was no response and this troubled Directress Gibbert greatly. It was very unlikely that Miss Thoma was still with the client. Few clients displayed such endurance and, also, the Erotika service was not cheap.

However, if Miss Thoma was not with the client and not at home and, if she had not turned in her receipts, the implications were ominous.

Helen Gibbert was fully aware of the dangers of the profession and she too had heard of the murders of Rosemarie Novak and Thi Ramanalonda. Summoning two employees of the company, twenty-eight-year-old Max Deggert and his senior by two years, Gerd Schulz, she told them to go to Iris's apartment, enter it one way or another and report by telephone on what they found inside.

Deggert and Schulz, pleasant-faced, young men with an astonishing muscular development, went off cheerfully and, after a short discussion with the housemaster at Iris's apartment building, telephoned from her apartment to say that Iris was not there and that her bed had not been slept in.

'Go to 48 Kaiser Strasse and speak with the occupant of apartment 12,' said Directress Gibbert. 'Be firm. He's her client from last night and he hasn't paid.'

Collection was one of the duties connected with Max's and Gerd's jobs and they were very good at it. This time, however, they called back a half-hour later to say that no one answered the door and that the building was not high class enough to have a superintendent.

'Go in anyway,' said Directress Gibbert, beginning to perspire. She was not a hard woman and she took a personal interest in the employees. Iris had been a good girl, simple, honest and a conscientious worker.

At the apartment house in Kaiser Strasse, Max and Gerd removed their jackets and folded them into pads over their shoulders. Competent professionals, they had no intention of damaging their working equipment.

This done, they took as much of a run as they could manage in the narrow hall, slammed their combined weight against the door and knocked it completely off its hinges at the first try.

The apartment was small with only two bedrooms. Iris was in the second one, sprawled on her back on the bed in the approved posture of her profession. She was in working uniform of stockings and high heels. The rest of her clothing lay neatly folded on a chair nearby.

She was, of course, quite dead, her throat crushed and her neck broken.

'It's our boy,' said the inspector, gazing down on the body which Dr Reich was engaged in examining. 'He's either gone completely off his rocker or he's tacitly giving up.'

The fact that the latest murder had been committed in an apartment, the occupant of which could be traced, meant that the case was essentially over even if the murderer was still at large.

'Name appears to be Libmann,' said the sergeant, digging through the papers in the desk in the living room. 'Achim Libmann, forty years old and, apparently, married.'

He held up a photograph of a smiling couple locked in a warm embrace.

'Young looking wife, but she's forty too,' he said. 'Why do you think he did it?'

'At the moment, I'm not so concerned over why he did it as that he doesn't do it again,' said the inspector. 'Call headquarters and read them a description so that they can get out an alert. He's probably still right here in Frankfurt.'

The sergeant carried out his orders and returned.

'What about the gorillas?' he asked.

Max Deggert and Gerd Schulz were waiting patiently in the patrol car downstairs. They had called the directress immediately following the discovery of the body and she had called the police. She had thought it best that they await the police's arrival so that they could explain the circumstances.

'Thank them for their co-operation and send them off about their business,' said the inspector. 'They've helped us solve a very nasty series.'

'If it is solved,' muttered the sergeant under his breath.

A man with a pessimistic nature, it had occurred to him that someone other than the official occupant might have had access to the apartment.

But no one had. Achim Libmann was picked up by a team of patrolmen making a routine check of the bars and taverns in the Entertainment District on the following evening.

He offered no resistance and made his confession to the three murders as soon as the inspector and the sergeant could be got out of bed and brought down to headquarters to listen to it. He had taken to killing whores, he said, because he hated them and he hated them because his wife was one.

She had become one only recently, on April 5th of that same year, to be precise.

Up until then, the Libmanns had been an unexceptional couple, married seventeen years, without children and, he had thought, as happy as most. They had not been wealthy, but they had not been poor either. Achim had a steady job in a textile firm with which he was reasonably content, although there was little opportunity for advancement.

However, on the afternoon of April 5th, a Saturday,

Achim had come home to find Pauline standing naked in front of the mirror and examining herself critically.

Asked what she thought she was doing, she had replied that she had come to the conclusion that she could make more money as a whore than as a housewife. She had what she felt was a saleable product and she was going to sell it.

Her thunderstruck husband demanded to know whether this meant that she was leaving him and she assured him that that was exactly what she had in mind.

Whereupon she packed her belongings and left and he had seen her only once since when she dropped by to pick up another suitcase. An important pimp was taking her to Monaco and Nice on the French Riviera where she would be introduced to some well-paying customers, she explained. She was already expensively dressed, expertly made-up and wearing jewellery which, if real, was worth roughly two years of his salary.

'I was bitter,' said Achim. 'I thought, here I work year in and year out for nothing and all a woman has to do is lay down and become rich. I didn't deliberately set out to kill those women though. It was just that whenever I got on top of one of them, it was like it was Pauline and I couldn't stop choking her.'

Achim Libmann was brought to trial on three counts of intentional homicide on February 27, 1987 and, his statements having been confirmed by Mrs Libmann upon her return from her business trip to the south of France, was accorded extenuating circumstances.

He was, however, sentenced to life imprisonment as the court appointed psychiatrists could not guarantee that he would not repeat his offences. Achim Libmann, it seemed, still had very strong feelings about whores.

8

BIRD-WATCHING IN SPAIN

It was Monday, September 29, 1986, when Detective Inspector Manuel Rogas was summoned to the office of a commissioner in the Department of Criminal Investigations of the Madrid police.

'We have here, Inspector Rogas, a rather curious report from the University of Madrid,' said the commissioner. 'I would like it investigated discreetly. Are you able to leave for Seville at once?'

The inspector was. Seville, nearly four hundred miles from Madrid in the extreme southwest of Spain, was not a place to which many would object being sent, particularly at this time of year.

'Good,' said the commissioner. 'Take your assistant and try to find out what has happened to Dr Ricardo Sanmesa who holds the chair for ornithology at the university. He was due to return from the National Park of the Guadalquivir on September 10, but he did not and they have been unable to contact him.'

'Ornithology?' said the inspector, a small, neat olive-skinned man with a thin, black moustache.

'The study of birds,' said the commissioner. 'Dr Sanmesa is preparing a scientific work on migratory birds and was given special permission to camp in the National Park.'

'Alone?' said the inspector.

'No,' said the commissioner. 'He is accompanied by his assistant, Miss Elena Duarte.'

'Elderly man?' ventured the inspector delicately.

'Dr Sanmesa is thirty-one,' said the commissioner. 'Miss Duarte is twenty-three. A former student, I believe. However, here is the information the university sent over. If you require anything else, you may contact the head of the science faculty directly. Report to me by telephone as soon as you learn something. No need to leave today.'

This final remark the inspector interpreted to mean that he was to leave the first thing tomorrow.

Returning to his office, he informed his assistant Detective Sergeant Juan Villamosa, that they were leaving for Seville the following morning and that he did not know how long they would be gone. He then telephoned his wife, told her the same thing, asked her to pack his suitcase and began going through the file sent over by the university, handing each sheet to the sergeant as soon as he had finished reading it.

There were only three sheets, one concerning Dr Sanmesa, one concerning Miss Duarte and the third concerning their mission in the National Park.

Most of the doctor's sheet was taken up with his academic qualifications, but it was also noted that he was unmarried.

Miss Duarte, it seemed, was not married either and, as the commissioner had suggested, was one of Dr Sanmesa's former students. She had previously accompanied the doctor on trips to France, Germany, Sweden and other parts of Europe.

'No wonder the commissioner wants it investigated discreetly,' said the sergeant.

The doctor's official mission in the park, a bird sanctuary taking in much of the delta of the Guadalquivir for which permission to camp was only granted under exceptional circumstances, was a study of rare migratory birds which would form a part of a forthcoming book.

They had left Madrid in the doctor's luxuriously appointed Ford camping car on August 14th and had telephoned the university upon their arrival on the 15th.

There had been one further call on September 2nd and nothing since. Telegrams and special delivery letters had been returned undelivered.

Attached to the information sheets were recent photographs of the young couple, both slender, dark, handsome and looking almost like brother and sister.

'Well?' said the sergeant, handing back the pictures. 'What do you make of it?'

He was a large man, loose-limbed and blond with little resemblance to the conventional concept of a Spaniard. The inspector frowned and tugged thoughtfully at his ear.

'What I like least is the reference to the "luxuriously appointed" camping car,' he said. 'There's a lot of poverty in those little villages down there. Something like that could be a great temptation to poor people.'

'Who might be willing to kill to get it,' said the sergeant, nodding. 'Why don't the Seville police handle the investigation?'

'They'll co-operate,' said the inspector, 'but it's the university that's behind this so it's up to us.'

'There could be worse assignments,' said the sergeant philosophically. 'I've never been to Seville.'

The trip down was made in the inspector's official but unmarked car and, after breaking their journey at Linares, they arrived in Seville on the afternoon of October 2nd. The weather was, of course, warm, sunny and bright.

The following morning, they reported to Seville's police headquarters, where they were expected, and were assured of the full co-operation of the Department of Criminal Investigation.

Having requested an area-wide search for the Ford camping car, the description and licence number of which they had brought down with them, they went to look at the place where it was last known to have been parked.

This was not far from the small port of Palos de

Moguer and the site had already been visited by the Seville police who had reported that someone had undoubtedly camped there but there was no indication of who of where they had gone. As no rain had fallen in the past few weeks, the traces left by the campers were still clearly visible and there were the prints of a great many bare feet.

'Some of these are definitely female,' said the sergeant, getting down on all fours to look.

'Miss Duarte, no doubt,' said the inspector. 'I don't think there's any question that this is where they were camped. The people in Palos de Moguer told the detectives who came out that it was a young couple in a Ford camping car and that they were here for close to a month.'

'And getting permission to camp in the park is almost impossible,' said the sergeant. 'You can see they were here for a long time from the amount of ashes where they had the grill.'

'Try to locate a latrine pit,' said the inspector. 'Maybe there'll be something of interest in that.'

The sergeant gave him a quizzical look and went off into the bushes, calling our after a few moments that he had found it, but that it had been filled in with sand.

'Go into Palos de Moguer and see if you can buy a sieve,' said the inspector. 'The bigger the better.'

'You're going to sift the latrine?' exclaimed the sergeant, popping out of the bushes in some alarm.

'The sand in the clearning, Juan,' said the inspector.

Being the estuary of the Guadalquivir river, the ground in much of the park was sandy, waterlogged and covered with vast fields of reeds. Although the camp site was some distance from the river and a small grove of bushes and trees had gained a foothold, the clearing in the centre where the bus had been parked was loose sand.

The sergeant drove off in the direction of Palos de Moguer and the inspector began crawling slowly over the clearing, outlining the location of the camping car, a table and chairs, a temporary shower and the grill by sticking sections of dead reeds into the ground.

He had just finished when the sergeant returned with two sieves and they began sifting the top layer of sand to a depth of four of five inches, starting with the fireplace and working out in concentric circles.

'Ah!' said the inspector, giving a sort of grunt of satisfaction.

'What is it?' asked the sergeant coming over to look.

The inspector held out the sieve. In the bottom lay a dozen small pebbles. Most were yellowish-brown, the colour of the sand, but two were deep brown, nearly black, but with a hint of red.

The inspector took one of the dark pebbles between his fingers and squeezed. It crumbled into dust.

'A drop of congealed blood,' said the inspector. 'Of course, it may be from an entirely innocent cause . . .'

If so, it was a very large, innocent cause. Carefully brushing the sand away with their fingertips, the detectives uncovered great crusts of dried blood, some more than two feet across.

'We'll need expert medical advice,' said the inspector, 'but I think that a quantity as large as this would represent a very serious, possibly fatal wound.'

'But to whom?' said the sergeant. 'Did he kill her or did she kill him?'

'Perhaps somebody killed both of them or, perhaps nobody was killed,' said the inspector. 'There may have simply been an accident and one drove the other to the hospital.'

But he did not believe it and a check of the hospitals in the area produced no trace of the missing couple.

In the meantime, samples of the dried blood had been taken to the police laboratory where they were found to be a mixture of venous and arterial blood of, at least, two people with different blood groups.

Two days later, the camping car was found on the

opposite side of Palos de Moguer nearly eight miles distant from the camp site.

'Stripped,' said the vehicle expert from Seville traffic section. 'Everything's been taken out that could be pried loose. Strange thing to do.'

'How so?' demanded the inspector.

'A lot of it was hard to get out and hasn't any value,' said the specialist. 'You couldn't sell it. You couldn't use it. Just a lot of work for nothing.'

The camping car was brought to headquarters and a team from the police laboratory went over it by the square centimetre. They found nothing, not a fingerprint, not so much as a drop of dried blood.

'That's why everything was taken out,' said the inspector. 'He wanted to get rid of the blood stains.'

'What for?' said the sergeant. 'They wouldn't help to identify him.'

'He doesn't think like that,' said the inspector. 'This is some poor devil who knows nothing about detection procedures. He just tried to get rid of everything.'

The discovery of the stripped camping car removed any remaining doubts as to the fate of Dr Ricardo Sanmesa and Elena Duarte. They had been murdered and the task of the police now was to identify the murderer and bring him to justice.

The inspector began the investigation by requesting an intensive canvass of the community of Palos de Moguer. The victims had shopped for provisions there and had, undoubtedly, had some contact with the local residents. The inspector wanted to know who these local residents were.

Almost immediately, reports of a local man who had spent much time at the academicians' camp were received. He was thirty-three-year-old Antonio Legones who rode almost daily in the National Park of Guadalquivir on a magnificent, white horse named Hidalgo.

Hidalgo was not Legones' horse, but the property of his employers, the owners of a nearby ranch called the

Manade de San Jose. One of the oldest and richest families in Spain, the park had originally been their property and, although they had donated it to the state, they still had the right to pasture their horses and fighting bulls there.

Everyone in the delta of the Guadalquivir knew Legones and Hidalgo, but their reputation stretched far beyond that, extendintg to such distant places as West Germany, Holland and Sweden.

Legones was, in fact, a major local tourist attraction.

Every summer great hordes of young, Nordic females came down to the warm sandy beaches where the Guadalquivir emptied into the Atlantic to bathe and sun themselves, generally stark naked, among the dunes. They were often romantically-minded maidens and, when a young, bronzed and extremely virile Spaniard appeared on a white horse, the vacation became successful beyond their wildest dreams. Antonio, said the villagers, was not quite as popular as the Alhambra, but it was close.

Taken into custody, he freely admitted that he had visited the professor and his assistant almost daily, but for business reasons. They had often rented riding horses from the Manade de San Jose.

According to Legones, Dr Sanmesa had said they would be returning to Madrid on September 10th and, when he passed by on the 12th and saw that the car was gone, he had assumed that they had left as planned. The last time he had seen them was on Monday, the 8th.

Legones' quarters at the ranch were searched, but nothing belonging to either Dr Sanmesa or Miss Duarte was found. He was consequently released.

However, he remained the inspector's prime suspect or rather, his only suspect. As far as it had been possible to determine, no one else had visited the camp site at all.

'It would help if we could locate the bodies,' he said, 'but I doubt that we ever will. The park is too big and the locals know it too well. It would take an army to search it thoroughly.'

'And the bodies may not even be in the park,' added the sergeant. 'They could have been thrown in the river and carried out into the Atlantic. Assuming that they were killed around the 10th September, it's been close to a month now.'

'We'll have to do the best we can without them,' said the inspector. 'I think that we can establish a supposition of homicide on the basis of the blood. The groups correspond to those of Dr Sanmesa and Miss Duarte. Then, if we could just locate some of the things from the van . . .'

This was, however, wishful thinking. If the murderer had disposed of the bodies so thoroughly that they could not be found, there was no reason to believe that he had done less well with the victims' belongings.

'But then,' muttered the inspector, frowning, 'why murder them if he didn't keep anything?'

'The girl?' suggested the sergeant. 'According to the people around here, Legones is a sort of super tomcat.'

'Well, maybe,' said the inspector doubtfully. 'But still, why murder? You read the background stuff that the commissioner sent down on Dr Sanmesa and the girl. They were a couple of intellectuals, modern, promiscuous, probably even socialists. Sanmesa wouldn't have objected if Legones wanted sex with Miss Duarte. He'd have asked to watch.'

'All right, maybe not Legones then, but somebody else,' said the sergeant. 'There must be some men so repulsive that even Miss Duarte wouldn't want to.'

'I doubt it,' said the inspector. 'I know the type. I still think Legones. After all, he does have a record.'

Antonio Legones did have a criminal record, but it was for a petty offence that had taken place when he was still in his teens.

Born of a miserably poor family in the town of Carmona, fifteen miles to the east of Seville, Antonio had dreamed like many other Spanish boys of becoming a famous matador and, at the age of sixteen, had sprung into the arena during a bull fight with nothing more serious than a handkerchief as a cape.

The bull had been better equipped and had laid open Antonio's left forearm to the bone so that, although prompt and heroic action by the professional bullfighters had saved his life, it was at first feared that he would be left permanently disabled.

He had, however, recovered with no more than a huge scar and had gone to Seville where he had worked at the market as a butcher boy.

Two years later, he had been caught stealing and had been sentenced to a year in prison. He had served nine months and, following his release, the social worker responsible for his rehabilitation had found him a job at the Manade de San Jose where he had been ever since.

He had had no further problems with the law and was highly regarded by his employers.

Although financially in a position to do so, he had never married, presumably because he found it unnecessary. As long as the Nordic tourists continued to come to the south of Spain, his romantic requirements were more than covered.

All of which made Antonio Legones a dubious suspect. If the motive for the murders had been neither money nor the charms of the doctor's assistant, what had it been?

The investigators were still trying to trace Antonio Legones' whereabouts on or about September 10th, a well-nigh hopeless undertaking with a cowboy galloping around an immense, sparsely populated swamp, when a development of which the inspector had long since given up hope occurred.

On Saturday, November 29th, Herminio Mariano, a construction worker who was employed during the week, went fishing the Guadalimer river which flows into the Guadalquivir near its mouth.

Working his way downstream, he had caught several

fish when he noticed a body tangled in the roots of a large willow growing on the bank. Approaching closer, Mariano saw that there were two bodies and that they were a hideous sight for they were in an advanced state of decomposition and were being fed upon by fresh water shrimp.

In his telephone call to the police, all that Mariano could say was that it was two humans.He could not even tell whether they were male or female.

For the Seville police, however, it was the bodies of Ricardo Sanmesa and Elena Duarte. There was no other couple missing in the area.

Inspector Rogas and Sergeant Villamosa were allerted and hurried to the scene, accompanied by a detachment from the Seville Department of Criminal Investigations and a police expert in forensic medicine.

The bodies were extracted with considerable difficulty from the tree roots and brought up on the bank where Dr Iganacio Lopez, a tall, thin, aristocratic-looking man who wore gold-rimmed glasses and a pointed beard, began the unpleasant task of examining them.

Understandably, considering the circumstances, the examination did not last very long, but the doctor was able to report that the corpses were those of a man and woman within the age group of Dr Sanmesa and Miss Duarte and that they had died of multiple stab wounds.

'I cannot estimate how long they have been dead,' said the doctor, 'or even how long they have been in the water. I may be able to when we have got them to the morgue.'

While he had been occupied with the examination, specialists from the police laboratory had been carying out tests at the place where the bodies had been lodged and had come to the conclusion that they been brought down by the current from somewhere higher upstream.

There was, therefore, no possibility of finding any clues there and, the bodies having been wrapped in plastic and placed in metal coffins, the party returned to Seville.

By that evening, Dr Lopez was ready with a preliminary report in which he stated that the bodies had been put into the water shortly after death and that this had been around September 10th. Dr Sanmesa had been stabbed fourteen times in the stomach and chest. Elena Duarte had been stabbed four times in the chest, once in the stomach and partially disembowelled. All of the wounds appeared to have been inflicted with the same weapon – a heavy, single-edged knife with a sharp point, some eight inches long.

'Nothing of any use to us,' said the inspector glumly.

'Except the identification,' said the sergeant.

The fingerprint experts had managed, despite the condition of the bodies, to obtain enough partial fingerprints for a positive identification and these had been sent to Madrid to be compared with prints taken from objects that Dr Sanmesa and Miss Duarte were known to have handled. The identification was not, therefore, as yet official, but it was assumed that it soon would be.

'Of course,' said the inspector, 'it does give us an indication of the motive. The man was in a rage and that means emotional involvement.'

'Or a panic,' said the sergeant. 'If they came back to the camp and found him rifling the van . . .'

'Damn!' said the inspector. 'It could have been that too.'

'We continue with Legones?' said the sergeant.

'We haven't anyone else,' said the inspector. 'Anyway, we know he visited them. He admits it himself.'

But this was a long way from proof of murder. The police had had no success at all in trying to trace Legones' movements on September 10th or any other day.

However, their persistence did eventually pay off, although in an unexpected manner. Legones, it was learned, had rented a studio in Palos de Moguer, a rather nice studio, on September 1st of that year.

'Now, why in the devil would he do that?' demanded the inspector. 'He lives at the ranch.'

'The young lady tourists?' suggested the sergeant.

'Wrong time of the year,' said the inspector. 'Anyway, he's been dealing with them in the sand dunes for the past ten years. Why change now?'

The sergeant was unable to answer, but when he came in to work the following morning, he said immediately, 'He was planning on getting married.'

'To Miss Duarte!' exclaimed the inspector who did not need to be told to whom the sergeant was referring. 'It wouldn't be the first such case. Legones is simple, uneducated and, despite the tourists, probably morally conservative. Miss Duarte was an intellectual, sexually liberated. He thought that if she had sex with him, it was true love, but she was merely entertaining herself. When she started to leave for Madrid, he lost his head.'

'But can we prove it?' said the sergeant.

Not without the help of Antonio Legones, but that was forthcoming. Rearrested and confronted with the investigators' theory of the murders, he turned red in the face with embarrassment and confessed.

He had met the Prof, as he called Dr Sanmesa, and Elena Duarte shortly after their arrival in the park, he said, and had struck up an immediate friendship. He knew the park intimately and the doctor was happy to have his services as a guide.

Elena had been happy to have his services in other respects. He had met her, as he had met so many of the Nordic tourists, sunning herself naked among the sand dunes and the result had been the same, the girl consenting to sex within an hour of meeting him.

She had taken him back and introduced him to the doctor and, after that, they had gone off nearly every day for sex in the sand dunes or hidden, little meadows that only Legones knew.

He had fallen deeply in love with her and had assumed that she loved him, but, when he arrived at the camp on the morning of September 10th, he had found the doctor busy packing in the camping car and Elena washing her hair, preparatory to leaving.

He had instantly declared his love, had asked Elena to marry him and had said that he had rented a studio in Palos de Moguer where they could live.

Elena, probably sincerely amazed, had said that she had no intention of burying herself in such a hole. She was going back to Madrid.

Legones had played his last card by threatening to tell The Prof about their sexual encounters, but Elena had merely laughed and called him.

'But I knew about it from the beginning!' Dr Sanmesa had cried. 'I know Elena. She does it all the time. In fact, I often watched you with the binoculars. Can't be watching birds all the time, you know.'

The young intellectuals had probably been laughing at the situation and not at him, but Legones had thought they were and, in an insane range, had stabbed first Elena and, when he tried to intervene, Dr Sanmesa.

Antonio Legones never retracted his confession nor did he make any attempt to defend himself. He was, consequently, found guilty on two counts of unpremeditated homicide and, on May 15, 1987, sentenced to thirty years' imprisonment.

Although he was accorded extenuating circumstances, his efforts to conceal the crimes worked against him as did his failure to display any trace of repentance.

'Don't expect remorse from me!' he snarled. 'The woman was a whore.'

'And all the German, Dutch and Scandinavian tourists?' chided the Judge.

'But they weren't Spanish!' exclaimed Legones in astonishment.

9

THE LADY DOTH RESIST TOO MUCH, METHINKS

It was not long before midnight on Whit Sunday, the Feast of Pentecost, and in the solidly Catholic town of Sankt Aegyd am Neuwald, there was music and dancing. It was May 19th, 1986 and spring had descended over the foothills of the Austrian Alps.

In the darkness of one of the side valleys leading away from the centre of town, an eighteen-year-old girl was running, panting, stumbling over the gravel of the narrow, unpaved road, crying hysterically.

She was naked except for a pair of short, beige socks, ripped and tattered by the sharp, split stones. From collar bone to naval, a splatter of fresh blood drew a red, sticky trail between her young, pink-tipped breasts.

There were houses along the road, dark at this hour, and she knew who lived in them. Sankt Aegyd am Neuwald is a small community of under twenty thousand residents and relatively isolated. Seventy miles to the northeast lies the capital, Vienna. The same distance to the north is Sankt Poelten and the Danube. There are no large towns nearby.

The garden gate of the first house was locked and she ran on to the next. This one was not and she flung it violently open, ran up the path to the front door and fell against the panels, hammering on them with her fists, whimpering hysterically.

There were sounds from inside. Although no light showed from without, Josef and Hertha Rath had been sitting in their living room, watching the late evening news on the television.

'Why Andrea!' exclaimed Josef as the light from the open door fell across the girl's face. 'It's Andrea Schoenbichler, Hertha. She's . . .'

'Naked,' said his wife, pushing him to one side and drawing the girl into the hall. 'And hurt. Get the cover from the sofa!'

Andrea was wrapped in the cover and taken into the living room. Hertha had seen by now that the blood on her body was not her own.

'Call my brother!' wailed Andrea. 'Call Hans! I've murdered Karl Groiss!'

The Raths exchange astonished looks. Karl Groiss, a thirty-two-year-old waiter, only lived some sixty yards down the road in a house which he shared with his mother. There was no conceivable reason they could imagine for Andrea Schoenbichler to have murdered him or even to have been in his house at such an hour.

However, whether they understood it or not, something had obviously happened and Josef immediately telephoned the police. In any case, he did not know where to reach Hans Schoenbichler.

A little agricultural community lost in the foothills of the Austrian Alps is not exactly a hotbed of crime and the Sankt Aegyd am Neuwald police force is small. At this hour of the night, there was no one in the Department of Criminal Investigation at all.

And there was scarcely anyone in the station. Slumped half-asleep behind the charge desk was a duty sergeant within six months of retirement who liked night duty because it left him free to work in his garden afternoons. He had been with the Sankt Aegyd am Neuwald police for over thirty years and, in all that time, there had been not a single case of homicide.

He was, therefore, uncertain as to how to deal with Josef Rath's telephone call. Sankt Aegyd am Neuwald presumably had a homicide squad, but he did not know who belonged to it, and more to the point, he did not know that a homicide had actually taken place. Josef Rath had said that Andrea Schoenbichler was in his house claiming that she had murdered Karl Groiss, but this seemed a highly unlikely thing to the sergeant. He had no idea who Karl Groiss was, but the girl, he knew, was a nurse at the local hospital.

Until he had more information than that, he was not going to turn out the head of the Department of Criminal Investigations, a man he had known for forty years and not one to be pulled out of bed in the middle of the night for nothing.

On the other hand, he could not simply let the matter slide. Some action had to be taken and all he could think of was to send the patrolman on standby duty at the station to investigate. He was a very young man with less than two months' service in the police and the sergeant regarded him as little better than half-witted, but he was all he had. He would have to do.

The Sankt Aegyd am Neuwald police budget does not run to many patrol cars and, in any case, the patrolman did not, as yet, have his driver's licence. He, therefore, made the trip to the Groiss home on one of the station's bicycles.

When he arrived at the house, he found it completely dark and the front door closed and locked. The sole indication of life was a reflection from the skylights in the roof against the night sky. The lights were, apparently, on in the attic.

The patrolman knocked timidly and, when there was no response, harder. He was nervous about knocking on people's doors in the middle of the night, but he was more nervous of the old sergeant.

After some considerable time and much knocking, there were shuffling sounds and Mrs Martha Groiss, the fifty-six-year-old, widowed mother of Karl, opened the door and stood staring at the patrolman in sleepy-eyed bewilderment.

'Has somebody been murdered here?' blurted the patrolman.

'Not to my knowledge,' said Mrs Groiss gravely. 'Have you been drinking on duty, young man?'

The patrolman was, of course, in uniform.

'No, no,' protested the patrolman. 'It's a man named Karl Groiss. We have a report that he has been murdered by Andrea Schoenbichler.'

'I do not know anyone named Andrea Schoenbichler,' said Mrs Groiss. 'My son's name is Karl. Perhaps you had better ask him about this. He sleeps up the stairs in the attic.'

She turned and led the way up the stairs with the patrolman following. When they reached the steeper stairs leading to the attic, she stopped and indicated that the patrolman should go on alone.

'I'm going back to bed,' she said. 'Karl can let you out.'

But Karl could not. The patrolman went up the stairs and came back down immediately. His face was white and his lips were trembling.

Mrs Groiss, who had been on the point of entering her bedroom, stared at him in astonishment and alarm.

'Where is the telephone?' said the patrolman, losing control of his voice so that it rose to a squeak. 'Something terrible has happened!'

Mrs Groiss gave a shriek of terror and ran towards the stairs which led to the attic.

The patrolman blocked her so violently that she was knocked off her feet and fell in a sitting position on the floor.

'No, no!' he shouted. 'You can't go up there!. Police orders! Go back downstairs!'

He seized the terrified woman and literally dragged her down the stairs to the ground floor. The telephone was in the living room and he held her in an iron grip while he dialled the number of the station.

The restraint was unnecessary. Mrs Groiss had ceased

to resist and had dropped apathetically down on to the sofa. The patrolman's appearance and manner evidence enough that what he had come to the house to investigate had, indeed, come to pass. Karl was dead.

The patrolman did not, however, want to say so in her presence and merely said that he was at the Groiss house and that the report received was confirmed. He needed reinforcements at once.

The desk sergeant was nearly as startled as Mrs Groiss had been, but he could recognize the urgency in the patrolman's voice and he immediately broke the connection, called the emergency ambulance and telephoned Inspector Anton Meier. Forty minutes later, the entire homicide squad of the Sankt Aegyd am Neuwald police was assembled at the house.

It consisted of no more than two men, the inspector, a burly, red-faced man with wavy, snow-white hair and a prominent jaw, and a sergeant of detectives named Peter Strauss who was normally concerned with petty larceny, narcotics and morals offences.

A third member of the squad, although not a police officer, was the Sankt Aegyd am Neuwald coroner, Dr Arnold Langbauer.

It was the first time in the history of the Sankt Aegyd am Neuwald police that the homicide squad had been assembled and they were all at something of a loss as to how to commence.

The inspector took charge.

'I expect you had better begin by examining the body, Arnold,' he said. 'I'll talk to Mrs Groiss and you go over to the Raths and take a statement from the girl, Peter. She's supposed to have confessed to the killing.'

The sergeant, a tall, lean, heavily tanned man with thin, hawk features, left without a word. He was, at best, little given to unnecessary speech.

The coroner, who was almost his exact opposite being short, plump, pink-cheeked and voluble, pulled on rubber gloves and got down on his knees beside the corpse.

It lay sprawled on the floor of a small entrance hall at the head of the stairs from which a door led into a sort of batchelor studio. The door was open and the lights were on. From the bed in the centre of the opposite wall a trail of blood led across the waxed floorboards to where the body lay.

Karl Groiss had been a handsome, athletic man with a small, black moustache and a round, cheerful face.

The face was not cheerful now, but contorted in the death grimace. He was completely naked and liberally smeared with blood which was still seeping from a gaping wound in the left side of his chest.

'Incredible!' said the doctor. 'He was apparently stabbed directly through the heart, but he lived long enough to stagger out here and pull the knife out of the wound!'

A large hunting knife stained with blood was gripped in the right hand of the corpse.

'His fingers are locked on it,' said the doctor. 'I can't pry them loose.'

'It's not important,' said the inspector. 'Look at the wall there! He seems to have slashed and stabbed at the wallpaper. What could that mean?'

'No idea at all,' said the doctor, 'but one thing is certain, this crime is connected in some way with sex. There's semen running out of the penis. He must have orgasmed seconds before he was killed.'

'It's not possible that he killed himself?' said the inspector. 'I don't know what we're going to present the examining magistrate with.'

The examining magistrate would be the judiciary official who decided whether a crime had taken place, who, if anyone, was responsible and whether the police should proceed with an investigation.

'Well, I guess anything is possible,' said the coroner doubtfully, 'but he'd have had to be crazier than anyone

I ever heard of. The knife was rammed into his chest to the hilt. If he did it himself, why pull it out again?'

'I expect it hurt,' said the inspector. 'You don't know him?'

The coroner shook his head.

'Neither do I,' said the inspector, 'but I think I've seen him working as a waiter at the Berthold tavern.'

'The ambulance is still waiting,' said the doctor. 'Do you think I could have them take the body over to the morgue now?'

The inspector hesitated.

'Better wait,'he said. 'We should photograph the body and the scene the way we found it and I don't know if Peter's brought the camera. Tell the ambulance they can go back to the hospital.'

He went off down the stairs to the living room where Mrs Groiss was sitting on the sofa with the patrolman holding her hand. She was staring unseeingly at the wallpaper and the inspector thought that she was in a state of shock.

'What do you know about this?' he asked as gently as was possible for a man whose normal speaking voice was a sort of gruff growl.

Mrs Groiss moved her lips silently a few times and then managed to bring out, 'Nothing.'

'Your son had a girlfriend?' said the inspector.

Mrs Groiss shook her head silently and abruptly broke into a veritable howl of anguish.

'The girls didn't like him!' she wept.

'Call Dr Langbauer,' said the inspector to the patrolman. 'This woman needs medical attention.'

The doctor came down, gave Mrs Groiss an injection and helped her up to her bedroom.

'She'll be out like a light for six hours,' he said, returning to the living room. 'Now what?'

'You stay here and look after things,' said the inspector. 'I'm going over to the Raths to see what happened to Peter. The statement shouldn't have taken this long.'

The sergeant was not, however, at the Raths.

'He took Andrea to the station,' bawled Josef. 'It's an outrage! She was the victim and he arrests her!'

'Groiss seems to have been something of a victim himself,' said the inspector. 'Didn't she tell you she killed him?'

'Well, yes, but . . . My God! Is Karl dead?' stammered Rath, crossing himself. 'What's happened? What's going on here?'

'That's what I'm trying to find out,' said the inspector and took his leave to go to the station.

Andrea Shoenbichler was seated in his office wearing one of Mrs Rath's dressing gowns. She had been crying and her face was streaked with tears, but she appeared to be calm and in control of herself. The sergeant was rewinding a cassette in the tape recorder.

'She wanted to make a statement so I thought I'd better take it immediately,' he explained. 'She admits she killed Groiss, but she says it was self-defence. He raped her and he was strangling her.'

The inspector picked up the telephone, called the Groiss house and when the doctor answered, asked him to come to the station.

'Miss Schoenbichler says that Groiss raped and strangled her,' he said. 'She should be examined as soon as possible so we have medical confirmation.'

'You'll have to take her over to my practice,' said the doctor. 'I can't carry out an examination at the station. Better have her mother present or some relative, at least.'

Mrs Anna Schoenbichler, Andrea's mother, was contacted and driven to the station by another daughter. No one knew where Hans was. He had been playing with his band, The Kobolds, at the Vogelleiter tavern earlier that evening, but had since gone off with the other musicians.

It was, by now, past two o'clock in the morning, but

the entire village was stirring. In such a small, close-knit community, news travelled fast. The story of the rape and murder had spread all over Sankt Aegyd am Neuwald and crowds began to gather in the town square and at the Groiss home.

In the meantime, the body and scene had been photographed and the corpse transferred to the morgue where Dr Langbauer was preparing to begin the autopsy.

The inspector, however, wanted first to hear the results of his examination of Andrea Schoenbichler.

'Was she raped?' he asked.

The doctor looked confused and slightly embarrassed.

'She was definitely subjected to intercourse,' he said. 'There was semen in the vagina and on the pubic hair.'

'That's not what I asked you,' said the inspector.

The doctor squirmed.

'It's not that simple,' he protested. 'She wasn't a virgin. There's a little irritation of the sex organs, but . . .'

'Can you swear in court that she was raped?' roared the inspector.

'No,' said the doctor.

'Indications of strangulation?' said the inspector.

'Some reddening of the skin on the throat,' said the doctor 'No serious bruising or finger marks.'

'I want an official signed report,' said the inspector.

He went into the outer office where Andrea was waiting with her mother and sister. They had brought clothing from home and she was fully dressed.

'You are charged with the unlawful killing of Karl Groiss,' said the inspector. 'I am releasing you into your mother's custody pending your appearance before the examining magistrate. You are not to leave the area and you are to hold yourself at the disposition of the police.'

All three Shoenbichlers broke into loud weaping and left the station clutching each other.

'The examination didn't support her story?' said the sergeant.

The inspector shook his head. 'Let's hear the tape,' he said.

It was not very long. She had, she said, gone that evening to the Vogelleiter tavern with her mother and sister. Her brother's band had been playing there and it was felt that the family should display solidarity.

At the tavern, she had been asked to dance by Groiss whom she described as a 'fat, old man in leather shorts'. She had not wanted to dance with him, but her mother had urged her to, saying that she had been watching Groiss and he had already been turned down by three other girls.

They had danced twice and he had invited her to the Berthold tavern, some fifty yards distant, for a cup of coffee. She had accepted and, after they had drunk the coffee, Groiss had asked her to come home with him.

She gone because he had told her that he had recently returned from Israel where he had taken a cure for psoriasis, a disorder of the skin characterized by rough, red patches, and she was interested as her brother-in-law had psoriasis. She had not been afraid because she knew his mother was living in the house.

He had taken her up to the attic where he had shown her pictures of nude girls which he said he had taken in Israel.

She had been nervous because he had locked the door, but she left it locked and put the key in her jeans pocket. He had laughed and asked if she did not trust him.

A little later, he had pulled a hunting knife out of the waistband of his trousers and had ordered her to strip. She had refused and he had pulled off her clothes until she was naked except for her socks.

Removing his own clothes, he had thrown her on to the bed, forced her legs apart with his knees and raped her.

While he was doing this, he had laid the knife on the dressing table beside the bed.

She had screamed and struggled in the hope that his

mother would hear and had threatened him, saying, 'Do you think I am going back to the tavern and will not tell anyone what you have done to me?'

He had replied, 'I'm not so sure that you will be going back to the tavern,' and had begun to strangle her.

She had seized the knife from the night table and stabbed at him blindly. It was only when he fell away from her that she saw the knife driven to the hilt in his chest.

She had run out of the room, down the stairs and to the nearest house.

'You suspect it didn't happen that way?' said the sergeant.

'Let's go over it point by point,' said the inspector.

'The girl was not a virgin. She knew what men want from pretty, eighteen-year-old girls. Yet she went to Groiss' house in the middle of the night to discuss psoriasis. The girl's not half-witted. She completed nurse's training.'

'Maybe she thought she could handle him,' suggested the sergeant. 'Equality of the sexes, that sort of thing.'

'Maybe,' said the inspector. 'But then, the locked door. She left it locked and stuck the key in her pocket. Where were her clothes when we were in the room?'

'On the back of a chair,' said the sergeant. 'His and hers.'

'But she's supposed to have run out of the room in a panic stark naked,' said the inspector. 'The door was locked and the key was in her jeans. Would she have to put them back on the chair after she got the key out?'

'Doubtful,' said the sergeant. 'There was the front door too. The patrolman said it was locked when he got there so she must have pulled it shut after herself. You wouldn't think a person in a panic would do that.'

'It's not a straight story,' said the inspector. 'She calls Groiss a 'fat, old man in leather shorts,' but he wasn't fat and, even to an eighteen-year-old, thirty-two is hardly senile. In the first part of her statement she seems to be saying that she didn't know Groiss from Adam, but when she ran into the Raths' place, she yelled, 'I've killed Karl Groiss!' and, on top of that, she says that she knew he shared the house with his mother.'

'She must have known him,' said the sergeant. 'You're going to ask for a murder indictment?'

'Not unless we can come up with a motive,' said the inspector. 'The first question the judge will ask is, "Why?" and we haven't any answer.'

'All I can think of is that they were secret lovers and they had a quarrel,' said the sergeant.

It was a logical theory and, indeed, no other was ever suggested. The only thing wrong with it was that it did not correspond to the facts.

Sankt Aegyd am Neuwald was a very small place. There was no such thing as a truly secret love affair and, certainly, not one involving Andrea Schoenbichler and Karl Groiss.

Both worked, meaning that their free time was limited. Both lived with relatives which reduced their personal privacy. Both were well known in the community and would have been noticed together. They never had been. In the end, the inspector was forced to accept that the only contact that had ever taken place between Andrea Schoenbichler and Karl Groiss was that on the night she had killed him.

In subsequent questioning, Andrea admitted that she had known Groiss' name, that he was a waiter at the Berthold tavern and that he lived with his mother. She did not know where she picked up the information, it was simply something she knew.

There was external confirmation of her statements too. She had gone to the Vogelleiter tavern unwillingly that evening. She had not wanted to dance with Groiss. Even the three girls who had refused Groiss' invitation to dance could be found.

Groiss had recently been in Israel for treatment of psoriasis and Andrea's brother-in-law did suffer from the same ailment. The pictures of nude girls were found in the night table in Groiss' room.

On the other hand, tests carried out with a female volunteer and a police officer showed it to be impossible for a woman lying on her back with a man on top of her to drive a knife to the hilt in the man's chest and equally impossible for her to take it from the night table without attracting his attention.

Andrea Schoenbichler was, therefore, indicted on an open charge of homicide and, on March 4, 1987, brought to trial. She pleaded guilty to homicide, but claimed self-defence. Groiss, she said, had been strangling her and, if she had not killed him, he would have killed her.

The prosecution charged that she had killed deliberately, but was unable to offer a plausible motive.

Faced with a great deal of conflicting evidence, the jurors deliberated for two days before deciding that Andrea had, indeed, acted in legitimate self-defence, but with excessive use of force.

On March 6th, she was sentenced to three years' imprisonment of which two years were suspended. As she had already spent over three months in pre-trial detention during the investigation, she was paroled a month later and sent home.

Since that time, the community of Sankt Aegyd am Neuwald has been divided into two camps consisting of those persons who believe that Andrea was totally innocent and those who think that she simply got away with murder.

10

THE PLUMBER, THE WHORE AND THE VIRGIN

As might be expected of a West German general practitioner, husky, pink-faced Dr Hermann May, a man with glasses as thick as the bottoms of water tumblers, did not normally see patients without an appointment in his practice at 27 Goethe Strasse in the city of Hannover.

And certainly not young women who charged through a half-filled waiting room, past the doctor's stupefied receptionist and into the inner sanctum at a quarter to eight in the morning.

'What does this mean?' shouted the doctor, hurriedly throwing a sheet over the shoulders of the half-naked woman he was in the process of examining.

'Help me!' gasped the girl. 'I've been raped!'

She was a beautiful girl with long, straight, white-blonde hair reaching nearly to her waist, but her eyes and nose were red from crying and she was trembling over her entire body.

Shock, thought the doctor. She's in shock.

'Would you get dressed and go to the waiting room, Mrs Wagner?' he asked his patient. 'I'm afraid this is an emergency.'

The woman hurriedly dressed and left and the doctor helped the girl on to the table.

She was wearing only a light cotton dress and shoes, although the date was September 18th of 1980 and the weather was beginning to turn chilly despite the autumn sun.

His examination revealed a mixture of blood and what appeared to be semen in the vagina and a hymen that had obviously been ruptured only a short time earlier.

Having collected samples and smears, he went methodically over the girl's entire body, taking note of numerous small bruises and two, large, black-and-blue marks on the insides of the thighs caused by clamping them over the hipbones of the rapist in a vain attempt to prevent penetration.

The indications were unmistakable. This was a clear case of the violent rape of a preciously intact virgin.

'Do you want me to inform the police?' he asked.

The question was legitimate. Not much more than ten percent of the rapes committed in West Germany are reported. The victim is intimidated by the thought of cross-examination in court. And, above all, there is the widespread belief that justice is rarely done in such cases. In an age where only crimes against property are severely dealt with, rape is often glibly described as 'a cry for help' and punished by nothing more than a little psychiatric counselling.

'Yes,' whispered the girl and fainted.

Dr May began, however, by calling the ambulance and having the girl transferred to the hospital. She was obviously badly shaken, even though not seriously injured physically, and she required care and, probably, psychiatric treatment which he did not have the facilities to provide.

While waiting for the ambulance to arrive, he revived the girl, told her that he was going to give her something to calm her nerves, did so and, as she once again lost consciousness under the effect of the powerful tranquillizer, telephoned the Criminal Investigations Department of the police.

Twenty minutes later, a sergeant of detectives appeared to collect the doctor's statement and a medical certificate attesting to rape. The amublance had by this time taken the girl away and all of the personal information spaces on the certificate were blank.

'Didn't you ask her name?' said the sergeant.

The doctor looked embarrassed.

'I didn't think of it,' he murmured apologetically. 'It was all so sudden . . .'

'It dosn't matter,' said the sergeant. 'I'll get the details from her at the hospital.'

But he would not, at least, not immediately.

'This woman is in a state of profound shock,' said the doctor in charge of the case. 'We cannot permit any questioning until we have had time to assess the extent of emotional damage. It will be, at least, two days and, probably more like a week.'

'By which time the rapist could be in Patagonia,' said the sergeant. 'Can't I, at least, ask her for her name and address so I can notify the next of kin that she's in the hospital? I understand she's a very young woman.'

'I'll see what I can do,' said the doctor. He went off and returned after a few moments.

'Her name is Tina Shuster. She's twenty years old and she lives with her grandmother at 71 Seehorst Strasse,' he said. 'She asks that we don't tell the grandmother she was raped. She's afraid it would kill her.'

The sergeant thanked him and set off for Seehorst Strasse which was on the eastern edge of the town. He was a compactly built, neatly groomed man, neither handsome nor ugly, and his manner was calm and businesslike. Hannover is a city of over six hundred thousand people. Rapes were not uncommon.

The woman who opened the door had to be in her sixties, but she did not look it. Had the sergeant seen Tina Shuster, he would have realized where she got the long, straight, white-blonde hair, the translucent complexion and the large, widely-spaced, china-blue eyes.

'Mrs Adelheid Hildenberg?' inquired the sergeant who had read the name on the mail box.

The woman inclined her head, polite but wary. Selling door-to-door is illegal in Germany, but some do risk it.

'Sergeant Manfred Peters of the Hannover Police,' said the sergeant formally, holding out his identification card. 'May I come in?'

He had deliberately omitted to state that he was from the Department of Criminal Investigations. Mrs Hildenberg was to believe that he was attached to the traffic department.

Still silent, but obviously bewildered and beginning to be frightened, she ushered him into a comfortable, middle-class living room.

'You are the grandmother of Miss Tina Shuster . . .,' began the sergeant.

Mrs Hildenberg turned pale and staggered back as if he had struck her.

'I knew it!' she whispered. 'When she didn't come home last night . . . Is she . . . ? Is she . . . ?'

'No, no, Mrs Hildenberg,' cried the sergeant hurriedly.

'She's perfectly all right. Just a slight accident, although she'll have to stay in hospital for a few days, but it's nothing serious.'

'Excuse me,' said Mrs Hildenberg faintly and sat heavily down in a chair. 'I was so worried . . . she's never spent a night away from home before . . . Was it a car?'

'Only a few bruises,' said the sergeant, not answering the question. 'May I ask you a few questions for the record?'

The much relieved Mrs Hildenberg proved co-operative, but not very helpful. She had brought Tina up, she said, her parents having been killed in a car accident when she was only fourteen months old.

'Does she have a regular boyfriend?' asked the sergeant, looking for a rape suspect. 'You say she's never spent a night away from home before?'

'Never,' said Mrs Hildenberg, 'and certainly not with

any boyfriend. Tina isn't like that. I know it's modern and progressive for young girls to be sleeping with just anybody who comes along, but I wasn't brought up that way and I haven't brought Tina up that way either. We both feel that she's still too young to become seriously involved with anyone. She does go out with young people, of course, but only in a group.'

The sergeant found all this mildly amazing. German girls of Tina's age were generally almost hysterically liberated as were women who looked like Adelheid Hildenberg, even if they were widowed and grandmothers. However, he did not doubt that the woman was telling what she believed to be the truth and, after obtaining the name of the company where Tina worked as a typist and the names of some of her girlfriends, he thanked her and left.

It was, by now, nearly noon and he returned to police headquarters, had lunch in the canteen and went up to the office of his immediate superior, Inspector Walter Busch, to report on what he had been doing.

The inspector listened rather absent-mindedly. He was a large man, very full in the middle, with a high complexion and very little neck.

'Probably carrying on an affair without her grandmother's knowledge,' he remarked. 'She'll be able to identify him once the doctor lets you talk to her. It wasn't some total stranger who attacked her on the street.'

'That's the way I see it too,' said the sergeant. 'She came home from work, changed clothes and went out again at around seven-thirty. She told her grandmother that she was going to have dinner with some of the girls from her office. She probably met this person with whom she was having the affair and he kept her prisoner in his apartment all night until she got out early this morning. I'll go over and take statements from the people where she works now. They may know who the man is.'

'Probably a waste of time,' said the inspector. 'Once

she calms down, she'll think twice about preferring charges and she'll be right. The defence would crucify her and, if the rapist served a year in jail, it would be a lot.'

The sergeant made no reply to this cynical remark, having heard similar before, and went off to carry out his duty like the honest civil servant he was. He did not feel that he was wasting his time. It was not his time anyway, but that of the state and the state required a methodical and serious investigation of a reported crime. That was what he was paid for and that was what he would provide.

The girls in the office where Tina worked were almost aggresively helpful and, upon being informed of what had befallen their colleague, immediately confirmed the sergeant's suspicions concerning a secret affair with an unidentified man.

Only it had not been an affair, they said, and they unanimously described Tina as being so morally conservative as to make Queen Victoria look like a swinger. Even a slightly off-colour joke and she turns red as a tomato, said the girls. We don't dare tell her what we do with our boyfriends.

'But the secret lover?' said the sergeant who could easily imagine what they did with their boyfriends, but was not interested. 'She never mentioned his name?'

The girls were not certain that she had known it. The initiative had been taken entirely by the man who was described as young, handsome, having a small moustache and being a natty dresser.

Since March or April of that year, he had waited outside for Tina to get off work. He had telephoned the office two or three times a day and he had sent huge bouquets of flowers. Indeed, one had arrived that very day. Tina had been permanently pink with embarrassment, but they thought that she had also been flattered - apparently flattered enough to accept a dinner invitation.

None of the girls in the office had been planning to meet Tina on the preceding evening as she had told her grandmother.

The sergeant asked to see the flowers, found the name of the florist on the wrapping and went to ask him the name of the customer who had been sending flowers to the office.

The florist said the man's name was Robert Bilden. He did not know his address, but he had often seen him on the street and had the impression that he lived in the neighbourhood. His description tallied precisely with that provided by the girls from the office.

The sergeant returned to police headquarters and got out the telephone book. He was looking for a Robert Bilden who lived reasonably near to the florist and to Dr May's practice. The girl, he reasoned, would have run into the first doctor's office she came to.

There was a Robert Bilden listed as living at 36 Weimar Strasse which was less than two blocks from the doctor's practice and the sergeant transferred his investigation to the Residents' Registry Office which contained the compulsory registrations of all residents in the city.

According to his registration, Bilden was a journeyman plumber, aged twenty-eight and unmarried, who had been born in a suburb of Hannover. A check of the police records showed no entry.

At this point, the sergeant went home for dinner, but returned at nine o'clock and began going through the bars and taverns in the area around Weimar Strasse. An unmarried man of twenty-eight could be expected to spend a good deal of time in such places and the sergeant wanted to learn a little more about him. There was no question of approaching him directly. At the moment, he was not accused of anything.

The sergeant was successful in the first bar he entered. Robert Bilden was locally famous and the mere mention of his name instantly produced a long string of anecdotes from the regulars.

Bilden was a lover to make Casanova look like a eunuch. No woman could resist him. His conquests were legion. His apartment was a hi-tech version of Sodom and Gomorrah with mirrors on the ceilings, pornography on the walls and the country's greatest collection of sex toys scattered around the floor. He had even seduced the chairperson of the local Women's Liberation Group, a grim veteran of the war between the sexes with the appearance and character of a pitbull.

Although ostensibly filled with admiration, it was obvious that the storytellers were really filled with envy and resentment. None of them was young, handsome and charming as Bilden was supposed to be. Their only candidates for seduction would be their own wives who probably wore long underwear, turned out the light before undressing and rationed them to once a fortnight.

Although it was hardly necessary, the sergeant checked on a few other taverns and, in those where Bilden was known at all, got much the same stories.

Well satisfied with his progress in the case, he went home, watched television for an hour and joined his wife in bed. She never turned off the light except to sleep, did not know long underwear existed and thought rationing referred to food.

'Bilden appears to be one of these men who regard women as a sort of challenge,' said the sergeant, reporting on the progress of the investigation to the inspector the following morning. 'He's like a mountain climber. He seduces them because they're there and the harder it is, the greater the challenge. If the story about the Womens' Lib chairperson is true, the man's a fanatic.'

'And, of course, Miss Shuster, with her antiquated moral standards, would have been the greatest challenge of all,' said the inspector, nodding. 'He must have thought he was dreaming when he ran into her. There's probably not another like her in all Hannover.'

'All Germany, I should think,' said the sergeant. 'I

haven't too much left to do before I'm finished with the case. I want to send a couple of men to Bilden's apartment house to see if we can find a witness who saw her enter or leave. We'll be ready then if she does prefer charges.'

The inspector found this a good idea and the sergeant was much gratified when the detectives returned with statements from two residents who had seen the girl entering Bilden's apartment at approximately eight o'clock Wednesday evening.

'Here we are,' said the sergeant, reading from the reports. 'Tall girl, dark, curly hair falling to the shoulders, impressive frontal development, heavy make-up, dressed like a whore . . .'

He came to a dismayed halt.

'That doesn't sound like the girl you described to me,' said the inspector.

'It isn't,' said the sergeant. 'Miss Shuster doesn't look anything like this. I haven't seen her myself, but, according to the doctor . . .'

'In short, you've been barking up the wrong tree, Manfred,' said the Inspector. 'Bilden didn't rape the girl. He had other company that night.'

'I guess he must have,' muttered the sergeant, considerably confused. 'But I don't see how . . . ?'

He picked up the second witness statement and began to skim through it.

'The other witness says here that the woman is a prostitute who hangs out in the Pink Pussy Bar,' he said. 'He knows her. Says she goes by the name of Helga Tallmann.'

The inspector tactfully averted his eyes and began shuffling through the files on his desk.

Such crass errors are not good for a civil service career and the sergeant spent two unhappy days reviewing the investigation and trying to determine where he had gone wrong.

He had still not arrived at any conclusion when he

was summoned to the hospital by the doctor who was looking after Tina Shuster. She was not yet fully recovered, but she was obsessed with the idea of filing criminal charges and was threatening to leave if she was not allowed to see the police.

To the sergeant's astonishment, she immediately named Robert Bilden as the rapist and said that the rape had taken place in his apartment at number 36 Weimar Strasse.

'I'm afraid that I can't accept that, Miss Shuster,' said the sergeant gently. 'We have evidence that Mr Bilden was entertaining a Miss Helga Tallmann in his apartment that evening.'

'Entertaining is right,' sobbed Tina bitterly. 'She raped me too!'

It took the sergeant some little time to digest this and still longer to accept even the possibility that it might be true. However, when Tina Shuster blushingly described certain aspects of Miss Tallman's anatomy which, if proved accurate, left no doubt that she had seen her in highly intimate circumstances, he was forced to abandon his theory that her mind had been affected by her experience.

That experience according to her tape-recorded statement, had been bizarre enough to affect the mind of a good many less chaste and more worldly maidens than Tina Shuster.

Bilden, she said, had begun courting her in March, but it had been May before she even consented to have cup of coffee with him in a café. Some of her girlfriends knew who he was and had warned her of his reputation.

He had, however, conducted himself like a perfect gentleman and the greatest intimacy he had attempted was to gallantly kiss her hand on parting.

'He really was terribly charming,' she said. 'He seemed like such a nice person.

'I told him that I didn't want to be seen with him because of his reputation and he said that that was all over. He had chased women because he was young and stupid, but now he was older and wanted to settle down with a nice girl and get married.

'I said I was too young to get married, but he said he would wait and he continued sending me flowers and waiting for me after work.

'During the summer, he began to ask me to have dinner with him in his apartment, but I always refused. I wasn't suspicious of him any more because he had always behaved so well, but I thought it improper.

'Finally, on the Monday before this happened, he asked me to dinner on Wednesday evening and said I didn't need to worry because his teacher from when he was in the fifth grade was coming too.

'I didn't tell grandma because I didn't want her to know I had been seeing Robert, but I thought nothing could happen if his old teacher was going to be there and I went.'

Bilden, it seemed, had gone to some lengths to avoid alarming his guest. He had taken down the pornographic pictures from the walls and had put away the sex toy collection. Only the mirror over the bed in the bedroom remained, but this room Tina did not see. Or, at least, not immediately.

The teacher had turned out to be rather different from what Tina had imagined. Helga Tallmann was only twenty-four years old and had been a prostitute for less than two years. Previously, she had been a secretary and had been one of Bilden's conquests at that time.

He had happened to run into her in the Pink Pussy Bar on September 3rd and had been given a free sample for old time's sake. She had asked how he was getting on with the girls now and he had replied that he was having trouble with the only intact virgin in Hannover who refused even to have dinner with him.

'I could come as chaperone,' suggested Helga. 'For a price.'

Unfortunately, Helga no longer owned any of the

clothes she had worn as a secretary. She was a professional prostitute and she dressed like one.

Tina had been, therefore, not a little astonished to find Robert's old teacher dressed up in a blouse with a neckline descending to the navel, a skirt scarcely wider than a scarf, black fishnet stockings with clearly visible pink, rose garters and six-inch high heels. Her make-up was in keeping with her costume.

None the less, the dinner went off decorously enough, but when it was finished, Robert suddenly cried out, 'And now for the main course!' which was apparently an agreed-upon signal for the supposed fifth-grade teacher flung herself upon Tina and began to remove her clothes.

Tina had tried to defend herself, somewhat handicapped by a sensation of total unreality, but Robert had lifted her on to the table and had held her while Helga subjected her to oral sex.

He had, presumably, assumed that this would put her in a receptive state, but it had, in fact, frightened and nauseated her.

Still fighting, but helpless against the man and the woman, she was stripped completely naked and carried into the bedroom. Spread-eagled on the huge bed beneath the mirrors, she was subjected to every form of sex that the imaginations of the prostitute and the plumber could devise.

Although this went on through the entire night, the only effect it had had upon her was one of disgust mingled with terror as she assumed that they would kill her once they had sated their lust.

Displeased by Tina's lack of co-operation and her inexpert technique in oral sex, which she was forced to perform on them alternately, they had cruelly pinched her over most of her body with special attention to the nipples and sex organs.

She had been raped by Bilden while Helga sat straddle over her face forcing her to oral sex by pulling her hair.

In what had apparently been a sort of sexual frenzy, the plumber and the prostitute had not confined their efforts to Tina, but had repeatedly engaged in sex between themselves, urging Tina to watch closely the proceedings in the mirror over the bed.

The orgy had continued throughout the night and had placed such physical demands upon the participants that, at a little after seven in the morning, Helga and Robert fell asleep exhausted.

Tina, who was expecting to be murdered, did not feel sleepy and, having seen where Bilden had hidden the key with which he had locked the apartment door, she slipped into her dress and shoes and let herself quietly out. She had run into the first doctor's office she passed.

Robert Bilden and Halga Tallmann were taken into custody and charged with rape, homosexual rape, assault, sexual assault and sequestration.

Both denied the charges, but Miss Tallmann was unable to explain how Miss Shuster could know that she wore a small gold ring through the left lip of her external sex organs or that she had a heart-shaped mole on her left buttock and she eventually confessed.

Although she confirmed Tina Shuster's statement in detail, she denied any responsibility for the acts. She had, she said, merely been acting according to the instructions of her client who had hired her for the job.

Having heard this statement, Bilden admitted that the charges were true, but said that it had all been Helga Tallmann's idea. He had been no more than a helpless bystander.

On June 22, 1981, after a trial held in camera, the court decided that both were guilty, but Bilden more so and sentenced him to five years' imprisonment. Helga was sentenced to sixteen months and fined thirty thousand marks.

11

A WAY WITH WOMEN

On the evening of Tuesday, November 11, 1986, Laura and Luigi Notaro received an unusual present – a dying woman.

The Notaros, who owned a small farm outside the southern Italian town of Maglie, did not at once realize that the woman was dying. They thought she was drunk or under the influence of drugs.

'Take care of her,' said the stocky man with a moustache, gave them a cheerful wave of the hand and drove away.

The dumbfounded Notaros stood staring after him for a moment and then turned towards the woman who had fallen to a sitting position in the dirt as soon as she had been helped, none too gently, from the car.

She stared back at them expressionlessly as if she did not know who they were or even what they were.

'Uh – madame . . . ,' said Notaro.

The woman began to cry. She was not a young woman, in her fifties or older, but she had once been beautiful and some of the beauty remained, although she was pitifully thin and very dirty. Her clothing was little better than rags.

'Help me get her into the house, Luigi,' cried Laura, her heart moved by the sight of a sister in distress. 'She's sick, terribly sick!'

Between them, they half-led, half-carried the woman into the farmhouse and laid her down on the living room sofa. She was gasping and choking as if she had difficulty in getting her breath.

'Heat some water,' ordered Laura. 'The first thing to do is to get the dirt off her. She looks like she's been sleeping in a manure pile.'

Luigi went to the kitchen to heat water and Laura began cutting off the woman's clothing with a pair of scissors.

From the kitchen, Luigi heard his wife cry out and he rushed back into the living room to find her standing beside the sofa with her fingers pressed over her mouth and her eyes round with horror.

The woman on the sofa had been wearing nothing but the dress which Laura had cut away. Beneath it, the body from neck to knees was covered with black bruises, angry red scratches and round, inflamed burns!

The Notaros did what they could, pulling away the filthy dress, washing gently the tortured flesh and trying to coax the woman to drink a little soup. She did manage to swallow two or three spoons of the soup and a little water but was unable to keep it down and immediately vomited it back up.

Although the Notaros had asked her name and whether she wanted them to call anyone, she had said not a word and they thought she was incapable of speech. Nor could she sleep, but lay with her eyes fixed on the ceiling, making convulsive, little movements with her hands, her body repeatedly shaken by terrible tremors.

The Notaros withdrew to the kitchen to confer.

'I think she must be in great pain,' said Luigi. 'She's been tortured, beaten . . . We should have taken the licence number of the car. We don't even know who she is.'

'I think we should call a doctor,' said Laura. 'She may be badly hurt inside. She could die.'

'It's late now,' said Luigi. 'The doctor isn't going to come out here at this hour and we have no way of getting her in to town. We'll have to wait until morning.'

The Notaros did not own a car. The income from the farm did not run to that. Although the land in the sunny, southern heel of the Italian boot is fertile, only the large landowners are rich. Luigi and Laura were hoping to become big landowners one day, but now they were still young and only just starting out.

Fortunately, it was November, not one of the busier months on a farm even in the south of Italy, for Laura insisted on sitting up with the woman and Luigi was unwilling to go to bed and leave the vigil to his wife.

They consequently spent the rest of the night in the kitchen, talking in hushed voices, keeping an eye on the sick woman through the living room door and drinking coffee to stay awake.

At a little after four in the morning, the woman began to give off low, rattling groans, broken by intervals when her breathing stopped altogether for what seemed minutes at a time.

The alarmed Notaros put more blankets over her and wiped her face with towels wrung out of warm water, but her condition worsened steadily and rapidly.

By five o'clock, it was obvious that something had to be done at once.

'She's dying!' wept Laura. 'You'll have to call the doctor.'

Luigi did not argue, but got on to his bicycle and rode swiftly into town where, after sustained knocking, he succeeded in bringing Dr Mario Brunelli's head out of his second-storey bedroom window.

The doctor, who thought that Notaro was drunk, told him to go away. Maglie is a small place, with a population of just over fifteen thousand, and medical emergencies at five in the morning are not common.

Luigi's explanation was so convincing, however, that the doctor agreed to come at once.

It was already too late. Upon their arrival at the farm, they found Laura in tears and a lifeless body on the sofa.

'She stopped breathing only a minute or two after

you left,' sobbed Laura. 'The poor woman! The poor woman!'

'But what is this?' exclaimed the doctor in horror, drawing the blanket back from the naked body. 'This woman has been tortured! Those are burns! Who is she? Why did you do this to her?'

The Notaros explained, but were not entirely believed.

'You mean that you never saw her before or the man either?' he said incredulously. 'He just stopped here, handed her over and left? Why did you accept her?'

'We didn't know what to do,' said Luigi. 'It all happened so fast. The car stopped and honked. We went out to the road. He pulled the woman out and she sat down in the dirt. He said, "Take good care of her", and drove away. You don't expect something like that.'

'I should think not,' said the doctor. 'If it's any comfort to you, I doubt that she could have been saved even if you'd called me immediately. She was obviously in a very weakened condition to begin with and I should not be surprised if she has suffered severe internal injuries from the beating.'

'What do we do now?' said Luigi. 'We have no experience in such things.'

'Call the *carabiniere*, of course,' said the doctor. 'This woman has been murdered.'

Actually, it was the doctor who called the *carabiniere*, the Italian rural police. The Notaros did not have a telephone.

However, the offices of the Criminal Investigations Department of the *carabiniere* were in Lecce, a town of nearly a hundred thousand inhabitants, thirty miles to the north of Maglie, and it was past eight o'clock before a homicide detachment arrived at the Notaro farm. As the circumstances had been described in vivid detail by Dr Brunelli, the detachment consisted of over a dozen detectives, specialists and technicians.

In charge of the detail was Detective-Inspector Luciano Rosso, a handsome, olive-complexioned man with very black hair, very black eyes and a carefully-trimmed, very black moustache.

His second in command, Sergeant of Detectives Silvio Antonelli, was equally dark, but more impressive than handsome. A squat, powerfully-built man, his moustaches were as fierce as those of a Corsican bandit and his eyes were deep-set and piercing.

As it turned out, neither he nor the inspector would have very much to do. Dr Brunelli had said in reporting the murder that it had taken place at the Notaro farm. A large detachment had, therefore, been sent to secure the evidence.

The specialists were, however, quickly able to determine that wherever the woman had been tortured, it was not at the Notaro farm. There are distinct differences in farm dirt and the dirt with which the woman's sole garment was saturated came from a farm, but not from the Notaros'.

In addition, the marks where the woman had fallen and the prints of her bare feet as she was led to the house were still visible in the soft dirt.

'Some one has been beating and torturing her for a long time,' said Dr Bruno Francese, the department's medical expert, 'and they have only stopped within the past twenty-four hours or less. Death took place less than four hours ago.'

'As a result of the torture?' said the inspector.

'More from the beatings,' said the doctor. 'Some of her internal organs are ruptured. She was already much weakened by undernourishment and she has a whole series of infections due to the lack of hygiene. I have never seen a human being in such a condition.'

'Nor I,' said the inspector, impressed by the doctor's manner. A tall, dignified man with a smooth, plump face and gold, pince-nez glasses, he was one of the most highly qualified experts in criminal medicine in the south of Italy.

'Can we have the autopsy report today?' said the inspector. 'No sexual indications, I suppose?'

'It was entirely sexual,' said the doctor. 'What other motive do you think he had? This woman has been in the hands of a sadist for years. Her condition is the result of satisfying his sexual needs.'

The party had brought the small trailer used for transporting corpses, usually victims of car accidents, with them and the body was wrapped in plastic and placed in it. The woman's dress, which the Notaros had thrown away behind the house, was put into another plastic bag. The Notaros' statements were tape-recorded and the party returned to Lecce.

When the body had been taken to the morgue, the face was cleaned and arranged into as life-like an expression as possible and photographed. The first task facing the investigation was identification of the victim.

'Which should also provide a suspect,' said the inspector. 'Once we know who she is, the identity of the murderer will probably become obvious. If he's been torturing her for all this time, she must have been living with him.'

According to the findings of Dr Frencese, it had been a long time indeed.

'Any bruises from old beatings have healed without trace,' he said, 'but the burns have left scars and some of these go back four years and more. They were all made with cigarettes or cigars.'

'Then, couldn't some of them be accidental?' said the inspector. 'I find four years of torture hard to believe.'

'It is very unusual for a woman to accidentally burn the lips of her vagina with a cigarette,' said the doctor.

The inspector gave an involuntary shudder.

'The cause of death?' he said, changing the subject.

'Ruptured spleen, ruptured intestines, lesions of the liver and kidneys, internal bleeding,' said the doctor. 'He used his fists and, probably, his boots on her. It's remarkable that she survived as long as she did. Time of death was around five this morning.'

It was late afternoon of November 12th and the doctor had just completed the autopsy. His findings were still being typed up for the official record, but in the meantime, he had come to make an informal report to the inspector in his office.

The sergeant was not present. Having been assigned the task of identifying the victim, he was supervising the distribution of the photographs of the face of the corpse and collecting reports from missing persons departments throughout the area. The dead woman's fingerprints had been taken so, in the event of someone answering to the description, a positive identification would be possible.

To the sergeant's surprise and dismay, his efforts produced no results at all. No woman in the age group and of the size and general appearance had been reported missing anywhere in the area within the past five years and there was no response to the information-wanted circulars bearing the dead woman's picture.

'It's possible that her sufferings changed her appearance so much that anyone who knew her can't recognize her now,' said the sergeant, 'but I have no explanation for the lack of a missing person report. Someone must have noticed that she had disappeared.'

'Not necessarily,' said the inspector. 'People in larger towns often go missing without anyone becoming alarmed. Sometimes, they assume that the person has moved without saying goodbye, more often,they simply don't care. People no longer look out for each other, not even down here in the south where we're a little less modern.'

'I've tried other age groups,' said the sergeant. 'Dr Francese says she was younger than she looked, around her middle forties. She hadn't passed menopause.'

The doctor had also found evidece of sexual activity within the twenty-four hours prior to the woman's death. Although he had been unable to recover any actual traces of semen, an abnormally high level of acid phosphotase, a by-product of the chemical breakdown of semen, had been found present in the vagina, mouth and anus.

'Considering that the victim has not washed in several years,' wrote the doctor with biting humour, 'the only suspects to be considered are those with a strong sex drive, an even stronger stomach and a deficient olfactory sense.'

The report had concluded with the observation that the victim had born several children who would now be fully grown up or nearly so.

'Which makes it the more puzzling that she was never reported missing,' said the sergeant. 'People normally notice it if their mother disappears.'

'She may be from some other part of the country,' said the inspector. 'Did you ever run a check with the records section?'

The sergeant had not and when he now did, the fingerprints from the corpse produced a local police file.

Her name was Giuseppa Santoro. She had been forty-five years old at the time of her death and she was on record with the Lecce police as an unlicensed prostitute.

'Strange sort of affair,' reported the sergeant. 'Here's the file. In the spring of 1982, some of the farmers out near Lequile complained that a woman living on a farm owned by a man named Antonio Cozzolino was engaging in prostitution.

'The farmers probably didn't mind, but she was collecting such crowds that it was becoming a local scandal and their wives may have got after them.

'It wasn't really the Lecce police's business and they let it slide until September of 1984 before they told Cozzolino, who was apparently getting all the money, to cut it out. The woman was brought in to Lecce and charged, but she was never tried and, after a couple of weeks, the charges were dropped and she was released.'

'But '82 to '84 falls within the period when Francese says she was being tortured,' said the inspector. 'She couldn't be working as a prostitute and be a prisoner of a sadist at the same time. And what about her children? Is she from Lecce originally?'

'Gallipoli,' said the sergeant, naming a town of some twenty thousand inhabitants on the Gulf of Taranto, forty miles to the south. 'I guess the children are there. According to her record, she was married in Gallipoli.'

'Go down there and see what you can find out,' said the inspector. 'And have that farmer she was living with brought in. I want to talk to him.'

The talk was not very informative. Antonio Cozzolino, a thirty-year-old bachelor, admitted that Giuseppa had lived at his farm from the beginning of May 1982 until September 1984, but said that he had had no idea she was prostituting herself until the vice squad told him to throw her out.

'I was sorry for her,' said the stocky, moustached farmer. 'Her husband kicked her out so he could marry a younger woman and her kids wouldn't do anything for her. She didn't have a place to stay so I let her have the spare room.'

'You were intimate with her?' asked the inspector.

'You must be joking,' said Cozzolino. 'Annamaria would have murdered me.'

Annamaria, it seemed, was Annamaria Reni, a twenty-seven-year-old, unmarried mother of four children, none of them, according to Cozzolino, by the same father and only the last by him. She had been living with Cozzolino since 1980 when her father had thrown her out for engaging in sex with casual acquaintances.

By a coincidence, Annamaria had produced her youngest on the same day that Giuseppa Santoro had died and had been in labour when Giuseppa's body was being carried to the morgue.

'Coincidences are supposed to mean something in a criminal investigation,' said the inspector, 'but I don't know what this one could mean. Did you locate any relatives?'

The sergeant had just returned after having been absent for three days. He had, however, not spent the entire time in Gallipoli.

'Six children,' said the sergeant. 'All legitimate and by her husband. It's true. He had six children by her and then threw her out and married a nineteen-year-old girl.'

'How could he get a divorce?' said the inspector. 'Remember? This is Italy.'

'He didn't bother,' said the sergeant. 'The kids are all grown up and poor as church mice. Mrs Santoro was living with the second oldest daughter up until May of 1982, but the daughter was married and had a child and it was a one-room studio apartment. She says it was a little crowded and that they were relieved when her mother moved out.'

'Does she know where she went?' said the inspector.

The sergeant nodded.

'She knew all about it,' he said. 'Mrs Santoro had a one-day job as a waitress at a farm wedding near Gallipoli and Cozzolino was hired to play the accordion there. They met. It was true love at first sight. She went to live with Cozzolino.'

'And where was Annamaria?' said the inspector. 'I thought she was jealous.'

'Not a sign of it,' said the sergeant. 'I talked to her kids. The oldest one is six, but he's better educated in sexual matters than most men of forty. He says that his mother, Cozzolino and Mrs Santoro all slept in the same bed when Mrs Santoro wasn't tied up in the barn. The kids all liked Mrs Santoro better than their mother.'

'But wait a minute!' protested the inspector. 'The boy was only four when Mrs Santoro left. Don't tell me his sex education started that early.'

'Probably did,' said the sergeant, 'but he's talking about 1986.'

'Mrs Santoro wasn't there in 1986,' said the inspector.

'Oh yes she was,' said the sergeant. 'She got kicked

out in September of 1984 and came quietly back on November 10th. She's been living in the barn ever since.'

The inspector digested the information briefly.

'In short,' he said, 'Cozzolino is our man.'

'Cozzolino,' said the sergeant nodding. 'Very violent type and, probably, a sadist. Mrs Santoro wasn't prostituting herself voluntarily. Cozzolino simply brought in the customers and they, more or less, raped her. They paid him. She didn't get a cent. I have a few of them who are ready to make statements in return for immunity from prosecution.'

'Bring them in,' said the inspector. 'It's your case. You solved it. You can wrap it up.'

The sergeant had been waiting for nothing else.

Antonio Cozzolino and Annamaria Reni were taken into custody that same afternoon and no less than nine of Giuseppa Santoro's former clients against her will submitted statements.

The most important statement of all, however, was that of Annamaria who said that she loved Antonio and would remain forever faithful to him and then proceeded to incriminate him in murder.

As the sergeant had already learned, Cozzolino had met Giuseppa at a farm wedding near Gallipoli in 1982. She had still been beautiful at the time, but, more importantly for Cozzolino, a sadist whose greatest pleasure lay in the domination of women, she had a docile, helpless manner which stimulated him greatly.

He had led her straight off behind the barn and Annamaria, who knew better than to oppose her lover in any way, had stood by while they engaged in sex.

Cozzolino had brought Giuseppa back to the farm, tied her to a chair, beat her half unconscious, forced her to the most disgusting sexual acts and left her without food or water until the following morning.

'I had to hit her too,' said Annamaria, 'but I didn't want to. I was afraid of Antonio.'

For over a year, Giuseppa had been subjected to daily

torture, but, being housed and fed however miserably, had made no attempt to escape.

'She was like me,' said Annamaria. 'She didn't have anywhere to go.'

At the end of a year, a salesman had dropped by to buy some eggs from Cozzolino and the talk had turned to women. Cozzolino had told the salesman that he had rather more than he could use and that if the salesman would like a nice girl cheap, he could arrange it.

The salesman had looked Giuseppa over and come to the conclusion that she was worth the price.

'She gave him a good time,' said Annamaria, 'because Antonio told her that she would be sorry for it if the customer was not satisfied and she knew what that meant.'

The salesman had been satisfied and had passed the word on with the result that Cozzolino soon found himself making more money from Giuseppa than from the farm.

However, the visit from the Lecce vice squad had frightened him badly as they had hinted that he could be prosecuted for procuring even if, as he claimed, he had known nothing of Giuseppa's business activities.

'Antonio is very law-abiding,' said Annamaria proudly. 'He's a good citizen.'

'Except for a slight tendency to torture women to death,' said the sergeant dryly.

Giuseppa, for a good reason it seemed, had mentioned nothing to the police about being tortured. She did not want Antonio sent to jail because she hoped to return to him. And, on November 10, 1984, she did, coming to scratch at the kitchen door like a dog that had been shut out and pleading to be let in.

She was in a terrible condition, having been sleeping in ditches and abandoned buildings and eating what she could steal out of people's gardens.

Cozzolino was, at first, adamant. The police had said

to get rid of her and he had done so. He did not want to risk any trouble with the police.

Giuseppa was, however, not a woman to be easily got rid of. Beaten to a howling pulp and dragged to the road, she came crawling back every time and it became a question of who would die first, she of the beatings or he of exhaustion from beating her.

In the end, he gave up and told her she could live in the barn. He had, in fact, rediscovered the joys of torturing Giuseppa and was more charitably inclined.

From November 10, 1984 to November 10, 1986 two years to the day, Giuseppa lived in the barn and earned her meagre keep as the sadist's toy before her apparently indestructible health started to fail and Cozzolino began to fear that she might die on his hands.

Being a man with a healthy respect for the law, he did not want any corpses on his farm and he had loaded Giuseppa into the car and had driven away with her. Annamaria had only learned what he had done with her from reading the newspaper.

The statements of Annamaria Reni and Giuseppa's former clients were quite enough for an indictment against Antonio Cozzolino, but there was also physical evidence found in his barn where a filthy sort of wallow showed where a suffering human had been chained for two long years.

Being left little choice in the matter, Cozzolino confessed and returned Annamaria's compliment by incriminating her. She had, he said, tortured Giuseppa as enthusiastically as he had.

As there was some evidence to support this statement, Annamaria was found guilty of complicity to homicide and, like Cozzolino, who was convicted of murder, sentenced to life imprisonment on May 8, 1987.

12

KEEPING IT QUIET

Corinne Dupont's date on the evening of Monday, February 2nd was, of course, a total disaster. She was not surprised. It had been nearly five years now since she had had anything like a normal date which was logical because she was not a normal woman.

She had not been one since that terrible day in June of 1976 when Patrick's best friend had come to tell her that Patrick thought it best that they did not see each other any more.

He had had a good reason, even if he had lacked the courage to tell her himself. He was happily married and the father of no less than seven children.

A large family, Corinne had thought dully. A large family.

It was all that occurred to her. She had not wept. The calamity had been far too serious for that. It was, quite simply, the end of her life, even if she continued to walk around and eat and drink and look like a living person.

Life without Patrick was manifestly impossible, although she had known him less than two years. They had met at the beach where Patrick was displaying his beautiful, bronzed muscles and, two days later, she had joyously surrendered up her virginity in a charming, little inn where it was possible to rent rooms discreetly.

She had been nineteen at the time and never before in love. It had been high summer, the glorious, golden summer of the French Mediterranean coast, and she had just exchanged her monotonous job in the shoe factory, where she had worked since she was sixteen, for the more cheerful and less demanding one of a chambermaid in one of the big hotels. Actually, the chambermaid's job paid less, but Corinne was pretty with large, soft, brown eyes, a cute fringe over her forehead and a neat, cuddly-plump figure so there were tips which more than made up the difference.

Now, she was twenty-six and it was winter. She still worked as a chambermaid in the same hotel and she was still pretty, but the appearance was deceptive for she was not a woman.

Not a real one, at least. Like the boy who swears never to wash the hand shaken by a sports idol, she had had no contact with any man since Patrick. She could not. The very thought revolted her.

But no one could see this and so she was often asked for dates, all of which turned out catastrophically. Sometimes she wondered why she accepted them. It was, she thought, because she had no reason for refusing without revealing the truth and that she could not do.

It had been no different on this cold winter evening of 1981. He worked at the hotel. He was a nice boy, a year younger than herself. Unmarried (with a twinge of pure agony in the region of the heart). There was no reason to refuse him.

'What would you like to do?' he had asked. 'The movies? A restaurant?'

'I would like to go to the Parc du Pharo' said Corinne, 'and watch the sea coming in.'

The Park of the Lighthouse lay on the southern tip of the entrance to the Old Port of Marseille, exposed to the fury of the winter storms. Its lee had sheltered great liners, rusty coasters, a thousand kind of sailing vessels, Roman barges, Greek triremes, Phoenician galleys and God knew what strange craft lost in the dawn mists of history. At night, when a storm was blowing in, it could be a too-old and haunted place.

She had not meant to put him off and he had not been

put off. The Parc du Pharo was, in fact, not at all a bad place to take a pretty girl for a little love-making and, perhaps, more. It was certainly private.

She had, of course, known what he had in mind. It was the same thing with all of them, but what else was she to do. If they went to the movies, he would be all over her and there would be an embarrassing scene. If he took her to a restaurant, it would be like obtaining money under false pretences. She could give nothing in return.

In the park, there would at least, be, no witnesses to any scene and the worst that could happen would be that she had a long walk home. She lived in the hotel and it was over a mile from the Parc du Pharo.

The evening went off practically by the numbers. They drove to the park in his little, old panel truck, very handy for lying down with the mattress on the floor in back. He proceeded to the laying on of hands. She informed him that she had come to look at the sea and nothing else. He tried persuasion, argument, finally, a little force. She got out of the car. 'You can go . . .' he had yelled, enjoining her to a physical impossibility, and had driven away.

Unoffended, she walked slowly down to the water's edge and stood looking out to sea. Except when the beam from the lighthouse flashed at its measured intervals, it was too dark to see anything.

The long, empty quay had been swept lonely clean by the Mistral, the sad, winter wind of the south, pouring inland like an invisible river, and lay featureless grey in the pools of light from the street lamps. To the right, Marseille, city of a million people, was a blaze of light.

There was no storm, but the waves were running high between the breakwaters, green-backed white-caps hammering and clawing at the stubborn shore.

It was a scene of aching solitude with nowhere a soul in sight, but she was not afraid. If you are already dead, there is nothing to be afraid of.

It was not quiet. The waves slopped and clashed against the cement walls of the quay, the branches of the leafless trees creaked and the Mistral whistled, whined, whispered and roared hollowly as if a giant were blowing across the neck of some monstrous bottle.

Because of the Mistral, she did not hear the motor of the big, black Renault R–20 as it slid slowly up behind her nor the sound of the stealthily opened doors.

The first indication she had that she was not alone were the hands gripping her biceps. They did not grip hard enough to hurt, but they sent a pang of fear through her such as she had never felt before and she screamed, instinctively, unthinkingly, the raw, throat-tearing cry of the human female in mortal terror of death or worse.

The wind took the scream, lifted it, enveloped it, made it its own and carried it many, many miles in over the plains of Provence. No one heard it.

Corinne did not scream again. She knew that there was no one to hear. Instead, she turned her head and looked at the men who were going to rape her. What else could they want? Chambermaids are not worth robbing.

There were four of them, all young, not unattractive, reasonably well-dressed, but with two or three days' growth of beard and thick, black, drooping moustaches. Like so many of the dwellers along the shores of the Mediterranean, they were stocky, lttle men, dark-haired, brown-skinned andbrown-eyed.

She saw all this with utter clarity as if her eyes had been transformed into a sort of camera and she thought, if I live through this, I shall never forget these faces.

With a feeling of astonishment, she realized that she wanted to live. She had thought she did not, but, now that her life was threatened, she wanted to live very badly. I must do nothing to frighten them, she thought. It was what the police were always urging rape victims to do, to co-operate. Better raped and alive than raped and dead.

But she had seen their faces! Was that not enough for

them to kill her? Adrenaline was pouring into her blood stream making her as wary as a cornered animal.

The men holding her arms said not a word, but pushed her in the direction of the car.

For an instant, panic got the better of her and she struggled wildly in their grip.

It was, of course, hopeless. The other two men moved forward and, between them they forced her into the back seat of the car. A man got in on either side of her. The remaining two got into the front seat and the car accelerated smoothly off down the Boulevard Charles Livon to turn left into the Corniche President J. F. Kennedy.

The direction frightened her. The high corniche running along the rocky headlands to the south of Marseille was a sinister place. Hardly a week passed without a report of a body found broken at the foot of the cliffs or tossing in the raging surf. It was the ideal place to get rid of a woman whom you had raped and whom you did not want to identify you.

Unreasonably, she was filled with anger. Why could the fools not wear masks? There would be no need to kill her then.

But wait! None of them had said so much as a single word. Could that not mean that they were concealing their voices? Perhaps, they did not realize that she had seen them back there on the quay. It was dark in the car. It would be dark wherever along the corniche they decided to stop and rape her. Perhaps . . . perhaps . . .

She had recovered a degree of optimism when the car pulled off the road, bumped over bare stone and came to a stop. In the light from the headlights, she could see that they were in a sort of natural little amphitheatre screened by a ridge from the road. One side apparently opened on to the cliff over the sea for there was nothing there, only darkness and the muted thunder of waves on the rocks far below.

To her astonishment and alarm, they began to pull

her out of the car. She had thought that they would rape her in it. Surely, the Mistral, now bearing scattered drops of icy rain that stung like buckshot, would discourage any normal person from sex outdoors.

If so, these were not normal people. Working as smoothly as a rehearsed team of acrobats and in what now struck her as an eerie silence, the four men set about raping her.

Draped over a rounded boulder in the pitiless glare of the headlights, her clothing was removed piece by piece until she was totally naked and only her shoes were left. Resistance was pointless and she offered none, but the men continued to hold her firmly, one on either side gripping an arm and a leg while the other two dealt with the undressing.

When they had finished, the men holding her released their grip and, for a moment, they stood silently around her, moving their hands in strange, quick patterns.

She could not imagine what they were doing. Was this some kind of occult ritual? Were the men members of some sect?

There was not long to ponder the matter for the men on either side once again grasped her wrists and ankles and drew her legs wide apart. One of the others stepped forward, unzipping his fly.

She had expected it to hurt. She was not sexually aroused and there would be no lubrication from her own secretions. In addition, it had been five years since she had engaged in intercourse. To her amazement, he entered her as easily as a knife sliding into butter and she realized that he was using an artificial means of lubrication. Rapists who thought of everything!

He was quick too. A half-dozen thrusts and he withdrew to relieve the man holding her left arm and leg.

The other three were repetitions. Quick, silent, lubricated. Almost before she knew what had happened and that it was all over, she was lying naked on the stone and the headlights were swinging in an arc over the rocks as the car regained the road.

Relatively painless as it had been, Corinne was left limp and exhausted, emotionally and physically drained as if she had just recovered from a long sickness.

The stone was, however, freezing cold beneath her back and it was beginning to rain harder.

Rolling off the boulder, she sat up and tried to collect herself. To her surprise, she realized that she was crying, deep, gasping sobs in which a great many emotions were mingled.

Above all, there was relief. They had not killed her. She was all right, not even injured.

But, nearly as strong as relief, there was outrage and anger. How could these men simply make use of her body as if she were some kind of convenience like a public toilet? She would see to it that they were punished for what they had done to her. She knew what they looked like. She could identify them. If she ever got back to Marseille!

A third and even stronger sensation came to overwhelm relief and indignation. It was fear.

She had, it was true, survived the rape, but would she survive the sequel? She was alone and naked in a near freezing temperature and strong wind and she had no idea of where the nearest house might be. That she was somewhere along the corniche meant nothing because she did not know whether there were any buildings there or not.

Cautiously, she began to grope for her clothing on all fours in the darkness. The first consideration was protection from the elements. Once she was dressed, she could get back out to the road and, even if no car passed, eventually make her way back to Marseille on foot.

Her handbag she found almost immediately. It was lying only a yard from the boulder on which she had been raped. There was, however, nothing in it that could help her. Putting the strap around her neck, she continued to crawl over the gravel and loose stones, struggling to control a growing feeling of panic. She could not find a single article of clothing!

Had the wind blown it away? Had the rapists taken it with them? It hardly mattered. The important thing was that it was not there and she was becoming terrible chilled. Her flesh was covered with goose pimples, every hair on her body stood upright and she was trembling uncontrollably.

Oddly, her knees felt warm and when she touched them, she found that she was bleeding. Some of the stones had sharp edges, but her fear had been so great that she had not felt the cuts.

It was impossible to remain there any longer. She would have to get out to the road as she was and hope for the best. The question was; where was the road? In the darkness, she had become totally disorientated and she no longer knew where she was within the little amphitheatre nor which way she was heading.

Near to hysteria, she crawled swiftly forward in what she thought was the direction of the ridge separating the amphitheatre from the road and, suddenly, her right hand was plunging down through empty air and the roar of the waves was loud in her ears. In her confusion, she had nearly crawled off the edge of the cliff!

Thrown off balance, she fell over to her right and her head struck hard against stone. For an instant, she thought that she was going to faint, but the fear of the sharp rocks and raging breakers in the darkness far below came to her rescue, giving her the strengh to roll back away from the fatal edge.

She had cut her head on the rock and blood was running down the side of her face. There were cuts on her breasts where she had flung herself down on the stones and her knees and hands were bleeding heavily.

Even so, her situation had improved for she had grasped something that she should have thought of long before. The Mistral was blowing straight inland off the sea. All she needed to do was go with it and it would bring her to the road.

But the road was the Corniche J. F. Kennedy and it was not much travelled at one o'clock in the morning. Nor were there a great many houses along it.

There was, however, an auberge, a small, country tavern, with the name of La Vache Qui Chante which means roughly At the Sign of the Singing Cow.

It has sometimes been noted that French auberges are often found in such improbable places that any custom can only come from the owner's immediate family and such an auberge was La Vache Qui Chante.

The owner was, therefore, not a little surprised when at twenty minutes to eight in the morning of February 3rd, a customer covered with blood, carrying a handbag and wearing shoes but nothing else, staggered through the door, croaked, 'A cup of hot coffee, please,' and fell unconscious on the floor.

Corinne had made it, much to the astonishment of the doctors at the hospital where she was taken following the tavern owner's hurried call for the emergency ambulance. On the basis of temperature, wind chill factor, exposure, emotional shock and loss of blood, she should have collapsed somewhere along the way and died.

As it was, she had nothing worse than superficial cuts and scratches and, by the following day, was recounting her experience to a Detective Sergeant Marcel Longuyon from the Marseille Police Department of Criminal Investigations.

The sergeant, a rather plump young man with soft, brown eyes and an unconvincingly fierce moustache, was sympathetic but faintly bored. In his profession, stories of rape were a very common occurrence.

By the time she had finished, however, his attention had been fully captured. From a professional point of view, this was a disturbing and unusual rape. Not because it had been a group of four men. That was unexceptional. It was the circumstances of the rape which were out of the ordinary.

The men had not been brutal with Corinne. They had carefully removed her clothing rather than rip it off her body. They had neither beaten nor tortured her. There had been no perversion, no oral sex, no anal sex, no forced female masturbation. They had taken a single turn each. And they had made use of a lubricating substance, believed to be vaseline, to render the process less painful. Remarkably considerate, methodical rapists.

Conversely, they had gone off leaving their victim naked in a near freezing temperature and strong wind on the edge of a cliff in total darkness over three miles from the nearest house. An act bordering on intentional homicide.

Finally, abduction and rape had been carried out with incredibly smooth teamwork. No one had seemed to be in charge, but the operation had gone off without a single word being spoken. It was difficult to see how such proficiency could have been attained without rehearsal or prior experience.

The most puzzling aspect of the case was, however, the strange movements of the men's hands which had so impressed Corinne.

'She thinks they're members of a sect,' said the sergeant, reporting on the interview to his superior, Inspector Denis Senault. 'She could be right'

'A sect for ritually raping girls?' said the inspector, who was large, round-faced and incapable of surprise. 'Well, why not? There are crazier ones. I think you've overlooked something though.'

The sergeant raised his eyebrows and waited.

'If you had abducted a girl with the intention of raping her,' said the inspector, 'and you had the choice between doing it in a nice, warm car or on an ice cold rock in the middle of a howling gale . . . ?'

'It wasn't a howling gale,' said the sergeant, 'but I see

your point. A man would have to be desperate to be even able to perform under such conditions.'

'Right,' said the inspector. 'And these men were not only able to perform, but they were quick on the trigger. They were desperate and that means they'll do it again. Only maybe the next time, the victim won't survive.'

'If they've already done it before, the cases should be in the records,' said the sergeant. 'The *modus operndi* is unusual enough that the computer should be able to fish them out.'

The inspector thought so too, but both he and the sergeant were wrong. There had been no similar case reported anywhere else in France.

By the time this had been determined, the sergeant and a squad of detectives had largely managed to verify Corinne Dupont's story.

The auberge was not the nearest building to the place where she had been left and she had walked and crawled nearly four miles that night. She had left traces of blood every foot of the way and the detectives were able to locate the amphitheatre, the cliff falling away to the sea and the boulder on which she had been raped. They found her scarf and her brassiere. The rest of the clothing was missing.

'No trace of the rapists,' said the sergeant. 'The ground is too stoney for tyre marks and they didn't leave a single potential clue. We went over the place by the square centimetre.'

'Then, all we can do is wait for the next one,' said the inspector, 'and hope that they'll be more careless.'

He did not think that there would be long to wait. An operation as successful as the rape of Corinne Dupont would encourage the rapists to an early repeat performance.

Perhaps, it would have, but, before that could happen, a potential suspect appeared and the case took on a decidely bizarre aspect.

Corinne, who was recuperating at her parents' home,

had called the sergeant in a state of great excitement to report that she had seen one of the rapists on television. He had been a guest on a local talk show.

There being no reason why rapists should not appear on television the same as anyone else, the report was taken seriously and the sergeant took into custody a short, stocky young man with a drooping, black moustache whom he then immediately released with apologies. The young man had been in the television studios taping the programme at the time that Corinne was being raped.

The sergeant went to tell Corinne this.

'I'm afraid you were mistaken,' he said. 'The man you saw on television is a deaf-mute and he was on the panel of a programme concerned with handicapped persons.'

'It was one of them,' insisted Corinne. 'He was making the same motions with his hands.'

'A gang of four deaf-mute rapists?' said the inspector. 'What next?'

'It would explain why they never said anything,' said the sergeant. 'Logical in a way. Deaf-mutes probably do have trouble finding girl-friends.'

'No doubt,' said the inspector,'but there must be hundreds, maybe thousands, of deaf-mutes in Marseille and how we're to find the right four, let along get an indictment against them, is beyond me.'

'You want me to drop it then?' asked the sergeant hopefully.

'Of course not,' said the inspector. 'Don't forget, they'll be trying it again soon.'

He was, however, once gain, mistaken. No further rapes by teams of four silent men who moved their hands in a curious manner were reported and the sergeant, steadily ploughing his way through the social security and handicapped associations lists, was beginning to narrow the field of potential suspects.

Even in a city of a million inhabitants, four-man teams of deaf-mutes were not common. In the end, there were only two whose whereabouts on the night of the rape could not be determined and the sergeant proceeded to arrests.

Taken into custody were Bernard Fabre, twenty-four, Guy Marchetti, twenty-two, Philippe Nowak, twenty-one, Jean Farsily, twenty-eight, and four other men who were subsequently released.

Fabre, Marchetti, Nowak and Farsily were all deaf-mutes and inseparable friends. None had a criminal record. All were small, stocky men with olive complexions and black, drooping moustaches.

Interrogated through an interpreter conversant with the sign language used by deaf-mutes, the four suspects began by proclaiming their innocence, but quickly broke down when confronted with their victim who unhesitatingly identified them.

Apparently sincerely repentant, they said that they had had great problems because of their handicap in finding girlfriends and had hit upon the idea of sharing one among them. They regretted having left Corinne in such perilous circumstances and had thought that there were houses much closer to where they had left her. They denied taking her clothes.

At their trial on May 14, 1982, they assured the court with tears in their eyes that they would never do it again, but the court apparently thought that, if they were let off this time, they might and handed down sentences of five years' imprisonment each.

Although Corinne reluctantly testified against them, saying that she would not want another girl to have to go through what she had suffered, she was forced to admit that she had found the experience beneficial. The physical and emotional ordeal had brought about such an alteration in her mental attitude that the affair with Patrick no longer seemed important.

She began going out on normal dates and is now happily married.

13

STARTING AT THE BOTTOM

The woman sitting upright on the bed had been pretty and she still did not look her thirty-seven years. She did look sick. Her pale cheeks were slightly sunken and there was a strange light in her grey-blue eyes. Her hair was the colour of oat straw and cut short.

'And you realized immediately, Mrs Elanson . . . ?', prompted Detective Inspector Oscar Andersson, inclining his massive, blond head attentively forward and holding out the microphone of the tape recorder in hands the size of squash rackets.

'As soon as the body was found,' said Albertina Elanson. 'It was the pipe. They had a picture of it in the newspaper. There was a deep scratch on the left side of the bowl. I'd have known it anywhere.'

The inspector remembered the pipe very well. It had been the most important clue in a case which had occupied the Criminal Investigations Department of the Linkoeping police for close to fifteen years.

Or rather the cases, for it was highly probable that the murderer of Anette Wernesson had also been the rapist of Marise Larson and a good half-dozen others, at least. The *modus operandi* had been identical in all cases.

Some of the rapes had taken place before the murder and the inspector had already been hunting the rapist when it took place.

The victims had all been young girls, adolescents, whose ages ranged from fourteen to seventeen. All had been blonde, but that was scarcely remarkable for a town in central Sweden.

According to the descriptions, the rapist was also blonde, very big and muscular. In Linkoeping, an industrial city of some eighty thousand inhabitants, producing, among other things, aircraft engines, pianos and furniture, there were several thousand young men answering to that description.

If the man's appearance was banal, his taste in sexual matters was not. Known to the police as the Chloroform Rapist, he anaesthetized his victims with a chloroform-soaked pad held over the nose and mouth before raping them anally. Never otherwise. Some of the Chloroform Rapist's victims had been virgins and they had remained so. Aside from a certain soreness, they recovered consciousness physically unharmed.

The exception was Anette Wernersson. Something had gone wrong there and the only thing that the inspector had ever been able to think of was that she had known the rapist personally, forcing him to kill her to avoid exposure.

As a result, the investigation had concentrated largely upon Anette's circle of friends, acquaintances and even relatives. A high proportion of sex offences are committed by persons related to the victim.

Either the theory was wrong or, perhaps, Anette had simply known too many people. She was a startlingly pretty girl, just sixteen years old, and it was impossible to say exactly how many people she had known.

A student in the local high school, she had gone to a youth centre on the evening of June 7, 1971, to listen to records with a group of friends of her own age. She had left at eleven o'clock to walk the mile and a quarter to her parents' home.

Anette had never arrived home and no one was ever found who admitted to having seen her after leaving the youth centre. She had vanished as if by magic.

Her parents, who had been out visting friends, had

not realized that she was missing until the following morning and even then were not greatly alarmed. Anette, they thought, had spent the night with a girlfriend.

It was nearly noon before they began telephoning her friends and past two o'clock before the police were called in. By this time, her parents had learned that she had left the youth centre at eleven o'clock alone and an immediate search was organized.

Although it continued for over a week, no trace of the girl was found and it was finally called off for lack of places to search.

The disappearance was not connected immediately with the Chlorofom Rapist as he had, so far, never hurt any of his victims except in the one place. Anette was, however, in the right age group and she had been very pretty.

She was far from pretty when she was finally found, entirely be accident, by a Mr Bjorn Andersson who was taking a walk in the forest near Linkoeping. It was the afternoon of August 2nd and, Anette having been dead for a week short of two months, decomposition was very advanced.

So much so, in fact, that she could not be identified by sight or by fingerprints. She had, however, had some dental work and this, together with the remains of the clothing and costume jewellery found on or near the body, was enough.

The body was autopsied by the Linkoeing police medical expert, Dr Sven Gregsson, who was unable to provide any information of use to the investigastion. Too much time had passed, said the doctor. He could fix neither a time nor a cause of death, nor could he determine whether she had been sexually violated.

'Much of the corpse has been eaten by birds, small animals and insects,' he wrote. 'What remains is nothing more than bones and rotting meat. At another time of the year, the body might have been better preserved.'

The summer weather had made the task of the police

examining the scene of the discovery of the body less difficult, but they had not been able to determine much either. They were not, for example, able to say whether whatever had happened to Anette had happened there in the forest or whether her dead body had simply been brought there for disposal.

The sole clue was a black, straight-stemmed pipe, much smoked and not a little battered, with the trademark 'Dollar' incised in the bowl. It was not an unusual brand and could be brought anywhere in Linkoeping. This one had obviously been brought a long time ago.

The only hope was that some one would recognize it from pictures printed in the newspapers and, although they did not mention it to the police, two people did.

One was the murderer. The other was frightened speechless.

'He wasn't home that night,' said Albertina. 'He often went out nights and never said where he had gone. I didn't suspect that he was the one raping those teenagers though.'

'Not even after you saw the picture of the pipe in the newspaper?' said the inspector.

'Not even then,' said Albertina. 'It didn't say anything about rape in the newspaper. It was just the girl that was murdered.

'We were having breakfast and I glanced over the top of the newspaper. He was staring right at me and there was something in his eyes that made my blood run cold.

'I couldn't stop myself. I said, "Where is your pipe?" and he said, "I lost it at work."

'I knew then that he had killed that girl.'

'You could have gone to the police while he was at work,' said the inspector.

'I couldn't prove anything,' said Albertina. 'You'd have had to let him go.'

The inspector did not reply. What she said was true. Her unsupported word that the pipe found near the body belonged to her husband would not have been enough to hold him.

There was no other evidence. Per Svenson, at that time twenty-four years old, was a perfectly respectable, young electrical equipment installer for a firm on the outskirts of the town. He and Albertina had married on May 11, 1969 and had moved into a comfortable cottage near Albertina's parents.

She had given up her job as a sales clerk in a men's clothing store, which was where she had met Per. His salary was quite enough to support both of them.

Per had no police record, no history of violence, and, if he was rather rough in his lovemaking, she had not found that too objectionable.

Albertina was, in any case, rather easy-going. Her father was an engineer with one of the local firms and she could have gone on to university, but she had preferred to leave school at eighteen and go to work. It gave her a feeling of independence, she told her parents.

She would see little independence once she was married. Per came and went as he saw fit and without explanation. When he felt like sex, which was often, he took it, whether she was in the mood or not. Curiously, perhaps, it was always straightforward vaginal intercourse. Per, it seemed, did not like variations in sex.

Nonetheless, Albertina was inclined to regard her marriage as successful up until the time of the discovery of the body of Anette Wernersson. After that, she lived in terror for she believed herself married to a monster, a murderer of young girls.

It did not occur to her that Per might also be the Chloroform Rapist, whose crimes had begun to attract much attention in the newspapers as the stories tended to increase circulation figures.

It had occurred to the inspector.

'Granted that we don't know how Miss Wernersson died or whether she was sexually assaulted,' he told his assistant, 'but the murder could easily have been a case where he kept the pad with the chloroform over her face for too long.'

'An accidental killing then,' said Detective Sergeant Lars Matson, 'but, even if it was indirect, the motive would have to be sex. There was no other reason to murder her.'

'Jealousy, if she had a boyfriend or got mixed up with somebody's husband,' said the inspector, 'but we've already checked that out.'

The sergeant remained silent. He was a tall, thin man, dark and haggard looking, and not someone who would be taken by many for a Swede. He did not see that it made little difference whether the murderer of Anette Wernersson was the Chloroform Rapist or not. There was no clue to his identity eitherway.

'The Chloroform Rapist is a compulsive sex psychopath,' explained the inspector, accurately interpreting his assistant's silence. 'He can't stop and every time he rapes another girl, we'll have another chance to catch him.'

'It was after the Larson girl was raped,' said Albertina. 'He drove me out to a house and he said, "That's her house. I know that you know, but, if you ever say a word, I'll gut you like a fish." I was so frightened that I couldn't answer him.'

The inspector knew what she was talking about. The girl had been called Marise Larson in the newspapers but that was not her name. She was only fifteen years old and rather slightly built and she had been anally raped so savagely that she had required surgery.

Otherwise, she had been no more harmed than the others and, like them, had been unconscious at the time. The rapist, a tall, blonde, muscular man, had pressed a cloth drenched in chloroform over her nose and mouth as he dragged her into the woods.

She had come to naked from the waist down and bleeding and had had a painful walk out to the road where she had been picked up by a passing motorist and taken to the hospital.

There, it had been possible to recover enough semen from her lower bowel to determine that the blood group of the rapist was B. This was the first time that this had been accomplished, but it only meant that men with other blood groups were excluded as suspects.

The inspector, who had been waiting for the next incident, went to interview Marise while she was still in the hospital, but obtained only another description of the rapist and his methods such as those already in the police files.

Marise had been on her way home from school on the afternoon of May 19, 1972, when a large, blonde man in a green car had pulled in to the curb beside her and had asked for directions. He had opened the door on the passenger side and, when she leaned in to explain, he had suddenly hauled her into the car and driven off.

He had not threatened her or, indeed, said anything at all after asking for directions, but it had not been necessary. Marise read the newspapers and she knew what was in store for her. Stiff with fear, she had noticed nothing, not the make of the car nor the licence plate number. All that she could tell the inspector was that it smelled like a new car.

Like her predecessors, she spent several days going through the police mug books, but was unable to find a photograph of the rapist.

With the exception of the identification of the blood group, the case provided nothing of value to the investigation. It did, however, confirm the inspector's prediction that the rapes would continue.

The total number of attacks was never ascertained. There were certainly many that were not reported.

'Usually between fifteen and twenty percent are,' said the inspector. 'Perhaps more in this case because the girls are all so young.'

'And, as we know of seven, not counting the

Wernersson murder,' said the sergeant, 'that would mean a total of thirty or over. How is it possible that we don't have a clue to his identity?'

It was a slightly foolish question. The sergeant knew the reasons very well.

The man's description matched that of thousands of young men in Linkoeping. There was no prior contact between rapist and victim to trace. The operation lasted such a short time that there was little likelihood of a witness. And the man's strength was such that the girls were as helpless as kittens in his hands. There was no possibility of resistance, no hope of escape, no time even to scream for help.

'He'll be raping them when we retire,' said the sergeant gloomily.

It sometimes seemed as if he were literally right. The investigation dragged on. The rapes continued at irregular intervals. On a few occasions there were vain hopes of a break in the case. An anonymous letter led to a suspect with a record of offences against young girls and there was, for a time, great excitement in the Department of Criminal Investigations when it was learned that he smoked a black, straight-stemmed pipe of the brand 'Dollar'.

Unfortunately, the subsequent investigation showed that he still had his pipe and, moreover, it was the only one he had had for many years.

'Wrong age group anyway,' commented the inspector. 'None of his victims had passed puberty.'

'And the wrong kind of sex,' added the sergeant.

The suspect specialized in female children around the age of ten whom he persuaded with gifts of candy, ice cream and money to masturbate him. He was not known to have ever attempted penetration and was believed incapable of it. He had, however, sometimes fondled his little victims' private parts.

There were several other reports concerning the pipe. It was, after all, a common brand. But all of the leads turned out to be valueless. During the entire period of fifteen years that the cases were under investigation, not once did the police have a valid suspect.

By the beginning of the 1980s, however, the rapes became less frequent and eventually ceased altogether, the last known anal rape with the use of chloroform taking place on September 14, 1982.

The victim this time was younger than usual as she was only twelve, but she was blonde and she looked older than she actually was. It was also a longer drawn out process and the girl recovered partly from the effects of the chloroform before it was over.

As the operation was intensely painful, she had begun to scream and struggle. The rapist had knocked her unconscious again with a violent open-handed slap to the side of the head and had fled without achieving orgasm.

'Getting old,' commented the inspector. 'He can't manage it any more.'

'It's a poor way to end a sex crime series,' muttered the sergeant in disgust. 'The rapist simply gets old and retires.'

But that was, apparently, what had happened and this would later lead to uncertainty as to whether Per Svenson really had been the Chloroform Rapist. In September of 1982, he would have been only thirty-five years old, too old to be a boxer or a high-performance athlete, perhaps, but still young for a rapist, many of whom continue their activities on into their seventies and, in exceptional cases, even older than that.

The twelve-year-old had, however, described him exactly as had all of the others, big, blonde, strong and, if she had estimated him to be middle-aged, it was because, by the standards of a twelve-year-old, thirty-five was middle-aged. Asked to indicate other middle-aged men, she had picked ones as young as thirty.

Even Albertina did not know.

'I used to go through his things when he was out,' she told Inspector Andersson. 'He had cut out the stories about the murder of Anette Wernersson from all the newspapers and he had them pasted into a scrapbook.'

'Did he have any clippings about rape cases?' asked the inspector.

Albertina shook her head.

'The only ones I ever saw were about Anette Wernersson,' she said.

By March 14, 1985, there had been no chloroform rape cases for over two years and the murder case of Anette Wernersson was officially classed as unsolved. The inspector had been reluctant to abandon the investigation, but there was nothing left he could do.

Then, on that Thursday morning, one of the Linkoeping newspapers received a long, anonymous letter in the mail. The writer claimed to know the identity of the murderer of Anette Wernersson and included certain details which indicated an intimate knowledge of the case. Although the editor did not think the letter was authentic, he handed it over to the police anyway.

It was a curious document, rambling, incoherent in places, and it did not name the murderer or anyone else other than Anette.

'It's obviously the work of a person who is seriously disturbed,' said the inspector, 'but he or she definitely knows more about the murder than what was in the newspapers. We're going to follow it up.'

'How?' said the sergeant. 'It isn't signed and there's no return address. The only name in it is the girl's.'

'We have the envelope with the postal district where it was mailed,' said the inspector. 'And it's written in longhand. If we can find the writer, we can make an identification by means of the handwriting. We'll start by getting an opinion on whether it was a man or a woman.'

'A woman,' said the graphologist unhesitatingly.

'Definitely a woman and, I think, one who has severe mental problems.'

'Enough to require her hospitalization in a psychiatric institution?' asked the inspector.

'I should think it very probable,' said the expert.

'Excellent,' said the inspector to the sergeant. 'Now, find out what is the nearest psychiatric institution to the postal district where this letter was mailed.'

There was one in the district itself and it was soon determined that the letter had been written there for it was on stationery provided for the use of the patients by the clinic.

At this point, however, there arose a problem. In the clinic were nearly two hundred people of whom more than half were woman. Most of these were wards of the court or the social welfare department and not legally competent to agree to questioning by the police.

There was a great deal of paperwork to complete and many authorizations to obtain and it was only on August 6, 1986, more than a year after the receipt of the letter by the newspaper, that the author was identified as Albertina Elanson.

Once identified, Mrs Elanson proved co-operative, although not always entirely clear-headed. She had been in the clinic since the beginning of December 1983 as the result of a complete nervous breakdown. Since then, she had been making slow, but steady progress and it was hoped that she could be released into the care of her family by the end of the year.

'Anyone would have had a breakdown,' she told the inspector earnestly. 'It's a terrible thing to kill someone, but, of course, I had to do it. He'd have killed me otherwise, sooner or later. He was getting more violent in bed all the time and sometimes he would put his hands around my throat when we were making love and squeeze until I couldn't get my breath.

'That night – I think it must have been in 1982 or, maybe, '83 – I'm still a little confused. It was spring though, I know that.

'He was sleeping hard. I think he'd had something to

drink. He didn't drink much so when he did, it had a strong effect on him.

'Anyway, he was alseep and I told myself, "It's now or never. If you don't kill him, he'll kill you." Besides, he had to be punished for what he did to that poor girl.

'So I took his belt and put it around his neck and I pulled as hard as I could and I kept on pulling until he was dead. After that, I don't remember what happened. I guess I had my breakdown and they brought me here.

'I'm not sorry I killed him. He was a monster.'

'Are you going to charge her?' asked the sergeant curiously when he had listened to the tape recording of Albertina Elanson's remarkable confession. 'After all, she was withholding information concerning a felony for fifteen years while we were breaking our heads with the investigation.'

'No point,' said the inspector. 'She's not mentally competent to stand trial. Besides, she doesn't have any first-hand knowledge of the crime other than the identification of the pipe. Her statements are unsupported.'

'So what do we do now?' said the sergeant.

'See if we can find some support for them,' said the inspector. 'What we want to know is whether Svenson was the murderer and or the rapist.'

The sergeant did not think there could be much support for Albertina Elanson's statements concerning the murder of Anette Wernersson and he was right. If Per Svenson had had a collection of clippings on the murder, it had long since disappeared and there was nothing else.

All that could be determined was that the pipe found at the scene of the discovery of the body was definitely his for it was recognized by several of the people with whom he had worked.

However, the simple fact that the pipe had been found near the body was no proof that Svenson was the murderer. It could have arrived there by another agent.

Identification as the Chloroform Rapist was more

successful. He had owned a green car at the time and some of the former victims were able to pick his photograph out of a selection of pictures of large, blonde men.

In the end, however, it was testimony from an unexpected source which provided final confirmation.

Albertina's family had, of course, been notified of her statements concerning her former husband and her confession to having murdered him. A few days after this notification, Albertina's younger sister by two years, Martina, came voluntarily to police headquarters and made a statement in which she said that her brother-in-law, Per Svenson, had raped her anally less than six weeks after the wedding. She had never told anyone because she did not want to disrupt her sister's marriage.

'Well, it looks as if the cases are finally solved,' said the inspector. 'Even if Svenson will never be brought to trial for them.'

'If he was guilty, he's been punished more severely than he ever would have been by any court,' said the sergeant. 'A horrible death. Why do you think she made that confession?'

'Confession between wish and reality, according to the psychiatrists,' said the inspector. 'She really believes she killed him.'

The investigations had shown that Albertina Elanson had divorced Per Svenson on March 16, 1983. The divorce had not been opposed and for a good reason. Svenson had been dying of lung cancer. He was a strong man and he had taken a long time to die, but, on July 7, 1984, after great suffering, he had breathed his last in the intensive care unit of the Linkoeping general hospital.

At the time, Albertina was already a patient in the psychiatric clinic on the other side of the city.

14

ONE FOR THE RECORD

Comfortably cool, naked and relaxed, twenty-eight-year-old Marie-Claude Pichon lay dreaming peacefully in the bedroom of her second floor apartment at 28 rue d'Anjou. It was the night of July 10, 1980 and in downtown Paris it was hot, but here, in the nearby town of Versailles, there was a breeze and the temperature at one o'clock in the morning was agreeable.

Abruptly, the darkness of the bedroom was replaced by the glow of the ceiling lights. Marie-Claude sat up in bed, roused from her sleep, confused, alarmed and immediately frightened.

Standing at the foot of the bed was a man, a tall, strongly built man. His head was covered by a hood with slits over the eyes and the mouth and he was wearing gloves. His right hand was stretched out in front of him and she thought he was holding something small in it.

There was a sudden, sharp click. A slender, gleaming blade shot out and Marie-Claude realized with terror that the object was a knife.

'I suggest that you co-operate,' said the man, his voice muffled by the hood. 'That way no one will get hurt. Are you on the Pill?'

The question so amazed Marie-Claude that she could only nod dumbly in reply. A sex maniac who wanted to know if his victim was taking the anti-baby pill?

'Good,' said the man. 'Let us begin with the foreplay. Get down on your knees. If you bite, I'll cut your throat.'

Marie-Claude followed orders. She had no choice.

Resisting a sex psychopath with a knife in his hand was suicidal.

The foreplay did not last long as the man quickly became excited, pushed her on to the bed and raped her, resting her ankles on his shoulders and arriving at his climax in less than a minute.

He then led her to the toilet, which was separate from the bathroom, deftly removed the door handle with a screwdriver and left her locked inside, frightened, indignant, but also relieved as it was obvious that he had no intention of harming her further.

As the toilet had no window, Marie-Claude was unable to escape and it was nearly noon of the following day when the concierge noticed that the handle of the apartment door was missing.

This was such a strange thing that she made no attempt to enter the apartment, but immediately called the police. A team of officers arrived in a patrol car, knocked on the door, rang the bell and, having received no response, tripped the lock and went in.

A few minutes later, they found Marie-Claude, chilled and stiff from sitting naked on the toilet for over ten hours. She was taken to the hospital where she was examined and enough of her assailant's semen recovered from her vagina to establish that his blood group was O.

She then went to police headquarters where she recounted her experience in detail to an Inspector Louis Mornay from the Versailles Police Department of Criminal Investigations and swore out charges of rape and burglary against persons unknown.

Until learning it from the inspector, she had not known that she had been robbed as well as raped. She had not had time to examine the apartment before going to the hospital, but the inspector's men had and they had reported that there were clear indications of a search for valuables.

And a successful one. Upon returning home, Marie-Claude found that she had been robbed of the equivalent of two hundred dollars and some cents in cash, jewellery to the value of over five thousand dollars, a portable radio, a small television set, a tape recorder, a hi-fi, several small kitchen appliances and numerous other compact and comparatively valuable items.

'An extremely sophisticated thief,' reported Sergeant of Detectives Charles Ardeche who had been in charge of operations at the scene. 'He did not remove his mask or his gloves once. He took only things that could be easily disposed of. And he used a pick or a skeleton key to get in. No damage to the doors other than the missing handles and we recovered them from the garbage can downstairs.'

He was a serious, young man, this sergeant of detectives, neatly dressed, clean-shaven and in perfect physical condition, but he was tired. An investigations sergeant in the suburbs of Paris puts in a great deal of overtime, most of it unpaid.

'Removing the door handles is a new twist,' remarked the inspector, tugging thoughtfully at the ends of his black, drooping moustache. 'I can't recall hearing of it before. It may be useful for establishing his profile. The rape was probably incidental.'

The sergeant nodded in agreement.

'She's a pretty woman and she was sleeping naked,' he said. 'The burglar just got carried away.'

That was also the opinion of Dr Bruno Dunoyer, a medical sex crimes expert attached to the department. A thin-faced man with sandy hair and huge, upswept, sandy moustaches, he had been called upon to help establish a profile of the rapist-burglar's *modus operandi* for the purposes of a search of the police records.

'Not in my line, really,' he said. 'The man's a burglar, not a sex psychopath. Rape wasn't the motive.'

It was one of the most monumentally inaccurate statements ever made by a police expert. Over the next six years, the Phantom Rapist, as he came to be known, would violate, at least, sixty more women. Even this incredible total was probably an underestimate. The rapist had kept no records and he could not always remember exactly where, when and whom he had raped.

The police records of unsolved rapes were more accurate, but there were, undoubtedly, many that were not reported at all. In the opinion of Inspector Mornay, the final figure could well reach a hundred or more.

However, on this dismal, grey, January day of 1981, he had still not fully grasped the extent of the operation with which he had been entrusted.

'He can't keep it up,' he said, shifting his very considerable bulk in his swivel chair and resting a stubby-fingered hand on the stack of files on the desk. 'Seven rapes and burglaries since the Pichon case of which five are definitely by the same man. Sooner or later, he's going to make a mistake.'

Although his voice was confident and his manner self-assured, he was actually more than a little worried. The Phantom had been keeping it up and with monotonous regularity. That it had been the Phantom in five of the cases, there was no doubt. All of the rapes had taken place in the suburban districts surrounding Paris. All had been by a man wearing a hood and gloves. All had been accompanied by burglary.

And, if that were not enough, the victims' apartments had all been entered by use of a picklock or a skeleton key and the door handles had been removed after the victim had been locked in the bathroom or the toilet.

'Some could be imitators,' said the sergeant gloomily, 'if any of the details had been published in the press, but we didn't release any and Miss Pichon says she was never even interviewed.'

'Why would she be?' grunted the inspector. 'Rapes and burglaries are a dime a dozen around here. She could have been murdered and, unless he did something spectacular to her, it wouldn't have got more than a couple of paragraphs.'

'He's not hurt any of them,' said the sergeant cautiously.

It was, of course, the fear uppermost in the two men's minds.

The Phantom was no sadist. He had not physically injured any of the victims. He had simply forced them to sex against their will under the threat of a switchblade or, in one case, a spray can of tear gas, sold widely in France for the purposes of self-defence.

But none of the known victims had offered any resistance. What would happen if one did? At the rate he was going, sooner or later, the Phantom was sure to run into a victim who would fight back. Would he use the switchblade then? Or was it merely bluff?

No one could say, least of all Dr Dunoyer who had been forced to concede that his original estimate of the Phantom's motives had been wide of the mark.

'He's not in the books,' he said. 'The behaviour is not that of a psychopath. No frenzy, no particular conditions, no specific type of victim. On the basis of the victims' statements, he's perfectly conventional male with a strong, but not abnormal sex drive.'

'But is he capable of killing?' said the inspector.

'Anybody is capable of killing, given the right circumstances,' said the doctor. 'You should know that better than I. There's no basis for a prediction.'

Nor for anything else. The Phantom's *modus operandi* was flawless. He introduced himself into an apartment somewhere in one of the dozens of districts around Paris without breaking the lock. If there was a woman alone in the apartment, he raped her and stole what he could find. He never removed his hood or gloves. He never left any trace of his identity. He never struck twice in the same street.

So far, the police had learned only two things about the Phantom. His blood group was O and he spoke with a Parisian accent. As this was true of roughly two million people in the area, the knowledge was not very useful.

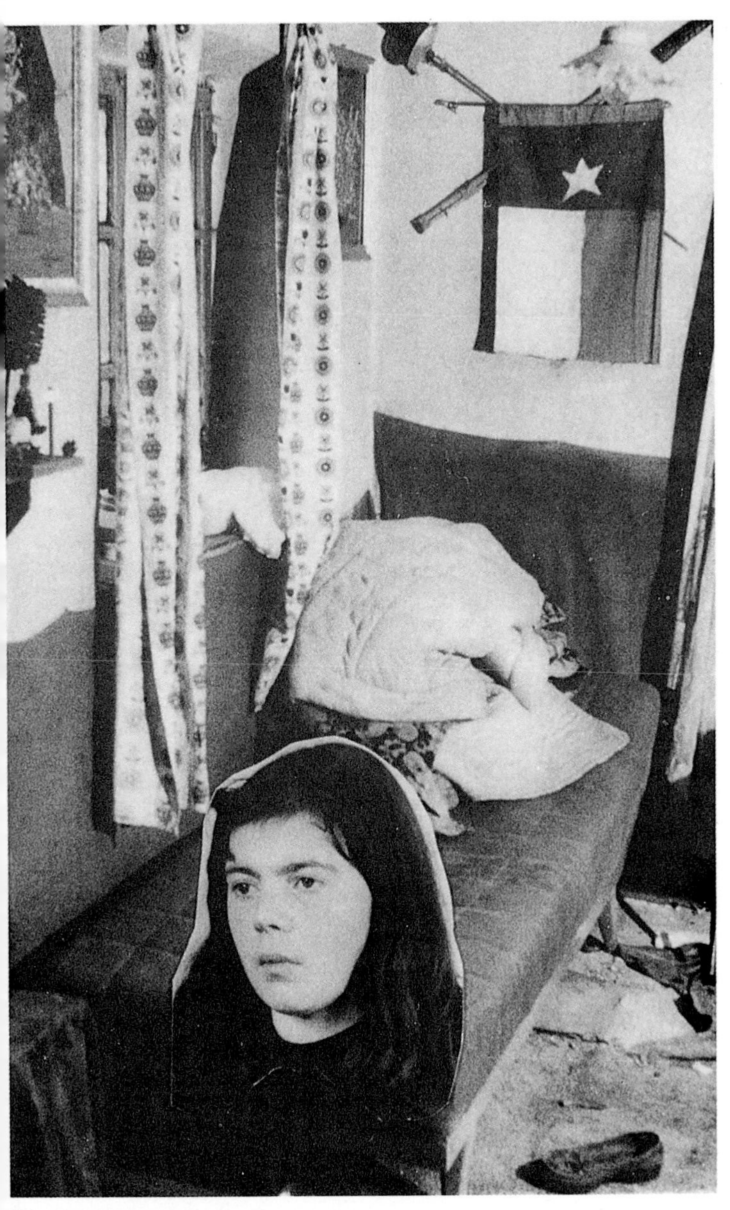

Elisabeth Adler and the bed on which she died
(Village Recreation Facility)

Wilhelm Padberg *(Village Recreation Facility)*

Jean-Claud Daillet *(Man's Best Friend?)*

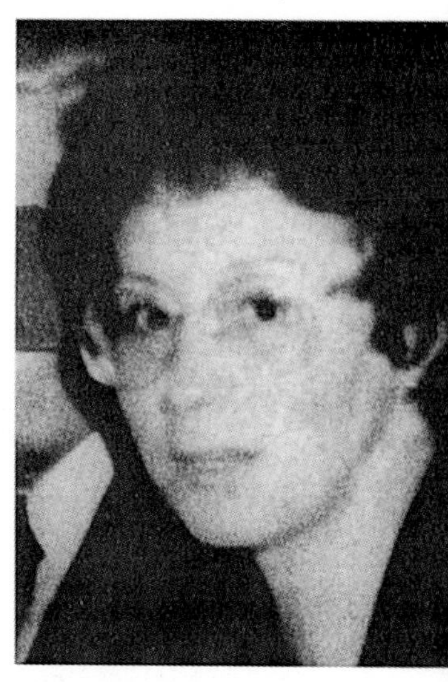

Nicole Daillet *(Man's Best Friend?)*

Maurice, the German shepherd dog *(Man's Best Friend?)*

The house where Dr Ulrich Koschwald tortured his 'girlfriends'*(A Male Supremacy Knight's Dream)*

Approximately two weeks later, on February 6, 1981, the police learned something else about the Phantom. He was health conscious.

On that Friday night, a Miss Paulette Jacques was asleep in the bedroom of her apartment at 46 rue Lanne in the northern suburb of St Denis when she was awakened by someone turning on the ceiling light. The figure at the foot of the bed was wearing a hood and gloves and was holding an open switchblade in his right hand.

There were, by this time, at least, a half-dozen women in the area around Paris to whom the figure would have been familiar, but it was not to Miss Jacques. The police had still not released any information on the series of rapes and burglaries. As the crimes invariably took place in the victims' own apartments, it would not have helped potential victims to avoid them and could have made the investigation more difficult.

Miss Jacques, however, rightly deduced that she was confronted by a sex criminal in her own bedroom and, although she was only nineteen, she instantly thought of a ruse to save not her virginity, which had been lost some time before, but her dignity. A modern girl with strong ideas on the subject of the equality of the sexes, she objected strongly to engaging in sex under coercion.

'You'd better use a contraceptive,' she said cooly. 'I'm under treatment for venereal desease.'

The stratagem was only partly successful. The Phantom did not rape her, but her forced her to perform oral sex on him, taking rather longer than usual to arrive at his climax. He made her wash her hands and brush her teeth first.

The outraged Miss Jacques was then locked in the toilet, the door handles were removed and the Phantom ransacked the apartment, making off with only a modest booty as Miss Jacques was not wealthy and had only recently moved in.

'She's certain he has a moustache,' said the sergeant, who had taken the victim's statement. 'While she was kneeling in front of him, he threw his head back and she saw it. She says it was thick and black.'

'Hardly an unusual colour for this part of the world,' observed the inspector, 'but every little bit helps. Try another run through the records section computer. Burgles, rapes, uses switchblade, big, burly, black moustache.'

The computer responded. File not found. Further information requested. The inspector had no further information and the Phantom continued to rape and rob at a brisk, steady rate.

He had still not physically injured a victim by the middle of September of 1982 when a Mrs Solange Millet, who was twenty-five years old and lived in the stylish suburb of St-Germain-en-Laye, was astonished and frightened by the sudden appearance of a man wearing a hood and gloves in her living room where she was watching television.

It was ten o'clock in the evening and Mrs Millet was alone in the house, her husband being temporarily absent on business.

The Phantom, who had raped other women in their living rooms when he found them there, produced a can of tear gas and told Mrs Millet to take off her clothes. Mrs Millet promptly did as she was told. She was five months pregnant and terrified that the rapist might injure her unborn child.

'Be gentle with me,' she pleaded. 'Don't hurt my baby.'

'Where is it?' asked the Phantom.

Solange Millet patted her only slightly swollen belly.

'Here,' she said. 'In here.'

To her amazement, the man in the hood made her a sort of respectful, little bow, put his can of tear gas back in his pocket and left the room without a word.

It was nearly an hour before the terrified woman ventured out of the living room, discovered that the man was no longer in the house and called the police.

Her description of a man wearing a hood and gloves tripped the alert which brought the inspector and the sergeant out of bed for the dozenth time and they drove to St-Germain-en-Laye, cursing the Phantom for invariably committing his crimes at night, although they were usually not pulled out until morning when the victim was found.

Unlike Paulette Jacques, Mrs Millet had escaped entirely. She had not been sexually abused and she had not been robbed.

'It was because she was pregnant,' said Dr Dunoyer. 'He's probably a family man.'

'A chivalrous rapist?' said the inspector. 'A sex criminal who respects mothers? What next?'

There was no answer to the question, but the sergeant ventured to point out that, if the Phantom did respect mothers-to-be, he had not been very respectful toward those who were already mothers. Two of his victims had been the mothers of babies and he had raped them next to the cribs, in one case, obtaining co-operation by threatening to harm the baby.

But threats were all that the Phantom had employed. Not one of the known victims had been so much as bruised. Was the rapist incapable of murder?

'Not at all,' said the doctor. 'If he ever has to actually injure one of them, he may panic and kill her. Every attack is a high risk situation.'

The inspector was fully aware of that and he was also aware of the fact that there were hundreds of unsolved homicides of women in and around Paris. Any of them could have been committed by the man in the hood. As the victim had not survived, there was no description of the killer.

'But there are no cases where the door handles were removed,' noted the sergeant.

'No need,' said the inspector glumly. 'He only removes them to lock the victim in and, if she was dead, it wouldn't be necessary.'

The rapes and robberies continued, steadily and at scattered points around the perimeter of the city, seldom within the city itself, and at irregular intervals, but averaging once every five weeks.

'Probably much more frequent,' theorized the inspector. 'They're not all being reported.'

'Statistically, two in ten,' said the sergeant, 'but that can't be the case here or he'd die of exhaustion.'

'I wish he'd die of something,' growled the inspector. 'Forty odd offences and all we've learned is that he has a moustache.'

The conversation was taking place in the inspector's office on the morning of Monday, June 4, 1984, and, in the suburb of Vincennes on the other side of Paris, twenty-four-year-old Claire Douillet was threading toilet paper through the ventilation grille of the toilet in her apartment at 57 rue Michelet.

Miss Douillet had tried shouting through the ventilation grille, but the apartment was on the fourth floor and no one had heard her. The toilet paper was her last chance to attract attention and save her from death by starvation.

Like so many before her, Miss Douillet, a remarkably pretty girl with a great mane of golden-blonde hair, had been awakened by someone turning on the lights in the bedroom where she was sleeping in a short and transparent nightie.

The nightie had been removed at the insistence of the man with the hood, gloves and switchblade and Miss Douillet had been raped. There had been no foreplay. The short, transparent nightie and her outstanding beauty had been quite stimulating enough without it.

She had then been ushered, almost gallantly, into the toilet, the door handles had been removed and she had been left to cry hysterically with humiliation and impotent rage.

It had been around three in the morning when she was shut into the toilet and, having soon stopped crying and regained control over her nerves, she had been trying ever since to get out.

She knew that it was now morning for she could see the gleam of daylight through the ventilator and she was hoping that someone would notice the toilet paper hanging down the side of the building and report it to the concierge.

If no one did, she was doomed. The apartment building was large and almost new, meaning that the tenants strictly minded their own business. Worse yet, she had only arrived in the Paris area a month earlier. She had not yet found a job and she knew no one. Eventually, no doubt, her relatives in the south of France would become concerned by her failure to answer letters, but, by then, it would be too late. Although there was water in the toilet, there was nothing to eat.

Fortunately, there was a light breeze in Vincennes that day and Miss Douillet's toilet paper banner floated straight out from the building in a very conspicuous manner so the she was released from her prison before nine o'clock.

It was over an hour before Inspector Mornay and Sergeant Ardeche arrived as they had had to go all the way around Paris and traffic was heavy.

They found no one at the apartment other than the concierge. Miss Douillet had taken a taxi and gone to the hospital, not because she was injured, but because she had not been on the Pill and was terrified of becoming pregnant.

The officers settled down to wait for her return. They did not think that she could furnish them with any useful information concerning the rapist, but they knew that it was one of their cases for the concierge reported that the victim had said the man was wearing a hood and the door handles were missing. At most, they expected a list of what had been stolen.

This Miss Douillet was able to provide and, to their gratification, it included several pieces of monogrammed silver which the young woman had inherited from her grandmother.

The monogrammed silver was important as it could be traced. No other leads being available, the inspector was concentrating on the search for items stolen in the burglaries. Some had already turned up, but it had not been possible to determine who had sold them. The indications were, however, that it was not a professional burglar.

Claire Douillet turned out to be one of the most valuable witnesses. Not only was there the matter of the monogrammed silver, but she was able to add a new detail to the Phantom's description.

'The end of the ring finger on his left hand was missing,' she said.

'He took his gloves off?' exclaimed the inspector incredulously.

The Phantom had not removed his gloves. Such a mistake was completely alien to him. He had, however, gripped Miss Douillet's ankle with his left hand as he pressed her legs nearly to her head in his favourite raping position and she had seen what none of her predecessors had noticed, that the empty tip of the glove finger was flattened and turned under.

'That's the reason for the gloves!' exulted the sergeant. 'It isn't simply fingerprints. A missing finger would make identification easy.'

'Well, not easy,' said the inspector. 'God knows how many men there are in Paris with a missing ring finger on the left hand, but it does help.'

Despite his caution, he was beginning to feel moderately optimistic. For the first time, enough details were coming in to make an identification from the records possible. Assuming that there was a record. The records section computer said that there was none. Nowhere in France and at no time since the records had been begun had there been a burglar who raped vast numbers of women, wore a heavy, black moustache and was missing the last joint of his left ring finger.

'So he's got no police record,' said the disappointed inspector grimly. 'The fellow's so successful that he's never been caught even once. You checked on Louby?'

Antoine Louby was the only name produced by the computer as being that of a known burglar who was missing the tip of his left ring finger. Unfortunately, he was short, thin and blond and, worse yet, he was in jail and had been for the past three years.

The sergeant nodded.

'He was in jail at the time of many of the offences and he wasn't out on leave. He's not eligible for leave because the last time he was given one, he didn't come back.'

Prisoners in European jails are often given leave for one reason or another. Not infrequently, they fail to return.

The inspector was back to where he had started with no suspect at all. There remained, however, the burgled items and an all-out effort was launched to locate them.

In the meantime, the Phantom continued to rape and rob, encountering on March 8 of 1985 his first serious resistance.

This was sheer bad luck for there should have no one in the house at 19 Avenue Gabriel Peri in the suburb of Gennevilliers at all, the twenty-seven-year-old woman who had occupied it having moved the preceding day. She had, however, left some of her possessions to be picked up later and her thirty-year-old brother, Jerome Dubois, was sleeping in the house to protect them.

Awakened from his sleep by someone turning on the lights in the bedroom, the startled Dubois found himself confronted by a tall man wearing a hood and gloves. Whether he was carrying his switchblade or not, Dubois was unable to say as, correctly assuming the man to be a burglar, he leapt instantly out the bed and charged him.

There was a scuffle during the course of which the

man's hood was torn away revealing his features. The man recovered it and immediately fled, pursued by the raging Dubois who was, however, too heavy to run very fast and quickly lost sight of him.

Although he did not suspect that this was a man who had, by now, committed a minimum of fifty rapes, he called the police to report an attempted burglary.

The mention of the hood immediately brought in Inspector Mornay, but Dubois' description added little to the known aspects of the man's appearance. He did, however, estimate his age as being close to forty.

'Strenuous way of life for a man of that age,' remarked the inspector dryly.

The incident with Dubois failed to discourage the Phantom for he raped and robbed another woman in Nanterre the following week. There were no clues.

Nor were there any in the weeks and months that followed up until late in 1986 when the patient tracing of the stolen items began to pay off. Several of the smaller appliances and some of the silver had been located in the possession of firemen stationed at Eaubonne in the Val d'Oise.

Questioned by the police, the firemen said that they had bought the things from Fire Chief Jean-Pierre Marsal, a forty-two-year-old married father of two grown children who had been decorated three times for bravery in fighting fires.

Marsal had no police record, but he did had a thick, black moustache and the last joint of the ring finger on his left hand had been bitten off in a brawl many years earlier.

Taken to police headquarters for questioning, his house was searched and a ring of skeleton keys, gloves, a hood, and a number of the stolen items were found.

The evidence was overwhelming and Marsal eventually confessed to sixty-one rapes and burglaries, give or take a half-dozen. As the police had suspected, Marie-Claude Pichon had been his first victim.

The only explanation he was able to offer for his abrupt conversion from fireman to champion rapist in May of 1980 was boredom. He had been recuperating from a torn Achilles tendon at the time and, having never had a hobby, he had looked around for something to do. The choice had been unfortunate for, on December 8, 1986, his avocation was terminated by his arrest.

By the time he is able to resume it, he may be too old. On June 5, 1987, having pleaded guilty to all charges, he was sentenced to fourteen years' imprisonment.

15

A HELPING HAND FOR BATTERED WIVES

The anonymous telephone call was one of twenty-seven received by the police that Monday in September of 1984. Copenhagen, the capital of Denmark, is a city of 650,000 inhabitants with twice that number in the extended urban area. Twenty-seven anonymous calls was below average.

Like all such calls, it was recorded and turned over to the relevant department for investigation, in this case, a newly formed section for dealing with cases of battered women.

Although radically liberal in many respects, Scandinavians beat up their wives as enthusiastically as anyone else and, this having become a burning issue in the press, the police had moved to do something about it.

Actually, they were only concentrating into a single department what had been previously taken care of by the various sub-stations throughout the city. Beating someone up, whether your wife, your girlfriend, your sister, your daughter, your mother, your grandmother or a total stranger, was assault. If a complaint was made, the police took action.

In this case, it was hard to see what action could be taken. The caller, a woman by the voice, had said that she had not only been beaten by her husband, but by a person who was supposed to be defending her and that he had raped her on top of it. She said she did not know the name, but she described the man. She then hung up.

'It would help a great deal if she had mentioned what organization he was working for,' said Inspector Sven Karlsson, the officer-in-charge of the unit, known unofficially as Beaten and Maltreated or BAM. 'Could be a social worker. Could be somebody from one of the private associations. Could even be a church worker.'

A huge, blond block of a man with cold, blue eyes and a very short haircut, the inspector did not regard anyone as being above suspicion.

'Average height, stocky build, blond, clean-shaven,' said his assistant, Detective Sergeant Otto Bergmann. 'We might have better luck trying to trace the clothes. Leather jacket, dark blue trousers and lighter blue shirt. Sounds almost like a uniform.'

'Well, see what you can do,' said the inspector. 'We have to investigate as much as we can regardless.'

The sergeant went off to see what he could do with the description in the personnel office of the social welfare department, the church groups and the private women's rights associations, all of which handled battered wives cases. He was not expecting to find anything significant nor did he. It did not upset him. He was fully aware that any other form of an assault charge reported anonymously would not have been investigated at all.

It was only when two further such calls were received in May and August of 1985 that he began to regard the matter seriously.

'It's a strang thing,' he told the inspector. 'The descriptions are practically identical so there definitely is some man beating up and raping battered wives, but why don't they identify themselves?'

'You're sure it's not the same woman who made all three calls?' said the inspector.

'Listen to the tapes yourself,' said the sergeant.

He pressed the play button on the tape recorder and sat patiently, a short, stocky man with a soft, drooping, brown moustache and a rough complexion, while the recordings ran through.

'All right,' said the inspector. 'It's three women and the reason they don't identify themselves is that they're from a social and economic level of society where they can't afford a scandal. They want this fellow stopped, but they don't dare use their own names.'

'Then, I fail to see how we're supposed to stop him,' said the sergeant. 'I've already run that description through every organization dealing with battered wives and there's nothing.'

'We'll have to wait,' decided the inspector. 'Sooner or later, if he keeps this up, he'll run into one who will tell us her name and we'll be able to get enough additional details out of her to identify him.'

As a matter of fact, someone was contemplating doing that at that very moment and, if she had done so, no further police investigation would have been necessary for Julie Kiel knew very well what the man's name was and where he worked.

The pretty, twenty-eight-year-old woman was, however, afraid. Not of her husband, although he had beaten her so savagely that she had ended up in the hospital which was where the affair with Niels had begun.

He had driven her home from the hospital and there had been, of course, no one in the house because her husband was spending the night in jail as a result of the complaint.

Niels had simply followed her into the living room, pushed her down on to the sofa, raised her skirt, pulled off her panties and entered her without so much as a word.

She still did not know why she had not resisted him. He was the only man she had ever had other than her husband and it had not even been particularly pleasant. She was still sore all over from the beating.

Illogically for a woman being, at least technically,

raped, she had worried about her appearance. Walter had blacked both her eyes and her nose was swollen. She had black and blue marks all over her and her eyes were red from crying. Perhaps, it was a subsconscious wish to revenge herself on Walter. She knew that he was as helpless as she. A scandal would ruin both of them and she was too attached to the comfortable life as the wife of an important businessman to think of divorce.

In any case, she had agreed to come to Niels' bachelor apartment the following day and she had been going there ever since. Walter probably knew, but there was nothing he could do about it. He was not anxious to be exposed as a wife beater, let alone as a cuckold.

No, it was neither Walter nor Niels that she was afraid of. It was the men who came to Niels' apartment to have sex with her while Niels watched or, sometimes, to watch while Niels subjected her to every humilating form of sex ever devised by the twisted mind of man.

She knew who some of those men were. They could break Walter and Niels like matchsticks with a single telephone call. If she went to the police over what was happening, they could and would break her too.

The affair had been going on since 1980 now and it was apparently going to go on forever. Although she had thought about it a thousand times, there was no way that she could end it. None of the anonymous telephone calls to the police were from Julie Kiel.

Curiously, it had never occurred to her that there might be others in the same situation. She thought that she was Niels' only mistress.

She was not though and, if Walter Kiel was leading an unhappy life in the suspicion, if not the certain knowledge, of what his wife was doing, Lars Asborg was in a permanent paroxysm of frustration and rage for it was not only his wife, but also his daughter who had become Niels' mistresses.

It had begun on a Tuesday evening, May 12, 1985, when he had administered a not exceptionally sound correction to his forty-year-old wife, Gertrude. Asborg, a prominent and successful lawyer, had been in the habit of using his fists on his wife for twenty years and she had never before sought help. Nor did she on this evening. Rather, it was Anna, their nineteen-year-old daughter, who had become frightened by her mother's screams and groans and had telephoned for help.

Help had arrived and Asborg had spent the night in confinement, but, to his boundless relief, there had been no official charge. Had there been, he would have been ruined. As a known wife beater, he would have been lucky to avoid disbarment. He had returned home, pleased at his narrow escape, and only then had learned that there would be a price to pay.

Gertrude's rescuer had returned during his absence and had made lover to her in Lars' own bed. He knew this to be true because Getrude had told him, going into considerable detail and obviously relishing every minute of it. She knew that he was completely helpless, unable to defend himself without ruinous consequences. She would continue the affair as long as she chose and he would never even dare to strike her again.

If Lars found this unthinkable, there was worse yet. Anna, it seemed, had been standing outside the bedroom door, listening to her mother and Niels make love and watching through the crack. When he had finished, she was waiting for him as he came out. She had changed into a totally transparent nightdress that reached barely to her navel and it would have taken someone far stupider that Niels not to realize what she had in mind.

It was a tribute to his virility that he could meet the challenge so satisfactorily as to be able to add mother and daughter to his collection of permanent mistresses.

Gertrude had not neglected to tell Lars about Anna, but the girl, who was apparently not overly attached to her father, had told him as well.

Since then, Lars' life had been a living hell. He was a proud and jealous man and, although he might have eventually accepted professional ruin in exchange for revenge, he was unable to bear the thought of public exposure of his wife's and daughter's sexual relations with Niels.

Although Gertrude and Anna knew about each other and, indeed, sometimes simultaneously occupied Niels' bed, Gertrude neither suspected the existence of Julie and an unknown number of other mistresses nor that Niels was continuing to rape and, not infrequently beat more severely than had their husbands, the women he was supposed to help. Like Julie, she thought that she and her daughter were Niels' only mistresses.

Anna, it seemed, gave the matter no thought at all. As she would later tell the investigators, she was not emotionally involved with Niels. It was merely that he was terribly good in bed.

In the meantime, calls continued to come in to the Battered and Maltreated unit and not all of the callers were as satisfied with their treatment as the Asborg mother and daughter or Julie Kiel.

Some were in tears and one woman sounded as if she were in agony. The battered wives man had forced her to anal intercourse, she sobbed, and she was bleeding. She was about to say more when there was the sound of a scuffle over the telephone and the dial tone came on as the connection was broken.

'Probably her husband,' said the inspector. 'Well, you have a lead now. Check with the hospitals and doctors in the city and see if any woman received treatment for injuries to the anus that evening. Let's hope that her husband let her go to a doctor.'

Perhaps he had. The sergeant was, in any case, optimistic for his investigations turned up no less than nine women who had been treated for injuries to the part in question on that evening.

In a community of over a million and a half, multiple cases of almost anything could be turned up.

The rest of the investigation was, however, inconclusive. As the sergeant quickly learned, the subject was somewhat delicate and attempted questioning of the women involved resulted in stoney silence, threats of suits for invasion of privacy and, in one case, near hysterical laughter.

'One of them could be the woman we're looking for,' he reported gloomily, 'but we'll never get the truth out of them. According to the doctors, at least five of them show signs of maltreatment in addition to the damage to their . . . uh . . .'

'Can you find out what their social and economic circumstances are?' asked the inspector. 'Discreetly, of course.'

The sergeant could. Eight of the women were from comfortable middle and upper-middle class families, but only six of them were married.

'Work on the married ones,' said the inspector. 'If it's fear of the consequences of exposure, it won't be the ones who aren't married and the one from a poor family would have nothing to lose.'

'How can I work on them?' demanded the sergeant despairingly. 'I don't dare question them unless we want a suit. The fellow probably never had contact with them but that one time. They certainly wouldn't call for help from that source again.'

He, of course, knew nothing about Gertrude and Anna Asborg or Julie Kiel.

'You know when they received treatment for their injuries,' said the inspector, 'and you can check that against calls for assistance received by the different battered wives organizations within the preceding twenty-four hours. Then,you can determine who answered the calls and check his appearance against the descriptions we have. Don't forget. He's always been described as wearing a leather jacket and a blue shirt and trousers.'

Considering the size of the city and the number of such cases taking place, this was obviously going to be an extended and difficult operation, particularly as there was little hope of co-operation from the victims themselves.

Both the sergeant and the inspector were aware, however, how important was the identification of this man who was abusing a position of authority and trust. Obviously, his actions were leading to emotionally charged situations which could end in a burst of uncontrolled violence.

Assuming that only a very small percentage of the cases resulted in an anonymous telephone call to the police, the man had preyed on dozens of women without risk of exposure and would, therefore, presumably continue to do so.

Sooner or later, one of the husbands would learn what had happened and the result could be bloodshed, either that of the rapist or of the wife.

Neither of the officers suspected that most of the husbands already knew.

The sergeant made little progress in his attempt to determine what organizations had been involved in the cases of the nine women who had had treatment, largely because the organizations themselves normally tried to keep such appeals for help secret. They did not want the women they were trying to help to suffer even worse for calling on them.

'The only ones on record are where the call was to the police,' he reported, 'and there are remarkably few of those that were followed up or were referred to us.'

'They all should have been' said the inspector, frowning. 'Send a circular round to all departments that any battered woman case they encounter should come to this office. They probably don't know we exist.'

The sergeant sent the notice round, but what was received two days later on November 7, 1985 was not a battered wife case, but a homicide. Or rather, it was a battered wife, but she was dead and so was her husband.

'Homicide has referred it to us because the woman

was apparently badly beaten and anally raped,' said the inspector. 'I'm waiting for the autopsy report now.'

The autopsy report confirmed the inspector's worst fears. The circumstances of the case were precisely what they had been anticipating.

'The subject is a woman of twenty-nine years of age,' wrote Dr Ingmar Westrom, the police medical expert who had carried out the autopsy. 'She was in good health and had never born a child. The cause of death was multiple fractures of the skull resulting from repeated blows with a heavy, sharp-cornered instrument. The time of death was approximately eleven o'clock in the evening of November 6, 1985.

'Examination of the body shows evidence of beating and maltreatment practised over a number of years. In addition, there are lesions of the sphincter and lower bowel indicative of anal rape. These are comparatively recent and were inflicted less than forty-eight hours prior to death.'

There was a second autopsy report on the woman's husband.

'The subject,' wrote the doctor, 'was a man of thirty-four years in good health, but slightly overweight. The cause of death was strangulation by a cord fastened around the neck and attached to a beam in the family garage.'

'The time of death was shortly after eleven o'clock in the evening of November 6, 1985. There are no indications of violence or a struggle on the body.'

There was a separate copy of the report by the homicide unit from the Department of Criminal Investigations.

'The victims are a man and wife, married since June 5, 1980.

'The murder weapon in the case of the woman has been established as a hatchet belonging to the household. It was found lying near the body and latent fingerprints present on the handle are those of the husband. Traces of blood and hair on the blunt end of the hatchet are identical to those of the victim. No signs of a struggle were found at the scene and the nature of the injuries indicate that the victim was struck down from behind.

'The body of the man was found hanging in the garage by a section of clothes line fastened in a slip noose around his neck and attached to a rafter. An overturned kitchen chair lay nearby.

'The conclusion is that the subject murdered his wife for an unknown reason and committed suicide. There is no evidence of the involvement of any third party.'

'But there was one,' said the inspector grimly. 'The fellow who's been beating up and raping the battered wives. The evidence is absolutely clear. She'd been beaten over a long period of time, undoubtedly by her husband. She called for help. The rescuer came, neutralized the husband in some way, raped the woman anally and, perhaps, beat her to force compliance. As soon as the husband was free, he killed his wife and himself. I think you'll find that they were in a position where exposure would have ruined him. It's exactly what I've been afraid would happen.'

'I see the names have been suppressed in the reports,' said the sergeant. 'Will we be able to get them so that I can try to trace the organization she called on?'

'They're here on a separate sheet,' said the inspector. 'The commissioner doesn't want them released until we find out what organization is involved. It's obviously going to be a great scandal.'

The sergeant was not convinced that it would be. Inexplicably, although it had had to be the same organization in all cases, no clue as to its identity had ever been uncovered and he feared it would not be in this case either.

He was quite right and, by the time he had confirmed this, it was Christmas day of 1985 and, once again, a battered wife was calling for help.

The call was received at four-fifteen in the morning

and, at four-thirty, Bank Director Hans Herning opened the front door of his luxurious villa on the outskirts of Copenhagen to find a stranger wearing a leather jacket, a blue shirt and darker blue trousers standing on the doorstep.

'We have a report of a woman in difficulty here,' said the man, holding out his official identification. 'May I speak to your wife?'

'Yes . . . uh . . . well, yes . . . of course,' stammered Herning. 'We were celebrating Christmas Eve last night . . . Had a little too much to drink . . . It's nothing, you understand?'

The man in the leather jacket gravely inclined his head and silently followed Herning into the living room.

Thirty-year-old Ingrid Herning was sitting on the sofa with her legs sprawled out in front of her. Her black evening dress had slid up over her thighs and it was obvious that she was not wearing underwear. She was very beautiful and very drunk.

'He hit me!' she moaned. 'He hit me!'

'Just a slap,' muttered Herning. 'It's nothing.'

He too was drunk, but he was becoming rapidly sober.

'I'm afraid that you had better come with me, Mr Herning,' said the man in the leather jacket.

Herning hesitated.

'We don't want any publicity about this, do we?' said the man. 'I can see to it that you won't be charged.'

Herning hesitated no longer. With a feeling of profound relief, he followed the official out to his car. Ingrid Herning remained alone in the house.

But not for long.

The first thing that Inspector Karlsson knew about all this was when he picked up the battered wives direct line telephone and was nearly deafened by someone screaming obscenities against the police.

It was a man's voice and the inspector's conclusion was that the caller was drunk to the point of brain damage, high on drugs or completely insane. It was not uncommon for the police to receive calls from such persons even at eight-thirty in the morning of Christmas Day.

He was about to hang up when, suddenly, a phrase in the flood of invective caught his ear. Although couched in extremely crude terms, the man had made reference to his wife being beaten and anally raped.

'Shut up!' roared the inspector in a voice of such authority that the man stopped dead in mid-curse. 'What is your name and address?'

The man, abruptly sober, gave it. Hans Herning. Twelve Avenue Dreyer.

Sergeant Bergmann was sent to investigate, but it was over an hour before he telephoned the inspector with a report and, when he did, it was in a voice sounding as if he had just witnessed the resurrection of the dead.

'What's the matter with you?' barked the inspector. 'Speak up. I thought you said the battered wives' rapist was a police officer.'

'He is,' said the sergeant. 'It's Chief Inspector Niels Falster from the residential night duty service. Herning has sworn out charges and I've just talked to Mrs Herning in the hospital here. She confirms what her husband says.'

The inspector snorted like a bull walrus surfacing, tried to say something, failed and laid the telephone receiver gently back down in the cradle. For some moments, he sat staring blankly at the wall. He knew his assistant. If he said that Chief Inspector Falster was the battered wives' rapist, it was because he was.

The inspector had been with Falster in the same class at the police training academy. They were both forty-two years old.

The remainder of the case was exceedingly painful to all concerned, the Hernings, the police and, above all, Chief Inspector Falster who had been in charge of the night service for twelve years and had been raping battered women for nearly as long.

The Chief Inspector had developed a foolproof system for taking care of his sexual needs which were apparently abnormal. His subordinates were under orders to refer all battered women reports to him for his personal attention.

If the parties were in circumstances where they could not afford publicity, he took the husband to the station and put him in a cell for the night, but did not charge him. He then returned to the couples' home wearing his uniform shirt and trousers and a leather jacket to rape the wife, using force if she resisted.

The husband was released the following morning and, even if he did find out what had happened, there was nothing he could do about it without being exposed as a wife beater.

For twelve years the scheme had worked, but one day Falster had to run into bad luck and Hans Herning was it. For Herning was no wife beater. He had never beaten his wife before and he had not beaten her on that Christmas Eve. They had both been drunk. There has been an argument and she had slapped him. He had slapped her back and she had called the police.

After her husband's departure with the police officer, she had fallen asleep and had awakened much later to find herself stark naked in bed with the inspector. She had begun to scream and struggle and the inspector had given her a black eye, a cut lip and a badly bruised cheek bone. He had then dragged her into the bathroom, draped her over the edge of the tub and raped her anally, causing such severe damage that she required three stitches at the hospital. She was lying in a semi-comatose state in the bathroom when her husband came home and found her.

The case aroused great interest in the press and many women came forward to testify, including Gertrude and Anna Asborg and Julie Kiel.

Chief Inspector Falster, realizing the hopelessness of his position, made a full confession to as many cases of rape and assault as he could remember and, on February

20, 1987, was sentenced to four years' imprisonment, a very heavy sentence for Scandinavia.

The spectators at the sex games in the inspector's apartment were never identified. A certain propriety has to observed in such matters and . . .

16

PERSONAL SERVICE BUSINESS

When Herbert Kavale saw the advertisement in the classified section of his favourite newspaper, he was understandably intrigued.

'Exotic, attractive, young couple seeks open-minded, generous friend for unconventional fun and games,' it read.

This was not a remarkable advertisement for a liberal, progressive society such as Austria, with the exception of the word 'exotic'.

That was, however, important. Herbert was fifty-five years old and a lifetime's preoccupation, if not obsession, with sex had inevitably led to a certain lassitude which exoticism might be hoped to counteract.

Herbert, therefore, wrote promptly to the box number given and was soon favoured with a visit which took place in his apartment at Rustenschach Allee 34 on the Prater Stern. The date was Tuesday, September 13, 1983, and Herbert did not emerge from his first encounter with the new friends entirely satisfied – in more senses than one.

Exotic, they undeniably were. Although he had assembled an extensive collection of North African and Middle Eastern experiences over the years, he could not recall having been on close terms with Egyptians before.

Young also. The girl said that she was sixteen and he believed her, but a delightfully developed sixteen, as tender and juicy as a ripe peach.

And, if that were not enough, they were absurdly

cheap. All they had asked was the equivalent of twelve dollars.

In short, a fairy tale come true for any aging satyr, but there was, of course, a catch.

Dahlia, the girl, did not want to go the whole way. She had let him handle the merchandise sufficiently to determine that it was top quality and she had let him look at it, but nothing more and her husband had refused to leave them alone together.

He had been left in a state of concupiscence of which he would not have believed himself capable.

Well, unless he was mistaken, all was not lost. Two hundred schillings did not go very far in Vienna. They would be back. Herbert Kavale was a shrewd judge of human avarice. The young Egyptians did return three days later

On Monday, September 19th, Helga Bessert, Herbert's cleaning lady, found his body when she came to clean the apartment. Although she regretted losing a comparatively well-paid job, she accepted the matter philosophically. She had thought for years that somebody would murder Herbert sooner or later.

'He couldn't keep his hands off anything female,' she told Inspector Josef Daggert, chief of District Four Homicide Section.

A pleasant, smiling woman of forty-six with the hips of a brood mare and the face of an amiable bulldog, she admitted that her employer had sometimes required services not normally connected with cleaning.

'But he always paid extra,' she said. 'He was a generous gentleman.'

He had apparently been more generous than he had intended this time.

'The apartment's stripped to the walls,' reported Detective Sergeant Franz Brenner, who had been going over the premises while the inspector waited for Dr Morris Scheidl to complete his examination of the corpse. 'And his car's not in the garage downstairs.'

'Get the plate number from the registry and issue an all-points pick-up on it,' said the inspector, wiping the top of his largely bald head with a handkerchief.

Although it was early autumn, the weather had been unseasonably warm and the inspector, who was considerably overweight and red in the face, did not stand up well to the heat.

The sergeant, who was dark, gaunt and wiry, was not affected by the weather and went off briskly to carry out his instructions.

'Well?' said the inspector, directing the question at the forensic medical expert who was bending over the corpse on the bed.

'Friday evening some time,' said the doctor. 'I can get it within a half-hour when I perform the autopsy, but say eleven o'clock for right now.

'Cause, strangulation with the bathrobe cord.'

The bathrobe cord was still knotted tightly about Herbert Kavale's neck. It and an undershirt were all that he was wearing.

'Died in the saddle?' asked the inspector. 'The cleaning woman says he was a super tomcat.'

'Looks like it,' said the doctor. 'I'll have to run some tests at the morgue, but there's a lot of dried secretion on the genitals and in the pubic hair and I doubt that it's all from him.'

'What do you mean by that?' demanded the inspector. 'Was he having it on with another man?'

'Women secrete too, you know,' said the doctor, straightening up and wiping his hands on a wad of gauze.

He was nearly as plump and rosy as the inspector, but he was not bald and he wore his dark-blond hair parted neatly in the middle, with sideburns halfway down the cheeks.

'Good enough,' said the inspector. 'I'll let the lab run over the scene and then we'll send him over to you. Be about two hours, I expect. We don't want to miss anything.'

The specialists from the police laboratory did not miss anything. All told, they recovered one hundred and six latent fingerprints from the apartment, most, judging by the size, feminine. They also found a modest collection of pornography and a stack of so-called contact magazines.

Most important of all, they found the advertisement for the 'exotic couple' which Hebert had ringed with red pencil.

This was immediately recognized as an important potential clue and the sergeant hurried to the newspaper in question where he learned that the advertiser was a Mr Ibrahim Allam who lived at 124 Czerny Ring. He no longer lived there, but he was remembered for he and his wife had omitted to pay the final two weeks of the rent before leaving.

'The girl's no more than a child,' the landlady told the sergeant. 'I wouldn't be surprised if they're not married at all. You can never tell with these foreigners.'

She did not, however, know what nationality they had been. Arabs of some kind, she thought.

The couple had lived at the address for less than two months and they had not registered with the alien residents' registry office as they should have done. There was, however, a previous registration under the names of Ibrahim and Dahlia Allam and, for the first time, the investigators learned that they were looking for an Egyptian husband and wife. For Ibrahim and Dahlia had been legally married in Cairo in September of 1982. The bride had been fifteen and the groom twenty-four.

Fortunately, the landlady at 124 Czerny Ring had not yet cleaned thoroughly her missing tenants' room and the fingerprint specialists were able to recover good prints of both the young Egyptians.

These were compared with those found in Kavale's apartment from which it was possible to determine that Dahlia had been in the shower and that both had handled most of the drawers and doors in the apartment in their search for valuables.

This physical evidence confirmed the Allams' position as the leading suspects in the murder of Herbert Kavale.

'Pity the body was discovered so late,' said the sergeant. 'It looks as if they made it over the border before we got out the pick-up order on the car.'

'I've already turned the information over to Interpol,' said the inspector, 'and they're issuing an international warrant. We should hear something soon.'

He was to hear something soon, but not about the whereabouts of the suspects. Rather, he received a file from the the West German police who had checked their records against the international warrant and had discovered that Ibrahim Allam was a former client.

Although he had been born in Egypt and held Egyptian nationality, Ibrahim had been brought to Germany at an early age by his parents and had attended school there.

In 1977, he had been nineteen years old and had fallen madly in love with the daughter of a fellow Egyptian, forty-two-year-old Ali Benfahdri.

Suleika, the daughter, had been only fourteen years old at the time and her parents had opposed marriage to Ibrahim, less on the grounds of immaturity than by reason of the fact that Ibrahim was little inclined to work and had no money.

Ibrahim had reacted to this rejection by knifing his proposed father-in-law to death in the middle of the street. There being a dozen or so witnesses to the murder, Ibrahim was quickly arrested, tried under the German Juvenile Crimimal Code, as he was under the age of twenty-one, and sentenced to eight years' imprisonment, two years less than the maximum.

Persons convicted of crimes, other than those against property which are punished savagely, normally serve about half ot their sentences. Ibrahim was released on February 9, 1981, promptly deported and prohibited from ever re-entering West Germany.

The German police had no further information, but,

according to the Austrian alien registration records, Ibrahim had remained in Egypt only a short length of time before marrying Dahlia and coming to Austria.

A query to the West Germans concerning Dahlia under her maiden name produced the information that she too had attended the German school system before returning to Cairo with her uncle. Her parents, it seemed, were dead.

Eventually, Interpol was able to come up with one more item of interest. Herbert Kavale's Toyota was found in the French port of Marseille. It had not been sold, but simply abandoned.

The car was gone over by fingerprint specialists from the Marseille police and the prints of both Ibrahim and Dahlia were recovered and sent to Vienna.

The case against the young Egyptians was well enough established to permit the issuance of an indictment and further investigation into the complicated affairs of Herbert Kavale ceased.

So did the investigation of the suspects for their whereabouts were unknown. The Marseille police were certain that they were not in Marseille. Although it is the second biggest city in France with a population of well over a million, Marseille boasts an excellent police force which is generally able to locate almost anyone. The Allams were by no means an average couple and, if the police could not find them, they were not there.

If their whereabouts were a mystery to the Vienna police, in New York City, the Allams were presenting the police with another kind of mystery.

They had arrived in New York on October 12th aboard the high seas yacht, *La Belle Friponne*, a name meaning The Handsome Hussy. They were not, however, the owners of the vessel nor did they know much about operating it. The owners, twenty-eight-year-old Jean Dupont and twenty-six-year-old Yves Despres, had been washed overboard in a storm, they said.

As the couple laid no claim to the boat and could

speak little English, the police did not keep very close tabs on them and, by the time they had contacted the French authorities and had determined that *La Belle Friponne* had set sail from Marseille on September 23rd with the two French yachtsmen aboard, the Allams had disappeared.

Unaware that there was an international warrant out for their arrest, the New York police did not worry a great deal about it. Nor did they need to for Ibrahim and Dahlia were, by now, in Chicago where they were the guests of still another Egyptian, Mr Mohammed Halouck.

Mr Halouck had met the Allams in New York and had brought them back to Chicago, but not with entirely altruistic intentions.

The fact was, Dahlia was not only attractive to ageing Austrian libertines, but to any red-blooded Egyptian and, possibly, other nationalities too. Halouck was thirty years old and unmarried.

As the Allams had told him of their problem in Austria and, perhaps, something of what had taken place on board *La Belle Friponne*, it had occurred to him that the situation might be turned to his own advantage. He had, therefore, suggested an exchange – his protection and help for them to remain in the United States in return for which Dahlia was to divorce Ibrahim and marry him.

Ibrahim was not very enthusiastic about this arrangement and even less over Halouck's insistence that Dahlia spend the nights in his bed so that they could become better acquainted while Ibrahim slept on a rug on the kitchen floor, but saw no alternative.

By October 14th, however, his emotions had passed beyond his control and, perhaps recalling his successful handling of the Ali Benfahdri affair, he made a determined attempt to stick a very long butcher's knife into his benefactor's stomach.

Halouck, forewarned by a knowledge of Ibrahim's

background, was, however, on his guard and took evasive action, escaping with no more than a slit shirt.

As it seemed probable that the deal was now off, he wasted no more time, but went to the police and said that he knew where they could lay their hands on a wanted murderer.

The police investigated, found that there was an international warrant out for Ibrahim's arrest, took him and Dahlia into custody and, on August 2nd, arranged for their deportation to Austria.

This was over the protests of the French police who were, by now, profoundly interested in learning how two experienced yachtsmen could have been swept overboard while their landlubber passengers remained safe and sound. The matter was the more mysterious in that weather reports showed no serious storms along the course followed by *La Belle Firponne* during her passage form Marseille to New York.

Ibrahim was not anxious to talk to either the French or the Austrian police and said, upon his arrival back in Vienna, that he knew nothing of all these matters and that he was being persecuted by the racist Europeans because he was a North African.

Dahlia was more co-operative and began by recounting her short, but not uneventful life's history.

She had, she said, been attracted to Ibrahim because he represented security to her. This was not as dubious a statement as it sounded. Dahlia's childhood, it seemed, had been so insecure that even Ibrahim spelled security by comparison.

Orphaned at an early age, she had been brought up strictly by her uncle who had, however, been more indulgent with himself as he had begun raping her shortly after her fifteenth birthday.

'He was opposed to my marrying Ibrahim,' she told the inspector, 'so we had to run away.'

She was apparently unaware that Ibrahim had not run

away on a previous occasion and that it had cost him four years in a German jail.

'After we were married, we came to Vienna,' said Dahlia, 'but we had no money and Ibrahim could not find work because of the racism.'

The inspector did not see fit to inform her that there were, at that moment, close to a hundred thousand non-Europeans working in Vienna, but waited patiently.

'We sold all my jewellery,' said Dahlia, 'and, when the money was all gone, Ibrahim thought of the idea of running an advertisement. We didn't like it, but how were we to live?'

The inspector continued his silence. He did not think that Mrs Allam expected a reply to her question.

'The old man was our first customer,' said Dahlia, 'but Ibrahim didn't want me to make love to him. He just wanted the money. The first time, all he would let him do was touch me, but then, we only got two hundred schillings and that didn't last but two or three days.

'So we came back and the old gentleman said that if we wanted more, Ibrahim would have to stay outside.

'Ibrahim didn't like it, but he wanted the money so he went and sat in the hall outside the apartment and the old gentleman and I made love.

'He was very gentle and very clever and, after we had finished, he asked me if I would like to take a shower.

'I said I would and while I was in the shower, I heard a terrible noise in the bedroom.

'When I came in, Ibrahim and the old gentleman were fighting and I tried to stop them, but Ibrahim pushed me away.

'I couldn't do anything to help so I went into the next room and put my clothes on. When I came back, Ibrahim had something around the old gentleman's neck and he was not moving any more.

'We went through the apartment and took everything that we thought we could sell. There was some money. I don't know how much. Ibrahim kept it.

'We took the car and left right away and, when we got to Marseille, we went down to the waterfront and we met two nice Frenchmen who agreed to take us to America in their boat.'

'Why?' said the inspector. 'Did you pay them?'

Dahlia cast down her eyes modestly.

'I think they liked me,' she said.

On the subject of the terrible storm in which the yachtsmen had been swept overboard, Dahlia was less helpful. She had, she said, been below decks and had seen nothing.

Confronted with his wife's statement concerning the murder of Herbert Kavale, Ibrahim not only confessed, but implicated Dahlia, saying that she had thrown him the bathrobe cord with which he had strangled the victim.

As a result, at the trial on March 8, 1985, Ibrahim was charged with unmpremeditated homicide and Dahlia with acting as an accessory to the fact of homicide.

Dahlia had consistently denied having thrown her husband the cord or having done anything except try to prevent the murder and, under cross examination, Ibrahim broke down and admitted that she was telling the truth.

'I wanted her to go to jail too,' he said gallantly. 'Who can say what she might be up to when I am in prison? It could be a long time.'

It could, indeed. Influenced, perhaps, by the fact that this was Ibrahim's second murder, the court accepted very little in the way of extenuating circumstances and sentenced Ibrahim to twenty years' imprisonment.

Even Dahlia did not escape entirely, but was sentenced to one year in prison for failing to come to the aid of a person in mortal danger. She should, said the judge, have run to one of the other apartments for help.

This was not, however, the end of the Allams' tribulations. *La Belle Friponne* had, in the meantime, been brought back to Marseille and police experts had recovered traces of blood and other clues from it which they believed to be sufficient to sustain a charge of homicide on two counts against Ibrahim and Dahlia. They will, therefore, upon completion of their prison terms, be handed over to the French authorities for further investigation and a possible new trial.

It may be difficult for Dahlia to maintain her innocence on the subject. Jean Dupont's credit cards were found in her possession when she was taken into custody in Chicago.

17

VILLAGE RECREATION FACILITIES

It was eight days to Christmas 1984 and the weather was awful. For close to a week, it had been alternately raining and freezing so that everything was coated with a half-inch of frozen sleet. The woods outside the town were filled with the sharp reports of tree limbs breaking under the weight of the ice.

'There are times when one appreciates a low crime rate,' observed Inspector Ludwig Krause, gazing thoughtfully out the window of his office at the wind-lashed square in front of the police headquarters building.

Actually, the crime rate in Regensburg, West Germany was low only by comparison with bigger communities, such as Munich to the south or Frankfurt to the north. For a rather quiet town of 140,000 inhabitants, the rate was normal.

'I just hope that things remain quiet here until after the holidays,' said Sergeant of Detectives Juergen Schulz. 'I hate it when something happens at Christmas time.'

He was a huge, slightly clumsy, young man, dark and hairy, and looking more like a bear that a police officer, but he had the soul of a poet.

'We still have the Wagner case running,' reminded the inspector, older, trim, neatly groomed, very much the German civil servant.

'Don't mind him,' said the sergeant. 'He wasn't the

type to celebrate Christmas anyway. Besides, we've had it under investigation for five months now and . . .'

The telephone on his desk rang and he picked it up.

'Sergeant Schulz, Homicide,' he said.

There was a few moment's silence while the inspector continued to gaze pensively out of the window.

'*Scheisse*!' said the sergeant. 'All right. We'll check it out.'

The inspector turned around and raised his eyebrows questioningly.

'Anonymous telephone call to the switchboard,' said the sergeant. 'Caller says there's a dead woman in the house at number 17, Schule Strasse in Suenching.'

'Good way to start off a Monday,' said the inspector. 'You're going down?'

Suenching was a village of some twelve hundred inhabitants fifteen miles to the southeast of Regensburg. It had no police department.

'Unless you'd prefer to handle it personally,' said the sergeant.

'No, I think I'd better stay here in case of any emergencies,' said the inspector. 'Give me a call as soon as you've determined whether there really is a corpse in the house.'

The sergeant, who had not hoped for a moment that the inspector really would answer the call personally, set off for Suenching, taking with him two detectives from the department. He did not think that he would need them for checking out the report, but he suspected that they would come in handy for pushing the car out of the ditch and, in fact, they did. Twice.

Considering the condition of the roads, the sergeant made good time. The anonymous telephone call had been received at four minutes to nine and, by nine-thirty-five, the police party was in Suenching.

Number 17 Schule Strasse turned out to be a single-storey, red brick cottage with a tile roof and a somewhat dilapidated fence around the small front yard. No one answered the sergeant's knock and the door was locked. According to the name of the mailbox, the occupant was Ms Elisabeth Adler.

'See if you can find an unlocked window,' said the sergeant, 'and, if so, come and open the front door.'

Because of his bulk, he was not enthusiastic about crawling through windows.

The detectives circled the house and reported that all of the windows were locked and so was a back door leading into the kitchen. They had been able to look into the kitchen through a glass panel, but the shutters were down on the rest of the windows.

The sergeant sighed and went to the car, returning immediately with a small, handy kit of tools with which he had little difficulty in tripping the lock.

'Oh, Oh!' said one of the detectives as a wave of stale stinking air poured out of the open door.

All three of the officers had immediately recognized the odour of rotting human flesh.

Elisabeth Adler was on a couch in a corner of the living room. She was naked from the waist down and, from the appearance of her body, had been a comparatively young woman. The face could not been seen as the body was lying on its stomach.

The room was in a state of disorder, not such as might have resulted from a struggle, but merely through carelessness, and it was dirty. There were dark splashes of dried blood on the wall, the floor and the bed covers and shattered pieces of what looked like a beer bottle lay scattered on the rug beside the couch.

The cottage was warm indicating that the central heating plant was in operation.

'Take a walk around the village and see if the woman has any relatives here,' said the sergeant. 'We'll need an identification.'

He went back to the police car, pressed the button on the radio telephone and was connected with the inspector.

'It's a homicide,' he said. 'Looks as if somebody knocked her brains out with a beer bottle. She's been dead a week or more.'

'I'll be right down,' said the inspector. 'How are the roads?'

'Like a bobsleigh run,' said the sergeant. 'I believe we'll need the full squad.'

The full homicide squad consisted of fourteen officers, most of them specialists of one kind or another. Usually, the services of less than half the squad were needed. A great many murders require little or no investigation, the identity of the murderer being immediately obvious.

It was possible that the identity of the murderer of Elisabeth Adler would become obvious once the investigation began, but the sergeant did not think so. If the body had laid there for a week or more without anyone reporting it, the circumstances were going to be obscure.

The homicide squad came down in two cars and two vans, skidding around on the icy roads with the headlights on. The weather had not improved and, as the morning wore on, it was becoming darker and the wind was rising. There was an ominous feeling in the air, as if some frightful catastrophe was about to break over the isolated, little village huddled on the bleak, winter plain to the south of the Danube.

The first step was the examination of the body by Dr Hans-Peter Fichtenbauer, the department's medical expert, who had come down in the inspector's car.

A short, plump, red-faced man who looked and was short-tempered, the doctor's examination was brief and his remarks terse.

'Dead over a week,' he said. 'Fractured skull. Anything else, you'll have to wait for the autopsy. Won't be much. Decomposition is advanced.'

He left the house and the inspector followed to where the squad was waiting in vans.

'All right. In you go,' he said. 'Do a thorough job of it. It doesn't look like it's going to be simple.'

The squad filed into the house carrying their equipment.

'Tentative identification,' said the sergeant. 'The neighbours' description of Elsabeth Adler matches the appearance of the corpse. According to them, she was thirty-two years old and unmarried. No relatives in the village.

'Boyfriend?' said the inspector.

'Apparently not,' said the sergeant. 'The people say they don't know of any.'

'In a place this size, that means she didn't have any,' said the inspector. 'We'll have to wait and see what the boys turn up.'

What the boys, otherwise known as the police technicians, turned up was a murder weapon and an incredible number of fingerprints.

'You'd think this was a railway station from the number of different prints,' said the specialist in charge of the detail. 'We've recovered a good two dozen latents and they aren't all old by any means.'

'And the murder weapon?' said the inspector.

'A beer bottle,' said the specialist. 'Broken to pieces. Weapon of convenience, of course.'

'Manslaughter charge at the most then,' said the sergeant. 'How do you account for all the fingerprints?'

'We think she was running a business,' said the specialist. 'This was a dirty woman. There's enough dried semen on that couch to starch all the shirts in Bavaria.'

'Oh come now!' said the inspector. 'Where would she get the customers? There probably aren't more than a hundred men in the age group here and ninety percent of them would be married.'

The specialist shrugged.

'Those are our conclusions,' he said. 'Maybe you can come up with something different.'

The detection specialists having completed their work, the body was wrapped in plastic and loaded into one of the vans for transfer to the police morgue in Regensburg.

The doctor and some of the specialists returned to Regensburg with the body and the rest of the party fanned out through the village, asking questions and trying to gain an insight into what kind of a person the dead woman had been.

Generally, an understanding of the victim's life led automatically to the identity of the murderer. It did not this time and the police party returned to Regensburg at seven in the evening considerably bemused.

Whether Elisabeth Adler had been running a business with her body or not, she had certainly had an extensive acquaintanceship among men of the village.

'Mostly forties and fifties,' said the sergeant gloomily. 'All of them married. Why in heaven's name didn't their wives suspect something?'

'Maybe they did,' said the inspector. 'But, sometimes, it's better to pretend you don't know something than to make a fuss over it. How many potential suspects do you have so far?'

'Eleven,' said the sergeant, 'not counting the wives. There's about twenty of them.'

'Hardly think it would be a woman,' said the inspector, frowning. 'The body was naked from the waist down. We'll have to see what Hans-Peter has determined.'

Dr Fichtenbauer had not determined a great deal, but he had completed the autopsy and the report lay on the inspector's desk.

'Time of death,' wrote the doctor, 'was the afternoon of Friday, December 7, 1984.' A closer estimate was not possible under the circumstances.

Traces of acid phosphotase, a by-product of the chemical breakdown of semen, had been found to be present in the vagina and oral cavity, but acid phosphotase also occurred normally in the body and this was, therefore, no proof of sexual activity.

Aside from the wound on the head, there were no signs of violence and none of a struggle.

The beer bottle had been swung with great force and the doctor was inclined to doubt that a woman, unless she were very large and athletic, would have had the strength.

'Beautifully vague,' remarked the inspector. 'This case is a real Christmas present. We don't know exactly what she was up to there in Suenching. We have a minimum of thirty-one potential suspects based on reports by people who are probably trying to get other people into trouble. We don't know exactly when she was killed or who she was with or what she was doing at the time. I think we'll sleep on this, Juergen.'

And sleep on it they did, but, unfortunately, the case looked no different in the morning.

The weather did. It was worse. The glare ice covering the roads had been, in its turn, covered by a thin layer of dry snow. Even with chains, travel by car was suicidal.

Nevertheless, an even larger detachment of detectives set off for Suenching that morning. Whatever the explanation for the violent death of Elisabeth Adler, it was in Suenching that it would be found.

Neither the inspector nor the sergeant regarded the case as murder. West German jurisprudence requires such elaborate evidence of wilful and malicious intent that the charge is rare. The murderer must be shown to have planned the crime in advance, to have derived benefit from it, to have been in full possession of all of his or her faculties at the time, not to have been emotionally upset, to have been over the age of twenty-one and to be liable, in the opinion of the psychologists, to murder someone else.

Obviously, on such a basis, most homicides are charged as manslaughter and the sole fact that the murder weapon had been one of convenience was enough to guarantee that this one would be too. Assuming of course, that the killer was caught. By the end of the day, most of the police party was inclined to doubt that he ever would be.

It was not that there were no suspects. There were far too many. In a community which numbered precisely three hundred and eighty-one males between the ages of sixteen and seventy, it could be shown that Elisabeth Adler had had some contact with, at least, one hundred and fourteen of them and, probably a good many more.

These did not include such innocent contacts as the postman or the butcher. They represented men reported to have been seen entering or leaving her house. For a young, single, attractive woman with no relatives in the area, this was a great many.

'She had to be running a business,' said the sergeant. 'Practically every able-bodied male in the village has been seen going in or out of her cottage and the reports are borne out by the number of fingerprints. What other reason could they have had for visiting her?'

'I don't know,' said the inspector, 'but, if she was in business, she didn't show much profit on the turnover. According to the accountant, her total worth doesn't amount to five thousand marks.'

'Maybe she told fortunes or maybe she made great cookies or . . . ,' speculated the sergeant, beginning to sound a little desperate.

'You're forgetting the couple of litres of semen the lab says was smeared over the couch,' said the inspector. 'The men went there for sex.'

'And she didn't charge them?' said the sergeant.

'Apparently not,' said the inspector, 'or, if she did, not much. Are all of our suspects married?'

'Nearly,' said the sergeant, running a pencil down the list. 'Edwin Hill. Fifty-four. Widower. Tobias Bockstiegl. Forty-four. Bachelor. Xaver Meindl. Forty-seven. Divorced. That's about it.'

'All right,' said the inspector. 'We'll work on them. Have them brought up here to Regensburg and we'll interrogate them formally.'

'Why the unmarried ones?' asked the sergeant curiously.

'They can talk without worrying about it getting back to their wives,' said the inspector.

And talk they did.

'We used to play strip poker and games like that,' said Edwin Hill. 'She loved that sort of thing and, if it went too slow, she'd cheat.'

'To win?' said the sergeant.

'To lose,' said Hill.

'Then, where did the money come in?' said the sergeant.

'What money?' said Hill. 'We didn't play for money.'

'You never gave her any money?' said the sergeant.

'Oh sometimes five or ten marks,' said Hill. 'As a present. She didn't need money. She was on social welfare.'

This remarkable statement was confirmed by Tobias Bockstiegl and Xaver Meindl. Elisabeth, they said, never asked them for money and they had never given her any.

'She just liked men,' said Bockstiegl.

Both he and Meindl had been less playful and more in a hurry than Hill. They had come to the cottage, had sex with Elisabeth on the couch and left.

'She wasn't satisfied with just straight sex,' volunteered Bockstiegl. 'You had to kiss her first.'

'On the mouth?' said the sergeant.

'No,' said Bockstiegl.

The unmarried witnesses, having made their statements were released. None of them had had any discernible motive for murdering Elisabeth Adler. Quite the contrary, as one of them said, there was now no form of entertainment in the village at all.

'I don't think we'll ever solve this,' said the sergeant in despair. 'It could have been any married man in the village or even from some other village for all we know.'

'I think we will,' said the inspector. 'It wasn't anybody from outside the village. She was strictly a local talent and Suenching is big enough that she didn't need to go outside. The killer is definitely one of the married men.

They're the only ones with a motive. She had a row with him. He picked up the beer bottle and hit her. Undoubtedly didn't mean to kill her and it was probably he who called the police.'

'I can see all that,' said the sergeant, 'But which one? We've got over three hundred potential suspects. How are we ever going to sort out the right one?'

'We can start by putting a little pressure on Hans-Peter,' said the inspector. 'He'll have to narrow down the period of the time of her death more than he did in the autopsy.'

'And then, we try to establish the whereabouts of all those three hundred odd suspects during that time,' said the sergeant. 'We should be finished by Christmas. Christmas of 1985.'

'Don't be bitter, Juergen,' said the inspector. 'Most of them will probably have been at work.'

He was, of course, right. Most of the adult men living in Suenching had been at work or just leaving it at the time of the murder.

This was fixed, with a good many reservations, by Dr Fichtenbauer as having been not earlier than noon and not later than six in the afternoon of Friday, December 7th.

It was possible to obtain some independent confirmation of the doctor's estimate. Two men were located who admitted to having come to visit Elisabeth at six and at eight-thirty that evening. They had both hammered on the door and called out her name, but there had been no response. As she hardly ever went anywhere other than to the local shops, by this time closed for the day, they had assumed that she had another visitor and had gone away.

There had been others who had called the succeeding days as well, but it had occurred to none of them that anything might be wrong. Elisabeth was, understandably, popular. For her to be engaged was not at all uncommon.

'I don't know whether the women in that village are super obtuse or super liars,' said the sergeant in some exasperation. 'Their husbands were running off practically to a man for fun and games with Miss Adler for years and not one of them seems to have known anything about it. No gossip, no scenes, no divorce suits. Normally, in a village of that size, you can hardly have it on with your own wife without everybody knowing the details by the time you get out of bed.'

'I suppose it could be because she didn't charge,' surmised the inspector. 'Those are country women, even if the husbands do work mainly in Regensburg. They might be more concerned over a raid on their husband's purse than on his virtue and if she showed no inclination to steal any of them . . .'

'Couldn't anyway,' said the sergeant. 'The village is solidly Catholic. Meindl got divorced and he's been practically ostracized ever since. So you think they did know?'

The inspector shrugged.

'It doesn't really matter,' he said. 'It's almost certain that it wasn't a woman. What we need is a male suspect.'

What he meant was a single male suspect. It was true that the vast majority of the potential suspects had been eliminated by the narrower estimate of the time of death, but there still remained over a dozen, all of whom had been known with certainty to frequent the dead woman and all of whom were married. All had been interrogated, but none had admitted to anything and there was no evidence to make one a better suspect than another.

The inspector was, however, convinced that the murderer was among them and interrogation continued, eventually producing not entirely anticipated results.

One of the potential suspects, forty-nine-year-old Wilhelm Padberg, a stone mason, six feet, two inches tall, said that he knew the identity of the murderer. He was sixty-two-year-old Karl Winschild. Winschild had wanted to abandon his sixty-eight-year-old wife, Hildegard, and go away with Elisabeth. When Elisabeth had refused, he had lost his temper and killed her.

Unfortunately, only three details of this statement were subject to confirmation. Winschild's wife was sixty-eight years old, her name was Hildegard and he had visited Elisabeth. His fingerprints had been found in her cottage.

But nothing more for Winschild had died only twelve days after Elisabeth and was not available for questioning.

'It could be true,' said the sergeant. 'Winschild was killed in a head-on collision with a panel truck. It was only two days after the discovery of Miss Adler's body. It's a well-known fact that a certain number of road accident deaths are really suicides. He could have been despondent.'

'Then, he took his time about it,' said the inspector. 'If you're going on the assumption that he killed her, then he didn't know about the death for only two days. He knew about it for twelve. Was he interrogated?'

The sergeant shook his head.

'He was due to be, but he was killed first,' he said.

'And the other one?' said the inspector.

'Fifty-one-year-old Adolf Fleiderer,' said the sergeant. 'Short, fat, married, three kids, all adult and no longer living at home. He says he saw Elisabeth Adler in the telephone booth on the evening of December 11th.'

'Which telephone booth?' said the inspector.

'There's only one public pay phone booth in Suenching,' said the sergeant, 'but Elisabeth Adler couldn't have been in it on December 11th because she'd already been dead for four days at that time.'

The inspector thought it over.

'Must be a case of mistaken identity,' he said finally. 'Whether he murdered her or not, there'd be no reason for him to make up such a lie. Unless he's more shrewd that I'd expect him to be, the statement clears him. It shows he doesn't know when she was killed.'

'He's not shrewd,' said the sergeant. 'So Winschild then?'

'Not Winschild,' said the inspector. 'Padberg.'

'Padberg?' said the sergeant.

'Shoving the guilt on to a dead man is an old one,' said the inspector. 'How would Padberg know all about Winschild's motives and actions if he didn't make the thing up? He's trying to put an end to the investigation before it gets any closer to home.'

'We've no evidence,' said the sergeant. 'Supposing he simply denies it?'

'He won't,' said the inspector. 'His conscience is already bothering him or he wouldn't have reported the murder to the police. Don't forget, he didn't kill her intentionally.'

And that, after a few hours of intense interrogation, was what Wilhelm Padberg said too.

He had been seeing Elisabeth for several years and was sexually dependent on her. At the same time, he loved his wife and was tortured by feelings of guilt over his infideilty.

This conflict had begun to have an effect on his virility and he was not always able to perform the sex act with Elisabeth. A normally tolerant girl, this was the one thing that she could not accept and she had taunted him, calling him a weakling and a eunuch.

In a fit of blind rage, he had hit her over the head with the beer bottle.

As the inspector had predicted, Padberg was brought to trial charged with manslaughter and, on November 21, 1986, was found guilty and sentenced to five years' imprisonment.

Dozens of Suenching reisdents were called upon to testify on their relationships to Elisabeth Adler, but, although there were many sore heads in the village following the trial, there have been no suits for divorce.

There is, it seems, safety in numbers.

18

TARTING IT UP IN TURIN

The profession of a prostitute is not an easy one and, particularly, not in an Italian city of over a million people such as Turin.

Not that there is any shortage of customers or money either. Turin, sometimes known as the Detroit of Italy, is rich with the payrolls of the great car manufacturing companies. But there are a lot of people competing for this money. In certain quarters, the whores stand nearly shoulder to shoulder along the pavement. Curiously, many are older women.

Linda Gallo was not old. On that Friday evening of April 6, 1984, she was only eleven days past her twenty-fourth birthday. She was also not afraid of the competition. A pretty, dark-haired girl with an eye-bulging figure, she was usually assured of more than her share of the business which, on this unseasonably warm, spring evening, was brisk. Linda had already turned five tricks, to use the jargon of the trade, at standard rates and was wondering if she might consider knocking off a little early when the brown fiat with the tinted window-glass pulled in to the curb.

'How much for the night?' inquired the driver, a young and stylishly bearded man.

'A hundred thousand lira,' replied Linda, quoting her regular fee of close to ninety dollars.

'Get in,' said the young man.

The studio apartment to which he took her was in an unfamiliar district. Like many big city people, Linda knew her own quarter perfectly and almost nothing about the rest of the city.

Besides, she was not paying much attention as the driver turned and zigzagged through the endless streets. Mainly, her thoughts were on how long her customer would keep her awake. A true professional, the sex was for her duty and not pleasure.

The studio was clean, modern and rather bare. Seating herself next to her client on the sofa, Linda began to unbutton his shirt in a businesslike manner.

'Wait,' said the young man.

He went to a shelf on the wall and returned with a stack of sex magazines such as were sold all over the city.

'Here,' he said. 'Look at this. And this. Does it excite you? I want you to enjoy it.'

Linda was touched. The young man seemed terribly gentle and sympathetic. He had obviously had little experience with professional women. Rather a sweetie, actually . . .

Well, why not? It was her last for the night anyway. She would play along, give him his money's worth, and, if she ended up losing some of her professional detachment, so what?

Rising to her feet, Linda went into an amateurish but highly effective strip routine, sliding her loose sweater down over her brassiereless breasts and following it with the black, leather mini-skirt scarcely wider than a belt. Stepping out of the half-dozen strings which constituted her panties, Linda lay down on the couch and arranged herself in operating posture.

The young man lay down beside her, but only for minute. Suddenly, he was on his feet and there was a leather dog-whip in his hand.

'Ah, you whore!' he hissed. 'Do you do it for the money? Or because you like it? There! Take that!'

The whip whistled down and cut a stripe across her naked stomach.

Linda screamed in agony and sudden terror. This was rough trade!

Rough trade. The prostitutes' term for the sadists, the perverts, the sex psychopaths who made their profession more dangerous even than that of a cab driver.

Of course, she had known that such monsters existed and that many a prostitute had died horribly at their hands, but, like car drivers, she had always believed that the fatel encounter could never happen to her. Others, yes, but not her. In that particular game of Russian roulette, the hammer would always fall on an empty chamber.

'Shut up,' said the man in a deadly, low voice. 'Or I'll kill you.'

He took a pistol out of his pocket and pointed it at her head. To Linda, the black hole of the muzzle looked as large as a wash tub.

Biting her lips in a violent effort of willpower, she remained silent while the man whipped her over the belly, the thighs and the breasts. Some of the lashes she was able to intercept with her arms, but that hurt nearly as much.

She was praying that the sadistic stimulation would bring on his orgasm and an end to the torture, but it apparently did not for, after a relatively short time, he threw down the whip and went to fetch a piece of electrical wire with which he bound her wrists.

He then dragged her to a full length mirror and shot a number of polaroid camera pictures of her red-striped body and tear-stained face.

Again, Linda hoped that this might be the end and, again, she was disappointed.

'On your knees,' ordered the man, unzipping his trousers.

Linda was far from inexperienced in the techniques of oral sex and this time she put her heart into it.

The man remained calm, snapping an occasional close-up of the activity.

When it was successfully terminated, he dragged her to the bed, beat her half unconscious with his fists and feet, raped her brutally vaginally and anally so many times that she lost count, beat her yet again and, snatching up the gun by the barrel, raised it high over his head. The gun swung downward and, for Linda, the lights went out.

When she came to her senses, she was lying, fully clothed with the exception of her panties, on the pavement, a yard from her usual beat. A colleague was bending over her with a concerned expression.

'What's happened to you?' she demanded. 'You're covered with blood!"

Linda was unable to reply. She was speechless with astonishment to find herself still alive. And not even seriously injured.

At the hospital, she was found to be suffering from a large number of bruises and cuts over most of her body, minor damage to the sex organs and anus as a result of the brutal penetrations and a four-inch cut on the top of her head where he had knocked her unconscious with the pistol butt. Her skull was not, however, fractured.

The police were, of course, notified and a sergeant of detectives named Franco Dangelo came to the hospital to take her statement.

She was able to provide a fairly exact description of the man's appearance, the colour and make of his car and the furnishings of the studio which had been on the third or fourth floor of an apartment building with no elevator.

Although she did not realize it, the sergeant, a pleasant-faced, young man with a tight cap of curly, black hair and a remarkable muscular development of the arms, took unusually great pains in recording a statement on what was officially a case of rape with violence.

There was a reason for this. On January 10th of that same year, another prostitute, forty-eight-year-old Annunziata Paffunda, had been found dead in a burned out car, her wrists bound with electrical wire. Although the corpse was in such poor condition that it could only be identified by means of the fingerprints, Dr Damiano Scorzatti, a police expert in forensic medicine, had been able to determine that the woman had been whipped and tortured.

As this type of homicide often signalled the beginning of a series of psychopathic murders, a special commission had been set up to investigate it and it was to this unit that the sergeant belonged.

'Strong parallels,' he told Inspector Mario Castelli, his chief, upon his return to police headquarters. 'The victim is a prostitute. She was whipped and tortured. Her hands were tied with electrical wire. About the only difference is that he didn't kill her.'

'And the age,' remarked the inspector, a comfortably plump man with a rather bland, smooth face in which two startlingly sharp, coal-black eyes made an incongruous appearance. 'A psychopath is normally age-orientated.'

The inspector knew what he was talking about. He was the department's top expert in abnormal sex crimes which was why he had been put in charge of the commission.

'I'll run the description through the records section computer,' said the sergeant, 'but I doubt anything will turn up.'

Actually, too much turned up. In a city of over a million people, there are a great many young men with beards and, like all other segments of the male population, a certain percentage of them have been arrested on sex-related offences. Having little else to go by, the computer could only indicate that it could be any or none of them.

'If it is a series, he should strike again fairly soon,' said the inspector, 'and then we'll have another chance.'

It seemed that it was not a series after all. Eleven

months passed and there had been no further report of a murdered or raped prostitute.

Or rather, there had been a great many such reports, but the perpetrator had been, in all cases, identified and cleared of complicity in both the Annuziata Paffunda and Linda Gallo cases.

As a result, the commission was disbanded – only to be called back into life on March 10, 1985, when a forty-seven-year-old prostitute named Addolorata Benvenuto was found near a dam on the Po river, her skull shattered by a nine-millimetre pistol bullet fired at close range.

This, in itself, would not have been enough to bring out Inspector Castelli and Sergeant Dangelo on a Sunday afternoon, but Addolorata's hands were bound with electric wire and she had obviously been whipped and otherwise tortured.

Fortunately, the similarity to the previous cases investigated by the commission was recognized in time and the body was not disturbed.

Upon their arrival at the scene, the inspector and the sergeant found Dr Scorzatti already present and engaged in an examination of the corpse.

The doctor, a small, almost frail man with a high forehead and a largely bald cranium, was looking very cross as he did not like being called out on Sundays.

'It probably is,' he called out before the inspector had the time to ask the question. 'Bound hands. Electrical wire. Whipped. Tortured. And there's semen in the vagina. Approximately the same age as the Paffunda woman.'

'Is the bullet still in her head?' asked the inspector.

'No exit wound,' said the doctor. 'I'll send it to Ballistics as soon as I get it out.'

'I'll be surprised if there's a record of the gun,' said the inspector.

He was not suprised. There was none.

The long interval between the murder of Annunziata Paffunda and Addolorata Benvenuto had apparently been no more than a delay. The series was now underway and, on March 18th, eight days later, the corpse of Giovanna Bicchi was pulled out of the Po river. She was naked and her hands had been bound with electrical wire. She had, however, neither been shot nor drowned.

'Strangulation,' said Dr Scorzatti. 'With a woman's stocking, probably her own. Considering how well-known she was, you should be able to locate someone who saw her with her last customer.'

In fact, several people, all fellow prostitutes, had. He had been young, in his early thirties, and he had worn a short, neat beard.

'Pitiful case actually,' said the inspector. 'The woman was sixty-four years old and out on the streets peddling her hips to support her son's drug habit. Everybody in the business knew her.'

'They should have,' said the sergeant. 'She was pounding the pavement before most of them were born. It's a marvel to me that she could earn enough to keep the boy in cigarettes at her age.'

'Tastes vary,' said the inspector. 'Look at how many makes of cars there are.'

'And even antiques,' said the sergeant. 'But, somehow, I don't feel that the analogy is all that exact.'

The commission continued its investigations, but, as anticipated, without success. The only information available was the description of the supposed murderer, who had now been christened the 'Devil of Turin' by the press, and this was not enough.

There was, however, good reason to believe that the man answering to this description was the murderer of Annunziata, Addolorata and Giovanna and the torturer of Linda Gallo.

Considering the short interval between the last two murders, the commission was braced for a veritable flood of crimes, but it was more than a year before another torture murder that could be, with some certainty, ascribed to the 'Devil of Turin' took place.

The victim this time was another prostitute in the high-risk age group. Her name was Maria Galfre and she was forty-four years old. She had been whipped, raped, tortured, mutilated and partially burned before being thrown naked into a canal, her hands bound with electrical wire.

'He's fixed on this specific age group,' said Dr Scorzatti. 'Three of the victims have been in their middle or late forties and he probably thought that the Bicchi woman was. She was well-preserved.'

'What about Gallo?' said the sergeant. 'If he took her for forty, we can start hunting for somebody with a white cane.'

'He didn't kill Gallo,' said the inspector. 'Maybe that's the reason why.'

As in the preceding year, the first murder was followed quickly be a second. On April 30th, the disfigured, raped and largely naked body of Maria Corda was found lying beside a stream. Like Maria Galfre, she was forty-four years old and the mother of three children. Like all of the other victims, she had been a prostitute.

Dr Scorzatti performed the autopsy and reported that the woman had been strangled with either stocking or pair of tights. The time of death was the preceding evening and the semen of the presumed murderer indicated blood group O.

This was of little help to the investigation other than to confirm that the case belonged to the series. No new elements were discovered.

Nor were there any witnesses, although reports were received of a young, bearded man seen in the vicinity of the street corner where Mrs Corda had had her station.

There was, in fact, no shortage of reports. With each new murder of a prostitute, the press roused itself to an even greater frenzy until every working member of the sisterhood saw the 'Devil of Turin' in any client under the age of seventy.

There were incidents. Innocent stockbrokers out for

a bit of fun were squirted with tear gas. Middle-level civil servants were bitten by guard dogs. Business executives with odd tastes were beaten up by pimps. Undeniably, there was a fall off in turnover, but there was also accompanying rise in costs as the operators refused to service the clientele in their cars and demanded to be taken to hotels.

'It is a total mystery to me,' said the inspector, 'how every whore in Turin can be watching out day and night and all we get is a description of a young man with a beard.'

'And a car with tinted glass,' said the sergeant.

'Anyway, we know that all the reports can't be of the same man because some are simultaneous in different parts of the city.'

'The usual hysteria,' said the inspector. 'They expect a young man with a beard so they see a young man with a beard. Well, maybe that's all for this year. He only struck twice last year.'

The inspector was too optimistic. Less than a month later, on May 22nd, Clelia Mollo was raped, whipped, tortured, mutilated and strangled to death.

The fifty-eight-year-old prostitute had feared exactly this and had no longer entertained customers in their cars. Instead, she had brought them back to her apartment and it was in her apartment that her body was found.

It was found by a colleague, a woman with normally sturdy nerves, who suffered a complete nervous breakdown and had to be taken to the hospital.

The inspector called a conference of the key members of the commission.

'This series of homicides has been going on for over two years,' he said, 'and we know no more about the murderer now than we did at the time of the Annunziata Paffunda case. Are there any suggestions?'

There was a profound silence. The commissioners, all experienced investigations' specialists, had been racking their brains for months in the search for any possible opening in the case and had found none.

'Is it the same man in all cases?' said the inspector. 'Or are some imitations? There's been immense publicity in the press.'

'The older women were all by the same man,' said Dr Scorzatti flatly. 'Marina Manna, perhaps. The other two, definitely not.'

Three other cases had been tentatively grouped with the 'Devil of Turin' murders. They were Alice Veronique Tirard, a French prostitute, who had been found strangled on April 7 1985; Manna Manna, found shot in the head on November 27, 1985; and Laura Mano, strangled and thrown into the Po river on March 30, 1986.

All had been raped, but only Miss Manna's hands had been bound with electrical wire and she had not been a prostitute or, at least, only an occasional, semi-professional one.

None of the three had been within the preferred age group for a 'Devil of Turin' victim. The oldest, Miss Manna, had been thirty-eight. Alice Veronique Tirard had been twenty-four and Laura Mano had been a teen-ager of fifteen.

The only real similarity in the cases was that the victims had been raped, whipped and tortured and that they were all unsolved.

'And Miss Gallo?' asked one of the detectives.

'Almost certainly the same man,' said the doctor. 'All the hallmarks without the murder.'

'Was it the same gun in the Benvenuto and Manna cases?' asked the sergeant.

'Nine-millimetre not on record in the Benvenuto case,' said the ballistics expert. 'The bullet exited and wasn't recovered in the Manna case. I understand that the entry wound was compatible with a nine-millimetre.'

'It was a nine-millimetre,' said Dr Scorzatti. He had performed the autopsy.

'Any luck with tracing a common contact, Franco?' asked the inspector.

Sergeant Dangelo had been in charge of a detachment attempting to trace the professional and personal contacts of the victims in the hope that there would be one man common to all of them.

'Nothing,' said the sergeant. 'We've found three or four men who patronized more than one of the women, but none of them is a valid suspect. You have to remember that these were women who had been prostitutes for over twenty years. Just to go back to the time of the Annunziata Paffunda case involves thousands of, more or less, casual contacts. It's impossible to identify even twenty percent of them.'

'Then, what we must do,' decided the inspector, 'is wait for a case that is reported soon after it happens. When we get one, we'll block off the entire sector and carry out an intensive check of every male in it.'

Most of the men present thought that it would be a long wait. In not one of the cases so far had the murder been reported much sooner than eight hours after it had taken place.

But seven was a lucky number, for the police, if not for the 'Devil of Turin'. When the seventh victim, forty-seven-year-old Maria Rosa Paoli, was strangled and thrown out of a car near a bridge over the Po on June 29th, the report was received within minutes at police headquarters. Fortunately, it was late at night and traffic was light. The police cordon went up in less than a quarter of an hour.

At shortly after midnight, a team of patrolmen manning a roadblock halted a brown Fiat with tinted glass driven by a bearded man. The description of the car and the driver checked with what they were looking for, but it was already the third such car and driver that had passed through.

This one's papers were completely in order and there

was nothing to be seen in the car other than a folded newspaper lying on the back seat.

According to his papers, the driver was thirty-two-year-old Giancarlo Giudice, an unmarried truck driver who lived on the other side of town. What, asked the patrolman, had he been doing in this district at nearly midnight of a Sunday?

'Looking for a girl,' replied Giudice calmly. 'I am not married and one has certain needs . . . you understand?'

'You found one?' said the patrolman.

Giudice shook his head.

'Unfortunately not,' he said. 'They are all too old and ugly.'

There were no more grounds for holding Giudice than for any of the others and the patrolman was about to wave him on when his partner, who had been peering inside the car, suddenly gripped him by the arm.

'Wait!' he said. 'Under the newspaper in the back seat.'

The patrolman opened the door of the car and unfolded the newspaper. Lying inside it was a black, nine-millimetre pistol.

A half-hour later, it was lying on Inspector Castelli's desk and Giudice was explaining that he had found it in a garbage can at Christmas time of the preceding year.

It was a story that could be true. The 'Devil of Turin' might very well have decided to get rid of the incriminating weapon and the police were certainly not in a position to prove otherwise. The very fact that it had been left lying so casually on the back seat of the car, covered only by a newspaper, indicated that Giudice had nothing ot hide.

A check of police records nationwide showed that he had never been arrested or charged and his employers described his as a hard-working, reliable employee who had been with them for over seven years.

On the other hand, Giudice apparently had no girl-friends and had never had one. He admitted this freely.

'You start having girlfriends and you end up married,' he said. 'I prefer whores. It's cheaper in the long run.'

'Middle-aged whores?' said the inspector.

'Young whores,' said Giudice firmly.

Linda Gallo, however, was a young whore and, when she was taken to Giudice's studio apartment, she said that she recognized it as the place where she had been raped and tortured.

Giudice said that she was mistaken. There were many such studio apartments in Turin and where were the pornographic magazines she described?

No pornographic magazines had been found in Giudice's studio and, once again, what he said could be true. There were many such studios in Turin.

'Without a confession, it's going to be difficult,' said the inspector, 'but we're going to ask for an indictment. He's the right age. He's got a beard. He drives a brown Fiat with tinted glass. He was found in possession of the gun that killed Addolorata Benvenuto. And Gallo swears it was his apartment. It may be enough.'

It was. The examining magistrate decided that the evidence was adequate to order Giudice held for trial on an open homicide charge.

Giudice then played his last card.

'I couldn't have done it,' he said. 'My aunt was one of the victims.'

Incredibly, this turned out to be true. Maria Corda, the fifth victim, was Giudice's aunt.

The defence backfired, however, for the subsequent investigation showed that Giudice's relationship to his aunt had been more that of prostitute and client than aunt and nephew. Giudice not only admitted this, but claimed that he had not thought much of Aunt Maria's services and had only patronized her because she gave him a reduced rate for being in the family.

However, having been indicted, he could now be held indefinitely and the incessant interrogation gradually broke down his resistance so that, on August 26, 1986, he made a full confession to the seven murders, including details known only to the murderer and the police.

On June 26, 1987, having been found legally sane and responsible for his acts, he was pronounced guilty on seven counts of homicide and sentenced to life imprisonment.

19

MAN'S BEST FRIEND?

The victim was handsome. A tall, well-built man of twenty-eight, his light brown, curly hair lay in a halo about his face and his full-lipped, generous mouth was curved upward at the corners in an amused smile.

The tiny but lethal hole in the left temple was hidden by the hair and only a red trickle of blood which had run down over the clean-shaven cheek betrayed its existence.

'Small calibre bullet,' said Dr Jules Pointin, coroner of the city of Beauvais. 'Point-blank range. The hair is singed.'

'Time?' inquired Inspector Paul Fregatte.

He was a compactly built man of fifty with greying hair and the olive complexion of southern France from which he had originally come.

'Within the last hour,' said the doctor, who was native to the region, some fifty miles to the north of Paris, and, with his sandy-brown hair, pale blue eyes and freckled cheeks, could have passed for German or Flemish.

'When does she say was the last time she saw him alive?' said the inspector, directing the question at a tall, loose-limbed man with imposing, auburn moustaches who was standing silently in the door of the bedroom.

'Nine o'clock, approximately,' said the Sergeant of Detectives Antoine Severeau. 'She left at that time to visit a girlfriend and, when she returned at eleven, she found him dead and called the police.'

He spoke with no particular intonation, but the doctor looked up sharply.

'You think . . . ?' he began.

The inspector laid a finger across his lips and tipped his head in the direction of the living room where the widow was sobbing and sniffling.

'We'll discuss that at the station,' he said. 'Call the desk and tell them to send over the lab crew, Antoine.'

'Anything special?' said the sergeant. 'Or routine check only?'

'Full investigation,' said the inspector. 'Signs of forceful entry. Missing valuables. Fingerprints.'

'She says the door was unlocked,' said the sergeant. 'Their savings are gone. Around four thousand francs in a tin box.'

'Which would have been well-hidden,' said the inspector. 'That could be an indication. If he didn't have to hunt for it, he must have known the family extremely well.'

The sergeant pulled down the lower lid of his right eye with an index finger in the European gesture of scepticism, but said nothing.

'We can talk in the car until the lab people get here,' said the inspector, leading the way out of the house.

The light dusting of frost over the top of the police car sparkled and gleamed like diamonds beneath the cold rays of the moon. It was ten minutes to midnight of November 18, 1978, and winter was arriving a little early in the north of France.

In the car, the three men lit cigarettes, settling down for an extended wait. Beauvais was a community of less than fifty thousand residents and the police laboratory was not manned at midnight on Saturday. The technicians would have to be called in.

'You think she did it, Antoine?' asked the inspector after a time.

'Who else?' said the sergeant. 'The spouse is always the first suspect.'

'True,' said the inspector. 'What kind of an impression

did she make on you when you were taking her statement?'

'About a hair's-breadth from hysteria,' said the sergeant. 'Either she killed him or she's mighty sorry to lose him.'

'Not the best situation for a woman to be in,' remarked the doctor. 'A widow with two small children.'

'They apparently slept straight through it,' said the inspector.

'They're asleep now,' said the sergeant, 'but the boy's only six and his sister's three. Kids that age are sound sleepers.'

'They'll be orphans, if she goes to jail,' said the doctor. 'I hope you're wrong about her doing it.'

'I hope so too,' said the inspector, 'but it doesn't look good. The door unlocked. Daillet asleep. Savings gone, but nothing in the house disturbed. And Mrs Daillet visiting her girlfriend. It's a little too pat.'

'We can check the alibi,' said the sergeant. 'It may not check out.'

'It will,' said the inspector. 'Believe me. It will.'

After a time, the technicians arrived and the inspector returned to his office, leaving the sergeant in charge of operations at the scene of the crime. The doctor went home. It would be an hour or two until the specialists had completed their work around the corpse, had photographed it for the record and had arranged for its transfer to the police morgue where he would perform the autopsy the following day. There was no particular urgency. It was highly unlikely that anything would be found that would be of use to the investigation.

Before leaving, the doctor gave Nicole Daillet an injection to calm her nerves and persuaded her to go to bed. She was obviously under great emotional stress and there was no point in her sitting up all night.

'Well?' said the inspector as the sergeant entered the office at a little after four o'clock in the morning. 'What did they find?'

'Nothing,' said the sergeant. 'The only recent prints in the house are from the Daillets. Nothing disturbed. The tin box with the savings was very well hidden . . . if it ever existed. No signs of forceable entry. No murder weapon.'

'Did they give her a paraffin test?' asked the inspector.

The sergeant nodded.

'She was about half-asleep,' he said. 'Pointin pumped her full of tranquillizers before he left. Negative.'

'She use rubber gloves to wash the dishes?' asked the inspector.

The sergeant nodded again.

'New pair in the kitchen,' he said. 'They tested negative too. There could have been another pair.'

'She'd have had to get rid of the gun and the gloves before she called the police,' said the inspector.

'She didn't have to call the police until she was ready to,' said the sergeant. 'Why do you keep looking for a third party? She did it.'

'Getting soft, I guess,' said the inspector. 'I feel sorry for her. She's a little woman, not pretty, wears glasses, and he was a handsome dog and a year younger. Probably had enough mistresses to make up a sewing circle and she couldn't stand it any more.'

The theory was logical, but it did not prove to be true. In a community as small as Beauvais, everyone knew who had mistresses and Jean-Claude Daillet had had none.

He had married Nicole Mouton, a comical name as it meant Nicole Sheep, six years earlier and very shortly before the birth of Sebastian. Sandrine had followed three years later and the marriage appeared to have been a happy one.

There had been no particular financial pressures. Nicole came from a large and poor family, but Jean-Claude was middle class and had received a training as an installer of television antennae. The job paid well and his employers described him as hard-working and dependable.

'If the motive wasn't on his side, then it must have been on hers,' said the inspector. 'She doesn't look it, but she must have a lover.'

'Must have,' agreed the sergeant. 'It couldn't have been a burglar. The reconstruction would look crazy. Daillet sound asleep in bed. Burglar enters. Shoots him in the head. Goes directly to hiding place of savings. Takes them. Departs.'

'It is crazy,' said the inspector. 'I never heard of a French family who told anyone where they hid the savings. And why shoot Daillet? He was asleep.'

'If there was only one person outside the family who knew where the savings were hidden, he'd have had to shoot Daillet,' said the sergeant.

'Then he'd have had to shoot Mrs Daillet too,' said the inspector. 'No. The only thing that makes sense is if she had a lover. Murdering Daillet would kill several birds with one stone. He'd get the money. He'd eventually get Mrs Daillet. And because she has a confirmed alibi, he'd draw suspicion away from her and, by association, himself. Very clever.'

'I think the explanation is more clever than the crime,' said the sergeant, 'but I'll see what I can do about identifying a lover for Mrs Daillet.'

Although he did not expect to be, the sergeant was almost immediately successful in identifying one of Nicole Daillet's lovers. Unfortunately, the identification only confused matters more than ever.

'I don't think you're going to believe this,' he told the inspector, 'but there's good reason to believe that Mrs Daillet has been intimate with a certain Mr Lucien Tessier.'

'Why shouldn't I believe it?' said the inspector.

'Lucien is fourteen years old,' said the sergeant. 'He's been telling his friends that he had intercourse with Mrs Daillet.'

'The boy's probably lying,' said the inspector. 'Lots of boys of that age brag about love affairs that never took place.'

'But not with women who look like Mrs Daillet,' said the sergeant. 'If you're going to boast about an imaginary affair, you pick on somebody beautiful.'

'But hell!' said the inspector with some irritation. 'Why would the boy murder Daillet? He couldn't marry his widow. His mother wouldn't let him.'

The sergeant shrugged.

'I think we should question him,' he said.

'All right,' said the inspector. 'Get hold of the juvenile section of the social welfare. They have to have a social worker present if we're going to interrogate a minor. Have to have the parents' permission too.'

For once, none of the formalities presented any difficulty and Lucien Tessier was brought to the inspector's office where he made a lengthy statement. He was not a very large or mature-looking boy and he was obviously frightened at finding himself in the hands of the police.

He had known the Daillets only by sight, he said, up until a few months earlier when he had encountered Jean-Claude in the street. Jean-Claude had engaged him in conversation and had asked him bluntly if he would like to have sexual intercourse with his wife.

Lucien had not known what to say. He was afraid that Jean-Claude suspected him of designs on his wife and he did not dare say yes. On the other hand, if he said no, it might be construed as meaning that he found Mrs Daillet unattractive.

He had, therefore, said nothing and Jean-Claude, taking silence for assent, had brought him to his house, ordered his wife to strip and suggested that they make love on the sofa.

Lucien had then engaged in intercourse with Mrs Daillet who had neither changed expression nor said so much as hello.

While the intercourse was taking place, Jean-Claude

had gone to the kitchen and had returned with a beer to watch television in the same room.

When it was over, he had asked Lucien if he found Nicole satisfactory and, upon being assured that he had no complaints, had said he could come back another time for more of the same.

Lucien had then left as it was nearly ten o'clock and his parents did not allow him to remain out late.

As Lucien's parents were not present when this statement was made, they were not upset, but the social worker, fearing there was something wrong with Lucien's head, demanded a psychiatric examination. One was carried out with the result that the psychiatrist not only pronounced Lucien as sane as anyone, but expressed the opinion that he was telling the truth. The boy had told him details of his experience which would scarcely have been known to a fourteen-year-old unless he had had intimate contact with an adult woman.

The bemused sergeant investigated Lucien's whereabouts on the evening of the murder, determined that he had watched television with his family until being sent to bed at ten-thirty and informed the inspector that he was not a potential suspect.

'Neither is Mrs Daillet,' said the inspector. 'We've practically grilled Miss Bourges and she swears that Mrs Daillet was with her all evening. She's lying, of course, but we can't prove it.'

Paulette Bourges was the twenty-seven-year-old girlfriend with whom Nicole had supposedly been on the evening of the murder and, if she continued to provide Nicole with an alibi, the police had little hope of obtaining an indictment.

'Or even without an alibi,' said the sergeant. 'We've turned up another of Mrs Daillet's lovers.'

'A member of the local cub scout troop, I presume?' said the inspector sarcastically.

Regardless of the psychiatrist's opinion, he had never believed Lucien Tessier's story.

'A sixty-year-old Algerian guest worker,' said the sergeant expressionlessly. 'She must be one of the great nymphomaniacs of all time.'

'That's ridiculous!' spluttered the inspector. 'A nymphomaniac wouldn't pick on adolescents and senior citizens. She'd want young, virile men.'

'Talk to him yourself,' said the sergeant. 'I've got him outside.'

The inspector did not talk to Hallal Benali, but he listened to him. Although a common labourer, he had been in France for many years and spoke good French.

'All right,' he said, after the Algerian had left. 'It's a straight story. They really did have intercourse in the car with her husband sitting in the front seat. He hasn't the intelligence to invent a story like that.'

'Must be some kind of a weird perversion,' said the sergeant, 'but I never heard of anything like that before. You heard what he said about her doing it with other guest workers?'

The inspector nodded.

'Put as many men on this as you need,' he said. 'I want to see every man she has had relations with here in this office.'

The office could not hold them! With no more than a superficial effort, the sergeant's men were able to produce fourteen Algerians, Moroccans and Tunisians, all guest workers and all one-time sex partners of the amazing Mrs Nicole Daillet.

Amazing, particularly, because, according to their statements, she had apparently taken no pleasure in the activity and had neither requested nor accepted compensation of any sort. All that she had asked was that they make a little cross on the palm of her hand with a ballpoint pen.

Her manner of entering into contact had been extremely direct. Unmarried guest workers in France are often housed in large barracks broken up into small rooms. Nicole had simply entered one room after another, raising the skirt of her dress and lying down on the bed or, if there was none, the floor. As she wore no underwear, her intentions were unmistakable.

Many of the men reported seeing her get into a waiting car after leaving the building and, on the basis of the descriptions, it appeared certain that the driver had been Jean-Claude Daillet.

'But never more nor less than three at a time,' said the sergeant. 'When she had got three crosses on her hand, she left. What in God's name do you think it means?'

'It has to be a perversion,' said the inspector. 'Or, maybe, the craziest sect that anybody ever dreamed up. The trouble is, the doctor says there isn't any such perversion and a sect would have more members.'

'I think we should drop it,' said the sergeant earnestly. 'Even if we got an indictment, she'd be acquitted on grounds of mental incompetency, assuming that it ever came to trial at all.'

'We can't drop it,' said the inspector. 'You know that. Bring her in. We'll confront her with all these people and see what she says.'

To his surprise, Nicole Daillet proved to be incredibly resistant to interrogation. Although formally identified by Lucien Tessier and all of the guest workers but two, she stoutly denied ever having had sex with any of them or even having laid eyes on them before.

Lucien, she said, was a schoolboy with a normal schoolboy's crush on an older woman. The guest workers were some kind of dirty foreigners. She could not tell one North African from another and they probably could not tell one French woman from another.

On the subject of sexual relations with her husband, she was, however, curiously frank.

Jean-Claude, she said, had been very virile. He had demanded sex immediately upon awakening in the morning and he had wanted it again after breakfast, usually simply bending her over the breakfast table and raising her nightdress in order to avoid being late for work. He had made love to her the first thing upon returning home and again after they had gone to bed.

'Four times a day?' exclaimed the incredulous inspector.

'More on weekends,' said Nicole.

'Did he beat you?' asked the inspector, searching for some comprehensible motive in this bizarre case.

'Never,' said Nicole. 'He had trouble with the police for beating Sebastian, but it was the neighbours who called them. They were just making trouble.'

The inspector already knew that Daillet had been given a two months' suspended sentence for beating his son in September of 1976. It was the only entry in his police record.

Probing for a weak point in the woman's stubborn defence, the inspector switched the subject to the children. Had they been fond of their father?

Nicole started to answer and then it was as if something in her mind had given way. The powerful emotions of love for her children, fears for their future and, perhaps, confusion over her strange marriage, caused the words to pour out of her in a great, half-incoherent flood.

It was too sudden and too much for the inspector to understand, but the interview was being taped and, after listening to it several times, two things became clear. Nicole was not admitting to any responsibility for the murder and she was terrified that her children might be sent to an orphanage if she were to go to jail.

'She'd confess in a minute if it wasn't for the kids,' said the inspector. 'She's from a social background where having them sent to an institution is the worst thing she can imagine.'

'What can we do?' said the sergeant. 'They will be sent to an orphanage if she's convicted.'

'Maybe not,' said the inspector. 'I'm going over to talk to the social welfare and then I'm going to see her family. She has a bunch of married sisters and brothers.

Maybe one of them would take the kids until she gets out.'

One of the married sisters would. In fact, even the unmarried brothers and sisters said they would look after the Daillet children if it should prove necessary. The Moutons were poor, but the family feeling was strong.

The inspector put it to Nicole straight.

'We know you killed your husband,' he said, 'and we know why you don't want to confess. But you needn't worry about the children. Your sister will take care of them and the social welfare will pay. I don't know what your motive for this was, but I suspect it was a good one and, if so, you're not going to get a very heavy sentence anyway.'

Nicole hesitated.

'Let me talk to my sister,' she said finally.

The inspector relaxed. The case was over.

'It was the dog,' said Nicole, approaching her confession with her characteristic devastating frankness. 'The children were getting older. They would have noticed.'

'The dog?' said the inspector uncertainly. There had been no dog in the Daillet house.

'Maurice,' said Nicole. 'He's a German shepherd. Jean-Claude's mother gave him to us for Christmas in 1975.'

'And?' said the inspector mystified.

'Jean-Claude was interested in sex,' said Nicole, making one of the great understatements of all time. 'He had me get down on all fours in the kitchen and he turned up my dress. Then, he rubbed sardines on my private parts.

'Maurice loved sardines so he came and licked them off.

'Jean-Claude kept doing that and, after a while, Maurice got excited. Jean-Claude helped him find the place so he could have sex with me.'

'You and the dog?' said the aghast inspector.

'Me and Maurice,' said Nicole. 'And then me and Jean-Claude. But Maurice wanted to do it all the time and not just with me, but with any woman who came into the house so we had to send him to a kennel.'

'But that settled the matter then,' said the inspector, still not grasping what the dog had had to do with the murder.

'Jean-Claude was talking about getting another dog,' said Nicole. 'He thought, maybe, we should get a Saint Bernard this time.

'I didn't think it was right for the children to see such things at home so I went over to Pont Saint Maxence on November 11th and bought a little gun.

'I had to wait until the 18th because I wanted Paulette to say I was with her that evening, but I was afraid to ask her before.'

This naive admission was clear evidence of premeditation and the inspector, in an effort to bolster the extenuating circumstances as much as possible, went to some lengths to establish the accuracy of her statements.

The kennel was located and Maurice gave an embarrassing, albeit incomplete, demonstration of his appreciation of the fair sex on the person of a female detective.

Nicole's statement that the crosses in her hand had been her husband's way of keeping track of her sexual activities was confirmed by Paulette Bourges who had been Nicole's best friend and confidante.

She had regarded Jean-Claude as a total madman and had often urged Nicole to divorce him. She, however, refused on the grounds that single-parent families were not good for the children.

Although it had been generally assumed that the trial would take place behind closed doors, Nicole, unembarrassed as ever over her unconventional love life, did not request it and emotionlessly related the details of her marriage to a packed and far from emotionless court room.

She was sorry that she had killed Jean-Claude, she said, but the Saint Bernard was the last straw.

'Who knows what it would have been after that?' she asked.

The court thought this a legitimate question and, on September 17, 1979, found her guilty of murder with premeditation, but with such extreme extenuating circumstances that she was sentenced to only two years' imprisonment.

Even this sentence was suspended and, to the cheers and some vulgar observations from the public, Nicole Daillet went home to her children, the only known murderess whose sole motive was to escape the embraces of a Saint Bernard.

20

A MALE SUPREMACY KNIGHT'S DREAM

Germans have great respect, even reverence, for their academic titles of which there was, up until recently, only the doctorate.

The holders of the title are often no less impressed. After a struggle lasting sometimes ten years and more, the newly annointed doctor is so astounded at his own achievement that he never forgets it.

He hardly could if he wanted to. His apotheosis into the ranks of the academicians has transformed him into another form of being having little in common with ordinary mortals. Henceforth, he will forever be addressed as Herr Doktor or, if he has two doctorates, Herr Doktor Doktor, plus any other official titles he may accumulate so that Lord Mayor Schmidt becomes Herr Oberbürgermeister Doktor Doktor Schmidt.

The distinction extends even unto his lawful spouse, if he has one, who is, consequently, addressed as Frau Doktor or, as the case may be, Frau Doktor Doktor, even though she may have left school at the age of eight.

German women greatly enjoy being addressed as Frau Doktor and reverently ushered to the head of any queue they may find themselves in. They will, therefore, overlook a great deal for the sake of the title. Up until the wedding, that is. Afterwards, things may be different. The modern German woman is liberated to an extent to make the legendary Amazons look like harem slaves.

The lordly doctor may, therefore, find himself sharing

bed and board with a person who bristles at the innocent command of, 'Pass the sugar.'

The sequel can be the divorce court, the hospital or the morgue, but some holders of the doctorate are more imaginative and there are startling variations.

Dr Ulrich Koschwald was a splendid specimen of German academician. Thirty-six years old, six feet four inches tall and thin as a drainpipe, he was not what would be called handsome by many. His sparse, slightly wavy, blond hair, which he wore in approved academic style down to his shoulders, covered only the sides and back of his head, the remainder being either bald or balding. His blue-green eyes tended to protrude and were magnified by the thick lenses of his steel-rimmed glasses, lending him the appearance of a frog peering through the bottom of a water tumbler. His gait was awkward and sometimes compared to that of a seasick bear. He was, however, immensely strong and a trained karate fighter.

A research scientist in the field of the sexual problems of married couples, he was attached to the university at Regensburg, a community of some one hundred and forty thousand inhabitants, located at the confluence of the Danube and Regen rivers in south west Germany.

As might be expected of a man of his standing, Dr Koschwald had been married twice and was the father of an eleven-year-old daughter named Gretel. He had also been divorced twice and was now having such serious problems with his current girlfriend that they had gone to seek the advice of a marriage counsellor.

'The counsellor said we either break up or fight it out,' said twenty-two-year-old Susanne Wagner upon their return to the doctor's home at Am Eichelberg 14 outside the village of Pillnach, 'so I am leaving.'

'But I prefer the other solution, my dear!' cried the doctor, delivering a shrewd karate chop to her midriff which left her paralysed with agony. 'Let us fight it out and may the best one win!'

Upon which, the doctor leapt upon Susanne like some sort of giant spider, handcuffed her, tore off her clothes, dragged her to the basement where, having suspended her in chains from a hook in the ceiling, he beat her to a howling misery with a rope normally used for securing calves and raped her no less than three times, the last time being a dry run, however.

Remarking that he had never before encountered such sensible advice as that given by the counsellor, the doctor went off upstairs for refreshments, dinner and a good night's rest.

Susanne spent an uncomfortable night. It was chilly in the basement and her wrists hurt terribly as her toes barely touched the floor. She was also sore from the beating and she was frightened nearly out of her wits as she was convinced that the doctor had gone mad and that release would come only with her death.

Actually, it was not going to be that easy. Susanne had become Dr Koschwald's slave on that afternoon of June 4, 1981 and it would be nearly a year before she regained her freedom.

The doctor much preferred Susanne as a slave to Susanne as a girlfriend. As a girlfriend, she had frequently been impertinent and disrespectful. She had once even put him out of the car she was driving and he had had to walk nearly a mile back to town. On another occasion, she had hit him over the head with a hairbrush.

It was this latter incident which had brought about the visit to the marriage counsellor, a visit which Susanne now regretted bitterly.

Being a scientist himself, Dr Koschwald regarded the pronouncements of a fellow-scientist as more infallible than those of the Pope and the counsellor's advice had opened the floodgates of a vast reservoir of fantasies which had been sloshing around in his head for a long time.

The doctor was, in fact, a closet reactionary, an unreconstructed advocate of male supremacy, and, particularly, with regard to sexual matters. As he confided to Susanne, he had always dreamed of keeping a woman or, better yet, several women as slaves.

He had even inquired into the possibility of becoming a Mohammedan so that he could legally marry four wives, but had been forced to abandon the project following legal assurance that he would be prosecuted for bigamy, regardless of his religion. Mohammedans living in Germany might have four wives, but they had to register three of them as cousins, sisters or scullery maids.

Thus balked, the doctor had resigned himself to never realizing his dream of a naked, slightly black-and-blue slave, snivelling and blubbering about the house and catering to his every whim, until he heard the counsellor's suggestion for dealing with Susanne.

As the counsellor later said, this was not exactly what he had had in mind, but rather a gentle and, possibly, erotic sort of wrestling match. Dr Koschwald's interpretation, he said, was exaggerated.

Dr Koschwald did not know this, however, and he was happy. Every day he beat, tortured and raped Susanne, sometimes bringing in his daughter, Gretel, to watch.

Gretel did not mention these performances to anyone. Perhaps, she thought that her father was engaged in one of his research projects and that Susanne was a married patient with sexual problems. Perhaps, she found them more interesting than television (notoriously dull in Germany). In any case, her thoughts remained her own for, being a minor, she could not be questioned by the police.

Gretel was, however, the only person, aside from her father, who knew what was happening to Susanne who had no relatives in the area and no friends close enough to concern themselves over her sudden disappearance.

The Koschwald household, therefore, settled down to a humdrum routine of work, sleep, meals, beating, torture and sex. The basement had thick walls and the house was well outside the village so Susanne's screams disturbed no one.

Susanne did not spend all her time in the basement. Sometimes she was chained to the kitchen stove or the radiator in the doctor's bedroom so as to be handy if he should wake up during the night and feel the need of entertainment. Sometimes she was even allowed to run free, the doctor assuring her that, if she made any attempt to leave, he would kill her in a particularly painful manner. She believed him and, being a modest girl, she was also loath to run off into the village stark naked. She had not seen so much as a handkerchief of clothing since becoming a slave.

Difficult as it is to break out of a rut, and, although her life could not be described as lacking in excitement, after nearly a year of this, Susanne became weary of the situation. The only incident in months had been when the doctor had broken his right hand when giving her a clumsy karate chop.

She therefore decided to forget about modesty and to escape. As for the doctor killing her, it would be, if anything, an improvement on what appeared to be a lifetime of unending torment.

Susanne did not know exactly what month it was, but she knew it was spring for the trees around the house were in leaf and the doctor had turned off the central heating. She would not, therefore, freeze to death if she managed to get out of the house and into the surrounding woods.

Actually, escape proved to be rather easy. The doctor, perhaps convinced that Susanne was content in her new situation, no longer kept such close watch on her and did not always hang her up in chains during the night.

On the night of May 24, 1982, after nearly a year of slavery, Susanne greased her hands with soap, slipped off her handcuffs and crawled quietly out of a window. She was afraid to go through the front door as it squeaked.

She was completely naked with the exception of a bath towel, illegally appropriated from the doctor's bathroom, but the night was warm and she set straight off through the woods, not heading in any particular direction, but simply away from the house. She was gibbering with fear and shaking so hard that she could hardly run.

The motorist who picked her up loping along the side of a country road thought that she was under the influence of some kind of highly potent drugs and he took her to the hospital.

There, she was given a bath, as she was remarkably dirty, her bruises were treated, she was given clothing and sent off about her business.

It was obvious to the doctors that she had been beaten and tortured, but she denied it and refused to let them notify the police. This was not regarded as unusual. Young ladies such as Susanne were frequently given demonstrations by their boyfriends of the inequality of the sexes and they frequently refrained from preferring charges either because they loved them or because they feared further demonstrations.

In Susanne's case it was fear and not love. Her cruel and humiliating treatment by the doctor had destroyed the tender feelings that she had once entertained for him and she would have cheerfully seen him hung.

That was, however, not likely to happen. German justice is lenient to the point of idiocy and it would be remarkable if her tormentor received more than a fine for his acts. He would certainly not be imprisoned or, even if he was, it would be only for a short time. All that it would do would be to put him in a bad humour and she had no doubt that he would hunt her down like a rabbit once he got out.

Susanne did not, therefore, say anything to the police or anyone else. She registered for welfare, found a small room in which to hide and went out no more than she had to.

While she had been hanging in chains in Dr Koschwald's basement, she had dreamed of lying in sunny meadows or in limpid, little streams that soothed her aching flesh. There were birds and flowers and someone gently stroking her hair.

Now, she suffered from ghastly nightmares in which she hung in her chains in the cold, dank basement and the gaunt, naked figure of Dr Koschwald, his eyes bulging wildly behind the lenses of his spectacles, bore down on her with the calf rope in his hand.

In the meantime, the doctor, hurt and annoyed at his slave's desertion, was not even searching for Susanne, but looking around for a more satisfactory substitute and, German university towns being invariably crowded with beautiful, young women, he soon found one.

Sabine Pauli was twenty-four years old and a student in his class on sexology at the university. A very beautiful girl with long, black hair, she was preparing a thesis on the sexual lives of Australian aborigines.

When the doctor invited her to have lunch with him at his villa, she was flattered. She did not suspect that she was soon to acquire personally more sexual experience than all the aborigines in Australia would ever dream of.

The doctor had come to the conclusion that where he had failed with Susanne was in being too soft and, although he allowed Sabine to finish her lunch, immediately after the dessert, he jumped upon her, tore off her clothes, chained her to the kitchen stove, cut off her hair, stuck an apple in her mouth and wrapped her head with plastic tape until she could neither see, hear, speak nor scarcely breathe.

He then dragged her to the basement, strung her up in chains to the hook in the ceiling, raped her several times and left her to contemplate the eccentricities in behaviour of university professors.

The next day, he gave her a bloody nose and two black eyes, following which he beat her nearly unconscious while screaming, 'This is the dream of untrammelled patriarchy and grovelling slaves without will!'

Being an academician, he made use of a large vocabulary.

Fortunately for Sabine's sanity, she did not suspect that she had had a predecessor who had spent nearly a year as the doctor's grovelling slave. Rather, she thought that her professor had gone suddenly and inexplicably mad. Her previous contact with him had been confined to dozing through his lectures where he managed to make even sex sound a dull subject.

Dull it was no longer. The doctor had lost all control of himself and torturing girls is, it seems, something like eating peanuts. It is moreish. For a time, it was a question as to whether the sex savant might not end by destroying his slave altogether.

Sabine certainly believed with each passing day that her last hour had come and, no doubt, it eventually would have had it not occurred to the doctor that he could double his enjoyment by doubling the number of his slaves.

He therefore simply seized one of the village girls who happened to be passing by, dragged her into the house, stripped her, gave her a sound beating with the calf rope, raped her to the best of his ability, which was not very much as he was rather worn out from his exertions with Sabine, and strung her up in the basement to grovel next to his other slave.

Nineteen-year-old Beate Koch was, if anything, more astounded at this treatment than either Susanne or Sabine had been. She knew who Koschwald was and that he was a prominent sociologist and research scientist at the university, although she did not know his precise field. His conduct was not what she had been led to expect from a university professor.

Sabine was unable to enlighten her. She knew no more about what was wrong with Dr Koschwald than Beate did.

This final addition to the collection of slaves without will was, however, a mistake. Beate was a local girl whose parents lived in the village and, when she failed to return home, they became alarmed and notified the police.

A sergeant of detectives named Willi Prutzig, who had a large nose, protruding front teeth and a sort of pageboy haircut, came out from Regensburg and talked to the parents, the neighbours and Beate's girlfriends in the village. None of them had any suggestions as to what might have happened to her.

The only thing he was able to determine was that she had left her parents' home at approximately three o'clock in the afternoon with the intention of visiting a girlfriend who lived in an even smaller community three-quarters of a mile away. She had not arrived there and, there being only one road between the two villages, it could be assumed that it was somewhere along this road that she had disappeared.

'Taken into a car, I should think,' said the sergeant, reporting on the results of his investigation to his chief, Inspector Joachim Borg. 'I was shown a picture. She's a very pretty girl.'

'If she wasn't so old, it could be white slavers,' mused the inspector, a spare, dry sort of man whose grey suit matched precisely the colour of his hair and moustache, 'but the North African market will hardly look at anything over sixteen. She have a boy friend?'

'More or less,' said the sergeant. 'Nothing serious, according to her girlfriends. There'd be no point in her running off with him. Her parents allowed him to spend nights in her bedroom.'

'Modern family,' said the inspector nodding. 'Well, what do you think? Is there a possibility of something serious?'

The sergeant hesitated.

'I think so,' he said finally. 'She wasn't expecting to disappear. She had dates with her friends and things like that. Could have been a hitchhiker hunter.'

Hunting hitchhikers was an all too common activity in West Germany and Europe, in general. With untold thousands of beautiful, young girls standing alongside the roads and getting trustingly into the first car to stop, a sex psychopath's greatest problem was in making a choice. Some hitchhiker rape series had involved twenty and more victims and there were murder series involving nearly as many.

'I wouldn't like that,' said the inspector who was fully aware of how difficult such crimes were to solve. 'See if you can find any witnesses to a vehicle on the road at that particular time.'

The sergeant thought this an unreasonable assignment, but, to his surprise, he was immediately able to locate a witness who assured him that no vehicle had travelled along the road in question within an hour of when Beate had passed down it.

Max Schelling owned a petrol station at the edge of the village and business was not particularly good. He had, therefore, been sitting in front of his station most of the afternoon and he had seen Beate, whom he of course knew, pass by. He was quite certain that no car had passed over the road in either direction for at least an hour afterwards.

As it would have taken Beate less than an hour to reach her friend's place, her disappearance became more mysterious than ever.

'Unless there was some kind of a psychopath running around on foot, she's either in one of the houses or out in the woods,' said the sergeant, 'but under what circumstances, I can't imagine.'

'Nor I,' said the inspector, 'get some search parties out along the road and I'll see what I can do about warrants to search the houses.'

Obtaining a warrant to search several houses with no grounds for suspecting that anything illegal has transpired in them is not easy in West Germany and the sergeant's search parties had long since scoured the woods and fields on either side of the road without success before the inspector was ready for the houses. However, by the time that he had obtained the warrants, it was late in the afternoon and the searches were put off until the following day which was May 4, 1984.

If Dr Koschwald's house was searched, Sabine and Beate would, of course, be found and released, but they did not even know that a search was being made.

Sabine, who had no relatives in the area, did not think that anyone would report her missing for a long time and, although Beate was certain that her parents would call the police once she failed to return home, she did not think that it would occur to them to look in the basement of a professor's house.

Hanging in their chains in the basement while the doctor, who had found dealing thoroughly with two slaves at a time physically demanding, slept soundly in his bed upstairs, the girls agreed that, unless at least one of them could manage to escape and get help, the mad scientist would eventually murder them. It was unthinkable, after what he had done to them, that he could ever let them go.

Fortunately, they were hanging close together and, after repeated highly painful efforts, Beate managed to lift herself enough by locking her legs around her fellow-sufferer to slip her handcuffed wrists off the hook in the ceiling. This resulted in a fall to the cement floor which nearly knocked her unconscious, but she was free, although her wrists were still locked in the handcuffs.

Struggling to her feet, she tried to lift Sabine down from her hook as well, but the terrified woman pushed her away with her feet.

'Run!' she hissed. 'Run and get help! If he wakes up and catches you, we're both finished.'

'He'll kill you if he comes down and finds me gone!' wept Beate, but she realized that Sabine was right and went off up the stairs as fast and as quietly as possible.

Susanne had known that the front door squeaked, but

Beate did not and she was horrified when it sent a high-pitched, rasping shriek echoing through the house.

Plunging through the door and into the welcoming darkness outside, she ran as fast as her bruised body would carry her in the direction of the village.

There were houses nearer and Beate knew who lived in them, but she no longer trusted her neighbours. If a university professor could torture her within an inch of her life, so could anyone. She therefore ran all the way home, falling frequently in the darkness and cutting her hands and knees.

When her father opened the door in response to her frantic hammering on it with the handcuffs, he could scarcely recognize her. She was naked, covered with mud and blood and hysterical.

'Sabine!' she gasped. 'Sabine! Save Sabine!'

But the Kochs did not know who Sabine was. Wrapping their daughter in a warm blanket, they called first the ambulance and then the police as they did not know how to get the handcuffs off.

Back in the house at Am Eichelberg 14, Sabine had heard the screech of the front door and her heart began to thud dangerously with fear. And with reason. A moment later, there came the dreaded sound of large, flat feet on the floor above. Dr Koschwald was coming downstairs to investigate.

In Regensburg, Sergeant Prutzig had been pulled out of a sound sleep by the duty officer in the station charge room. He was listed as having the Beate Koch disappearance under investigation and the Kochs had just telephoned to say that their daughter had returned home in a deplorable state.

To the sergeant, it sounded as if the girl had just escaped from a sex psychopath and he ordered the roads in the area blocked off, told the duty sergeant to call out Inspector Borg and left for Pillnach in his own car.

By the time he got to the Kochs' house, the ambulance had already arrived and the paramedic who had come with it had succeeded in calming Beate enough for her to make a coherent statement – which, however, no one immediately believed.

'She's on drugs!' said the sergeant. 'A university professor holding girl slaves in his basement?'

'She's not on drugs,' said the paramedic. 'She's in shock and look at the marks on her. She's been beaten.'

'Save Sabine!' wailed Beate. 'He'll kill her! He's killing her right now while you all stand around and talk!'

The sergeant hesitated no longer.

'I'm going to the house,' he told the paramedic. 'The first police that arrive here are to follow me.'

At 14 Am Eichelberg, Dr Koschwald opened the door in response to the sergeant's thumb on the doorbell looking very out of sorts.

'Go away,' he said. 'What do you want?'

'Regensburg Criminal Police,' said the sergeant, producing his official identification. 'We have a report that you are holding a young woman in your basement against her will.'

'Nonsense,' said the doctor. 'She has no will.'

This was an ill-considered assertion and the sergeant promptly informed him that he was under arrest, handcuffed him to the radiator in the hall and went quickly hunting the stairs to the basement.

Sabine was hanging motionless and limp in her chains, her eyes closed. She had been badly beaten and burned in many places with cigarettes and the sergeant thought that she was dead.

She had, however, merely fainted when she saw the grotesque figure of the doctor descend the stairs and advance upon her and that had, perhaps, saved her life.

The doctor was a reasonable man. There was no point in torturing someone who was unconscious. They would not feel it.

He had, of course, been very annoyed and disappointed by Beate's desertion and, as he later told the court, he could not understand it. The girls had been creatures without will. How could they run off without his consent?

If Dr Koschwald could not understand Beate, the psychologists who studied him while he was awaiting trial found some difficulty in understanding him. They were, however, in agreement that he had known what he was doing and that there was a substantial risk that, given the opportunity, he would do it again.

Susanne had, in the meantime, come forward and, after she, Sabine and Beate had all made their statements before the court, Dr Koschwald was found guilty on three counts of sequestration, aggravated assault and rape and, on May 22, 1986, sentenced to five-and-a-half years' imprisonment.

He was taken off still proclaiming his innocence. The charges were all lies, he said. The entire affair was a plot by the women's liberation movement.